Heidegger & Jaspers

Heidegger & Jaspers

Edited by

Alan M. Olson

Temple University Press

PHILADELPHIA

Temple University Press, Philadelphia 19122
Copyright © 1994 by Temple University
Published 1994
Printed in the United States of America

The paper used in this publication meets the minimum requirements of American
National Standard for Information Sciences—Permanence of Paper for Printed Library
Materials, ANSI Z39.48-1984   ∞

Library of Congress Cataloging-in-Publication Data

Heidegger and Jaspers / edited by Alan M. Olson.
    p.   cm.
   Includes bibliographical references and index.
   ISBN 1-56639-114-8 (hard). — ISBN 1-56639-115-6 (pbk.)
    1. Heidegger, Martin, 1889–1976.   2. Jaspers, Karl, 1883–1969.
 I. Olson, Alan M.
 B3279.H49H3425   1993
 193—dc20   93-9674

For Edith Ehrlich, Leonard Ehrlich, and George Pepper:

Pioneers in the Founding and Development of the

Karl Jaspers Society of North America

Contents

Acknowledgments

I wish to extend my heartfelt thanks to Dr. Mutie Tillich Farris for her gracious permission to publish her father's essay "Heidegger and Jaspers." I also wish to thank Dr. Alan Seaburg, Curator of Manuscripts at the Paul Tillich Archive at the Andover Library, Harvard Divinity School, for his helpful assistance in securing this permission.

Heidegger & Jaspers

Introduction: A Dialectic of Being and Value

Alan M. Olson

THE PUBLICATION of Victor Farías's *Heidegger et la nazisme* in 1987 was a controversial event in the usually placid world of philosophy. And while the general consensus may be that Farías's book is flawed, even deeply so, his unabashed critique of Heidegger has provoked one of the more extensive moral reflections in the history of recent philosophical publication.[1] As one surveys the extensive literature on *l'affaire Heidegger*, however, it becomes evident that scant attention has been devoted to any sustained analysis of the lifelong but troubled association of Martin Heidegger and Karl Jaspers. This is unfortunate because their relationship not only provides valuable historical and biographical information, but is a source of insight, as Joseph Margolis reminds us, regarding the moral responsibility of intellectuals and the nature and purpose of philosophy itself. The relatively recent publication of Jaspers's *Notizen zu Heidegger* and their *Briefwechsel*, combined with the even more recent appearance of the correspondence between Karl Jaspers and Hannah Arendt,[2] provides the occasion for redressing this scholarly deficit in a sustained and hopefully informative and constructive manner. This collection of essays is the product of that effort.[3]

During the organizational phase of this research, I somewhat serendipitously came across a lecture on Heidegger and Jaspers by Paul Tillich given at the Cooper Union in New York City in 1954. This essay, published here for the first time,[4] is highly representative of the views of many, if not most, of Jaspers's and Heidegger's intellectual contemporaries during the 1950s. As our lead essay, Tillich's reflections provide a sense of historical context for the current discussion by reminding the reader that even during the time Heidegger was at the peak of his influence as a philosopher, his colleagues were not blind to the questionable implications of his politics. And while Paul Tillich, like Hannah

1

Arendt (as Leonard Ehrlich reminds us in his essay), here identifies Heidegger as a "great thinker" and Jaspers as a "noble scholar," this diminutive attribution of intellectual virtue also enables Tillich to amplify the larger moral significance of what might be termed the danger of Being's seduction of value—especially during times of great political and social crisis, when individuals are most prone to diminish the importance of immediate moral concerns for the sake of an alleged "greater good."

The events of recent decades confirm the accuracy of Tillich's observations and provide a productive basis for rethinking the scholarly significance of Jaspers in ways that heretofore have been overlooked. Indeed, Heidegger and Jaspers provide a case study for understanding the perennial conflict between Being and value, as understood and avowed by these two thinkers, in terms of the projects of fundamental ontology and speculative metaphysics, respectively. For example, Heidegger's stinging critique of "values" in his "Humanismus Brief" (1947), namely, that "thinking in values is the greatest blasphemy imaginable against Being," strikes a quite different note for perceptive readers today than it did even a decade ago. The Achilles' heel of ontological pursuits intent upon disclosing "the lighting of Being," as Tillich suggests, lies in the self-exempted removal of the thinker from the moral and ethical considerations that might call into question the value of this kind of inquiry. Indeed, the tendency toward the deconstructive privatization of philosophizing, as Tillich recalls, was precisely the point of Nicolai Hartmann's critique of Heidegger's "subjectivism"—in spite of Heidegger's constant railing against post-Enlightenment subjectivist epistemologies. Ontological quests, then, sometimes provide warrants for the assumption that the thinker is somehow justified, a priori, in overturning tradition—that is, justified in not seeking justification on the grounds that the authentic thinker is driven by the higher but functionally useless purpose of "letting Being be."

Many scholars believe that Kant saves Jaspers's metaphysical reflections from ethical and moral paralysis in this regard, for throughout his career, Jaspers clearly and unequivocally viewed Kant as the "nodal point" in modern philosophy and devoted himself to rescuing what he considered to be the authentic spirit of Kant. It was not speculative metaphysics, Jaspers argued, that Kant repudiated, but ontology[5]—including the obscurely mystical medieval realism that seems to drive the Heideggerian quest for fundamental ontology. Jaspers, as William Blattner indicates, always regarded Kant's understanding of the "limit situation" as the primary metaphysical clue for developing a moral philosophy grounded in the mystery of freedom—in contrast to Heidegger's dissolution of these limits in order to stand once more in the "neighborhood of Being." As a consequence of Heidegger's incessant repudiation of value theory and actual transgression of value, Karl Jaspers, like Eric Voegelin, ultimately viewed Heidegger as a kind of shaman with mystifying, seductive powers regarding "the magic of the extreme."[6]

It is interesting to note, therefore, that while neo-Kantianism represented the establishment enemy for both Jaspers and Heidegger during their early periods, as Karsten Harries points out, Jaspers was primarily interested in getting beyond the formalism of the neo-Kantians and not beyond Kant. Heidegger, by contrast and as Hans-Georg Gadamer has written, always felt compelled "to get beyond Hegel" and, as such, beyond the entire tradition of German Idealism. In order to "get beyond" Hegel, he had to "get behind" him "by thinking more radically, deeply and comprehensively" everything that Hegel thought.[7] Thus Hegel, the "consummation of Western metaphysics," and not Kant, was Heidegger's principal object of overcoming; for with the publication of *Sein und Zeit* (1927), as Gadamer observes, Heidegger had already "transformed the final and most powerful form of neo-Kantian thought, Husserl's phenomenology, into philosophy"—in other words, he had transformed phenomenology into something more than a purely transcendental logical method, and in so doing, Heidegger "draws close to Hegel."[8] While Klaus Brinkmann here argues that Heidegger fails in this regard, Heidegger's effort probably helps to explain why the neo-Kantian Heinrich Rickert (1863–1936), who, while at Freiburg, directed Heidegger's *Habilitationsschrift* on Duns Scotus's theory of categories, remained Heidegger's ally. However, once at Heidelberg, after replacing Windelband in 1916, Rickert became the erstwhile enemy of Jaspers because, as an "untrained" philosopher with a medical background, Jaspers recalls, he was perceived as bent on overturning the neo-Kantian position Rickert most clearly and unambiguously represented.[9]

In the same vein, it is instructive to note some of the particulars regarding the enthusiastic reception of Heidegger during his Marburg years (1923–1928)—precisely the period when, as Walter Biemel points out, it had become entirely evident that "the old neo-Kantianism had lost its influence." This loss of influence is perhaps best symbolized by the death of Paul Natorp in 1924. During the previous year, Natorp had been chiefly responsible for recruiting Heidegger to Marburg on the strength of his work on Aristotle.[10] The members of Heidegger's impressive coterie of liberal Protestant colleagues and students at Marburg (including the likes of Rudolf Otto, Nicolai Hartmann, Paul Friedländer, Rudolf Bultmann, Paul Tillich, and Hans-Georg Gadamer) were themselves breaking out in various ways from the legacy of neo-Kantianism and, as a consequence, were deeply fascinated with Heidegger's phenomenological explorations of fundamental ontology. Nevertheless, one must remember that Heidegger accomplished this not only as an incipient expert on Brentano and Husserl, but primarily as a classicist and medievalist amidst the then-burgeoning interest in classical, medieval, and romantic culture at Marburg. For at the time of his arrival in Marburg, Heidegger was known for his work on Aristotle, Albertus Magnus, and Duns Scotus; he was, in short, a Catholic philosopher in the midst of a faculty comprised of what, at the time, was arguably the most distinguished collection of Protestant thinkers at the oldest Protestant university in Germany. Founded by Philip of Hesse in 1527, Marburg was the university forever memorialized by way of the Colloquy in 1529 between Luther and Zwingli—the debate that established definitively the philosophical boundaries between Catholics, Lutherans, and other Protestants regarding the nature of sacramental presence and, a fortiori, the dim prospects of any future Protestant natural theology or, for that matter, any future metaphysic. It is reasonable to assume, as Biemel also suggests, that given the obvious political and religious differences between Heidegger and his colleagues, he probably initially pondered, on accepting his appointment, the prospect of being something of a strange prophet in a strange land. But since the philosophical and theological faculty was in the midst of a full-scale rebellion from its liberal Protestant, neo-Kantian past, Heidegger had little cause for alarm—nor was he forced to confront (as might have been the case at Berlin or even Heidelberg) Jaspers's deeply held Kantian conviction, out of the nominalistic austerity of Luther, that "the God who meets us in nature is the God of wrath." There can be little doubt, I think, that the orbit of Heidegger regarding what Stephen Erickson calls the "space of transcendence" is heavily textured by the deconstructed language of the God knowable in terms of the *ens realissimum*, whereas Jaspers's orbit is nominalistic language where God, as the *ens singularissimum*, is known only through the language of the moral law.[11]

This admixture of religious and cultural factors suggests that Farías was on to something important in beginning his study of Heidegger as a Catholic youth in Messkirch and as a Jesuit novice in Freiburg. We forever remain the prisoners of our earliest childhood impressions regarding religion and values—or the lack of the same; and these influences are particularly free to play themselves out in philosophy. But while Farías is correct in suggesting that Heidegger was deeply impressed by a very specific form of German religious ethnocentrism, the philosophical and theological implications of this influence are developed inadequately. For the most telling significance of Heidegger's background, I suggest, consists not in locating the roots of his religious and political consciousness in the conflict between Catholics and "Old Catholics" or in advancing the dubious proposition that Catholics are inherently more anti-Semitic than their Protestant Christian counterparts. The significance rather lies, I think, in recognizing that Heidegger, like many rural south-German Catholics, probably resented deeply the liberal-Protestant, social-democratic, modernist-cosmopolitan, north-German domination of culture, politics, and national identity after the Enlightenment. Thus when Heidegger elevates, as he does in the "Humanismus Brief," the "primordial world-historical" vision of "homelessness" through the "Remembrance" of the Swabian poet Hölderlin, and sets this against the "mere cosmopolitanism" of Goethe as something far more "significant" with respect to the meaning of authentic *humanitas*, we also have the basis for a quite stunning contrast to the liberal humanistic attitude of the north-German Karl Jaspers. Heidegger in fact concludes this oblique observation by saying that because Hölderlin was so much more "the shepherd of Being" than the court poet Goethe, "those young Germans who knew about Hölderlin, when confronted with death [during World Wars I and II], lived and thought something other than what the public held to be the typical German attitude."[12]

Because Heidegger was a south-German Catholic thinker of the highest rank, therefore, he probably believed that the problem of German national identity or *Being*, if you will, had much to do with the gradual usurpation of Catholic influence in the nineteenth and early twentieth centuries, and that the ineptitude of the Weimar Republic represented the decadent culmination of the shift of power from Catholic to Protestant, from south to north. This shift is symbolized politically by the bookends, so to speak, of the 1848 Revolution, namely, Metternich and Bismarck; but it really was a shift that stretched back much further, beyond Frederick the Great and even Luther, through the history of ideas, into Suarezian Thomism and the desperate attempt of the Church to shore up essentialism against the onslaughts of Scotist, Ockhamist, and Baconian nominalism. What was Luther and, indeed, what was Kant and the whole of nineteenth-century German philosophy if not the Protestant working-out of nominalistic *techne* and subjectivist individualism—a working-out that was, a fortiori, the "covering up" of Being? And what was the Reformation and its aftermath if not the turning back of Aristotle by the Pauline-Augustinian version of nominalism instantiated in the *Freiheitsprinzip* of Luther and the commencement of the secularized individualism that would reach its culmination in the twentieth century? To be sure, onto-theology, for Heidegger, commenced with Plato; hence, Heidegger's invitation to reconsider the origins of philosophy out of its pre-Socratic obscurity. Had Heidegger located the "forgetfulness of Being" in the high and late middle ages, which may have been closer to his real intentions, he would not, needless to say, have enjoyed much of a hearing among his Protestant or, indeed his Jewish, colleagues.[13]

One of the more prominently identified reasons for the estrangement between Jaspers and Heidegger is usually located in their differences regarding the place and purpose of the university in the Germany of the 1930s. However, such differences remain superficial, as Krystyna Gorniak-Kocikowska suggests in her discussion of Jaspers and Heidegger on Schelling, unless they are perceived against the horizon of the quite different philosophical vocations of these two thinkers, as these vocations are informed by the meaning of *freedom*. Thus, while both Jaspers and Heidegger, in contrast to many, if not most, of their philosophical contemporaries, made highly influential public pronouncements on the ideas of a university and the civil society, it is the conception of freedom implicit in each that sets them apart. Jaspers's initial statement on *Die Idee der Universität* (1923), published shortly after his first major philosophical work, *Psychologie der Weltanschauungen* (1919), reappeared in expanded form after the war in 1946, and again in 1961, under the same title, in collaboration with Kurt Rossmann.[14] Heidegger, of course, presented his controversial rectorial address on the "The Self-Assertion of the German University" (*Die Selbstbehauptung der Universität*) to the faculty of Freiburg University on May 27, 1933. A regional sensation when first presented, the published text of this address was formally withdrawn from circulation on orders of the *National Socialist Democratic Party* (NSDAP) when the disillusioned Heidegger resigned after ten months as the chief academic officer of the University of Freiburg.[15]

Following the war, of course, and to the chagrin of many of his devoted followers, Heidegger remained conspicuously silent with respect to acknowledging any personal moral culpability for his rectorial address—especially his nationalistic references to the primordial power of "blood and soil" and the "bond of service." Had he dealt with these matters directly and forthrightly, as Marcuse suggested and as Derrida and others have observed, the current scrutiny of his works probably would not be taking place. Certainly it is true that apart from his administrative activities in 1933–1934, Heidegger scarcely ever dealt directly with mundane political matters, remaining aloof from the "sound and fury" in the streets, as is not unusual among philosophers and intellectuals generally. For this reason, many of Heidegger's supporters are inclined to view his political activity as a "misstep" along the lines of the maxim "Fools rush in where angels fear to tread" and that Heidegger, for a moment, at least, was a fool to be duped by the Nazis. Others, less forgiving, including Tom Rockmore and Leonard Ehrlich, contend that

Heidegger's originary work in ontology, however oblique and obscure it might be at times with respect to matters of praxis, has a fundamental political and social implication, and that this implication is negative and morally destructive.

Jaspers, in contrast to Heidegger, was a highly visible and much more conventional moralist throughout his academic career. This was especially true after the war, when he was elected an honorary senator of the reconstituted University of Heidelberg and was also asked, by the Americans, to be the minister of culture—a position he declined in view of his advancing years and his imminent move to Basel. Furthermore, and as we see from his correspondence with Heidegger, Jaspers had mixed feelings about these righteous expectations—as would any citizen given the agonizing circumstances and apocalyptic proportions of the German defeat. As the extremities of Nazi brutality became apparent, however, Jaspers gave voice to what is perhaps the most famous postwar philosophical reflection by a German thinker, namely, Die *Schuldfrage* (1946), in which the moral culpability of all Germans, including intellectuals, is forthrightly acknowledged.[16] Following this, Jaspers continued to deal with a variety of moral and ethical questions having a bearing not only on the future of German and European civilization, but world civilization. Responsive to the obvious dangers of the Cold War but also its inevitability in the face of the terrorism of Stalin and his successors, Jaspers was particularly concerned with the foreboding prospect of thermonuclear holocaust, which he addressed with great perceptiveness in his highly acclaimed Die *Atombombe und die Zukunft des Menschen: Politisches Bewusstsein unserer Zeit* (1958). Here, and in a host of books and treatises wherein he explored the urgent need for moral and spiritual reawakening, Jaspers continued the amplification of themes already established in his highly successful Die *geistige Situation der Zeit* (1931),[17] which, by 1965, had gone through eleven editions. Like Heidegger, Jaspers was a major player in the exploration of basic issues in philosophical anthropology, or the philosophy of man, as it was then called, that so dominated academic discussion during the "time between the times." Unlike Heidegger's esoteric ruminations in fundamental ontology, however, Jaspers's philosophizing on the "grounds of possible Existenz" is exoteric, that is, driven by the desire to communicate in the spirit of liberal humanism, including the "illicit progressivism" it may pressupose, as Joseph Margolis suggests.

Whatever one ultimately makes out of the quality of the personal friendship shared by Jaspers and Heidegger, it was sufficiently close to command the exchange of at least 157 letters, the record of which is now available for public scrutiny through Hans Saner's edition of their *Briefwechsel* (1990). The extremity of their postwar alienation was evident, however, when Jaspers suppressed, in 1957 and until after Heidegger's death, the publication of the section in his "Philosophical Autobiography" containing his personal reflections on Heidegger. Thus when the new "augmented" edition of the Paul Schilpp *Festschrift* appeared in 1981, Heidegger and especially Jaspers scholars were curious to see what Jaspers could have said in 1957 that could not be revealed publicly for nearly twenty-five years.[18]

Those familiar with the philosophical positions of both Jaspers and Heidegger cannot fail to be struck by the extent to which these materials, including Jaspers's *Notizen zu Martin Heidegger* (1978), represent a veritable minefield of philosophical, political, and psychological nuance—only the traces of which are directly evident in the *Briefwechsel*.[19] To make sense of these allusions, one must again recall the nature of their philosophical rivalry during the early years—a rivalry that, at least from the standpoint of Jaspers, was fated not only by the politics that separated them during the Nazi years, but also by their disproportionate recognition as scholars after the war. For at the beginning of their scholarly careers, Jaspers and Heidegger initially shared the common belief (as in the case of Schelling and Hegel—and with a not altogether dissimilar outcome) that they were destined to rejuvenate German philosophy by breaking the bondage of the "dull, threadbare, authoritarian neo-Kantian scholasticism," as Jaspers disdainfully called it, dominating late-nineteenth- and early-twentieth-century German philosophy. As such, both Jaspers and Heidegger believed that they were charting the waters of a newly creative philosophical science and "renewing the *Gestalt* of German philosophy" to the grandeur of its previous existence.

Our essayists explore various aspects of this background, including how both Jaspers and Heidegger, during the tempestuous period during and following World War I, were inspired by common sources in their quest for philosophical originality (namely, Nietzsche, Kierkegaard, Schelling, Husserl, and the romantic German poets and mystics), and how both dedicated themselves to publishing "first works" that the rest of the philosophical world could not safely ignore. Nevertheless, when Jaspers published his *Philosophie* in 1932, Heidegger, six years younger than Jaspers, had already presented *Sein und Zeit* to the world in 1927. As Hans-Georg Gadamer (Jaspers's successor at Heidelberg) observes, Jaspers's three-volume magnum opus, while not "stillborn from the press," so to speak, did not receive the attention it properly deserved. This neglect was due in large measure to with the manner in which Heidegger's *Being and Time* had successfully riveted the attention not only of the philosophical world but the academic world generally.[20] Compared with the "ground-breaking work" of Heidegger, Jaspers's *Philosophie*, published in a three-part form reminiscent of both Kant and Hegel, seemed to his more hostile critics (including Heidegger, who already, in 1919, had severely criticized his *Psychologie der Weltanschauungen* in an unpublished review he shared with Jaspers) an existentialized repristination of German Idealism. As a consequence, Jaspers had to content himself with taking an academic "back seat" to Heidegger. But what probably troubled Jaspers even more following World War II, as Heidegger's philosophical star continued its remarkable ascent, was the psychological pain of coming to terms with the realization that his suppliant position would continue indefinitely, Heidegger's politics notwithstanding. Thus even after the *Katastrophe*, it must have seemed to Jaspers that moral resolve counted for little—especially in academe, as European and American intellectuals alike preoccupied themselves with the formal concerns of analytical philosophy, on the one hand, or flirted with neo-Marxist or primordialist ontologies, on the other. Such options, in Jaspers's view, simply diverted attention from the exigent challenge of "authentic philosophizing on the grounds of possible Existenz," which, for him, always meant moral philosophizing in the spirit of Kant. One cannot fail to detect, as Harold Oliver notes, the hint of deep psychological resentment in Jaspers's personal reflections regarding these issues. Nor can one escape, in the related context Tillich mentions, the sarcastic moral irony embedded in the reflections of Hendrik Pos regarding Heidegger's alleged "snub" of Ernst Cassirer during their 1929 encounter in Davos, Switzerland, as the postwar elevation of Heidegger as the prophet of Being continued.[21]

Questions of Being and value, of course, are both meaning questions, but the modes in which such questions are raised are sometimes disjunctive, as clearly tends to be the case between Jaspers and Heidegger. Therefore, while Jaspers and Heidegger each viewed the university as the morally constitutive institutional agency in Germany after the demoralizing defeat of World War I, they did not agree on *how* this moral reconstruction might best take place or *what* its implications might ultimately be in terms of actualization. Jaspers conceptualized his convictions rather strictly along the lines of the Humboldtian model of a university equally dedicated to both education and research. He also held rather strictly to the Kantian notion that only individuals, not societies or collectivities, can be enlightened—a position not far from Luther's conception that "the good man does good works; good works do not make a man good." Little by way of "moral resolve" is to be expected, therefore, from the university as a corporate entity. Thus when Heidegger embraced the *Führerprinzip* as the means of transforming the essence of the university, Heidegger's "resolve," in the rectorial address, as Tillich observes, becomes highly conspicuous as contrast to what "moral resolve" can be adduced from his otherwise elusive analyses of Being.

The moral pessimism of Max Weber probably served to adumbrate Jaspers's views as to what was and was not properly within the legitimate purview of the university; indeed, after Kant, Weber is the most constant influence in the philosophy of Jaspers. During the years following World War II, Jaspers's critique of *Katholizität*, combined with his relentless critique of totality (which not only influenced Hannah Arendt but also served to endear Jaspers to many conservatives), reinforces his earlier suspicions regarding the messianic pretensions of some intellectuals. Jaspers never tired, therefore, of warning against the usurpation of the independent authority of the university and the thwarting of due process through the nationalistic intrusions of the state. Indeed, Heidegger's repudiation of Jaspers's defense of pacifism within the context of academic freedom, in his first essay on "The Idea of the University," as "the most irrelevant of irrelevancies" was a portent of things to come, whether with respect to the alienation of sentiments between Jaspers and Heidegger or, far more significantly, the disaster that was soon to envelop the entire world.

Like John Cardinal Newman a century earlier, Jaspers believed that the university must be "supra-nationalistic and supra-political" in order to preserve its educational mission in the service of truth. A basic difference between Jaspers and Newman, of course, had to do with the latter's conviction that sponsorship by a supranational hierarchical ecclesiastical institution with its own political agenda might provide this kind of independence.[22] Such an alliance, for Jaspers, is fundamentally in conflict with his Kantian views regarding the freedom and moral autonomy of the individual self-consciousness, however benevolent and well-intentioned the moral authority of the sponsoring institution might appear to be. For Heidegger, on the other hand, the cherished ideal of a wholly detached, autonomous, academic freedom in the service of truth was identical with the elitist-modernist illusion he denounced in his rectorial address. There are no rational or historical grounds, he argues, for assuming that the independence of the research university will provide an island of sanity and hope during periods of national crisis. On the contrary, "there are times," Heidegger says to Jaspers, "when one has to choose" between insular, self-serving notions of academic freedom, on the one hand, and the pursuit of knowledge in the service of what one perceives to be the greater good, on the other.[23] Of course, Heidegger believed that such a choice must be guided by what Heidegger identifies, in his rectorial address, as a "spiritual" apprehension of the "essence" of truth. Unfortunately this "essence," rooted in Heidegger's primordialistic, pre-Socratic understanding of *aletheia*, as both Leonard Ehrlich and Tom Rockmore point out, remains hopelessly obscure. Thus when Heidegger asserts that "Spirit is the primordially attuned resoluteness towards the essence of Being,"[24] such oracular utterances, however mystically sublime they might be, could easily be distorted in the service of their opposite, as indeed turned out to be the case.

These differences do not diminish the fact that both Jaspers and Heidegger were deeply concerned with coming to terms with secularism and the power of technology. On the imminent dangers of technological massification and the deadly implications of "instrumentalist rationality" becoming the lodestar of academic self-understanding, they are entirely agreed.[25] How one might deal with these problems, especially in their advanced, late-modern form, is another matter, and this probably is where a major difference between Heidegger and Jaspers lies. For in the case of Jaspers, morally defensible answers regarding the problems generated by science and technology can arise only through the "loving struggle of communication," that is, in the spirit of dialogical mediation, a notion to which Habermas is deeply indebted. Heidegger, who did not have Jaspers's scientific background and who sometimes seemed to Jaspers grounded in some obscure form of "medieval scholasticism," had considerably less faith in dialectical-dialogical processes. For if the goal of modern academic inquiry is "value free" science, Heidegger asks, how can there be anything like authentic dialogue, since the goal of true dialogue is some kind of intellectual and moral conversion. Heidegger, like Nietzsche, pushes toward a higher, transformatory sense of value—a transformation consistent, he believes, with true *Wissenschaft*, namely, the value-transformed apprehension of Being become manifest in the call to the "spiritual bond of service."

It is at the point of remedy, then, that the conflict between questions of value and questions of Being becomes clearly manifest in Jaspers and Heidegger; and it is a conflict that seems to originate, as Klaus Brinkmann argues, in profound disagreement regarding the nature of the *good*. Given this disagreement, it is not surprising that Jaspers and Heidegger have quite different and conflicting conceptions of freedom and Transcendence, and that these conceptions, given the benefit of hindsight, might be identified with the social and political consequences they seem to entail.

We remain with the question as to whether such dire consequences can be avoided today and in the immediate future. Given the collapse of the dialectic of ideology that has dominated nearly a century of category formation and analysis, do we now have a unique opportunity to develop, in Jaspers's phrase, more encompassing conceptions of freedom and the good that can lead us to more constructive conceptions of praxis? Have we moved beyond the "noumenal sources of privilege and validation" that Joseph Margolis finds objectionable in Heidegger and Jaspers; and are we ready for yet another assault on the "single paradigm of rationality" proposed by Klaus Brinkmann? And what of the role of consensus when such projects are performed within the context of the advanced, liberal democracy? Is it possible even to begin to develop actualizable conceptions of the good during a time in which institutional life has been so devaluated, a time when fewer and fewer people actively identify with what Alasdair MacIntyre calls "the tradition constituted, tradition constituting" universe of critical moral discourse?[26]

The quality of ethical life, as Hegel well understood, depends very largely on the strength and vitality of the institutions of the civil society through which we are given to ourselves. Obviously, neither Jaspers nor Heidegger ever encountered anything like the free-market version of deontological liberalism that increasingly characterizes the advanced postindustrial state. It is clear that both Heidegger and Jaspers were fearful, in their respective ways, that radically deontological approaches to ethics and moral philosophy bereft of the numinous dimensions of "the essence of reason," whether through a "default of thinking" or remaining oblivious to "ciphers of Transcendence," might lead to severe deformations of value. But it is also clear, especially in the case of Heidegger, that "heeding the call of Being" through quasi-archaic modes of renunciation (or what Paul Ricoeur has called "the direct route to ontology") has tremendous risks as the alternative to working out, publicly and prudentially, formally and dialogically, the thorny and seemingly irreconcilable questions of value and Being that appear anew in every age. Indeed, Heidegger's fear of "massification," whether on the American or the Soviet model, led precisely to the uncritical small-scale actualization of the quasi-ontologically grounded nationalism that became synonymous with a terror unparalleled in human history.

Heidegger's arguably "deconstructive manipulation"[27] of the phrase out of Plato's *Republic* (497 d. 9) in the final line of his rectorial address—"All that is great stands in the storm,"—perhaps provides the final irony in this regard, since he neither offered any real criteria for the discernment of "authentic greatness," nor could he foresee how seemingly insignificant, even trivial, rhetorical assertions might be caught up in the vortex of an utterly demonic whirlwind. In this regard, it may be well to heed the superlatives in the utterance of the corporal from Linz when he confidently asserted that "the great masses of the people. . . . will more easily fall victim to a great lie than to a small one." To the horrible truth inherent in this cynical assertion we might might append what seems to be the only available moral conterposition, namely, Jaspers's conviction that "philosophy alone yields clarity against the perversions of reason."[28] By this, Jaspers does not mean that reason itself is perverse; he means rather that many of reason's constructions are perverse, and that this is most likely to happen when the dialectic of value and Being is sundered. Only philosophical faith can hold this dialectic together, and by this he means a faith that is not ready-made nor likely to issue from philosophers who consider themselves members of an "isolated priesthood" in the service of Being. Just as the mature Hegel, in one of his most prudent moments, said that philosophy has to do with "comprehending one's time in thought," so also Jaspers understands that philosophical faith is discovered ever anew on the grounds of possible Existenz and always in the mediating spirit of dialogue.

NOTES

1. Victor Farías, *Heidegger et la nazisme* (Paris: Éditions verdier, 1987). See the English translation by Paul Burrell and Gabriel Ricci, edited by Joseph Margolis and Tom Rockmore, *Heidegger and Nazism* (Philadelphia: Temple University Press, 1989). For a partial list of recent publications on *l'affaire Heidegger*, see the bibliography following Chapter 10 below.

2. See Karl Jaspers, *Notizen zu Heidegger*, ed. Hans Saner (Munich: Piper Verlag, 1978); *Martin Heidegger/Karl Jaspers Briefwechsel*, 1920–1963, ed. Hans Saner (Munich: Piper Verlag, 1990); and *Correspondence, 1926–1969: Hannah Arendt and Karl Jaspers*, trans. Robert and Rita Kimber (New York: Harcourt Brace Jovanovich, 1992).

3. In their earlier forms, the essays contained herein (with the exception of Tillich's) were delivered in conjunction with the annual meetings of the American Philosophical Association Eastern and Pacific Divisions, in 1990–1992, and the annual meeting of the Society for Philosophy and Existential Phenomenology in 1992.

4. I would here like to thank Dr. Mutie Tillich Farris for the permission to publish her father's lecture as the lead essay in this collection. I would also like to thank Dr. Alan Seaburg, director of the Tillich Archive at the Andover Library, Harvard Divinity School, for his kind assistance in securing this permission.

5. See Karl Jaspers, *Kant*, ed. Hannah Arendt (New York: Harcourt Brace Jovanovich, 1962).

6. See Eric Voegelin, "Wisdom and the Magic of the Extreme," *Southern Review* 17, no. 2 (Spring 1981): 235–287.

7. Hans-Georg Gadamer, *Hegel's Dialectic: Five Hermeneutical Studies*, trans. P. Christopher Smith (New Haven: Yale University Press, 1976), pp. 100–116.

8. Ibid., p. 102.

9. See Jaspers's "Philosophical Autobiography," in *The Philosophy of Karl Jaspers*, ed. Paul Schilpp (LaSalle, Ill.: Open Court, 1957), pp. 3–94. I cite this as a

somewhat ironic alliance since Heidegger clearly presented more of a repudiation of Rickert's value theory than Jaspers did. Had Rickert lived beyond the "turning" of Heidegger, he would, no doubt, have reassessed his position. See also Jaspers's preface to the fourth edition of *Psychologie der Weltanschauungen* (Munich: Piper Verlag, 1971).

10. Walter Biemel, *Martin Heidegger*, trans. J. L. Mehta (New York: Harcourt Brace Jovanovich, 1976), pp. 9–16.

11. Adherence to the primacy of the moral law was what make Kantianism popular to many Jewish thinkers since natural, that is, ontological, speculations into the nature of Being, are idolatrous. See William Kluback's analysis of work of the neo-Kantian Hermann Cohen in this regard, in *The Idea of Humanity* (Washington, D.C.: University Press of America, 1987). See also Karl Jaspers, *Chiffren der Transzendenz* (Munich: Piper Verlag, 1970), and the strength of his tribute to the biblical "personal" cipher of God as distinct from the "incarnate" cipher drawn from the mystery cults.

12. See "Letter on Humanism," in *Basic Writings of Heidegger*, ed. David Farrell Krell (New York: Harper and Row, 1977), p. 219.

13. For other aspects of Heidegger's problems with modernity, see Tom Rockmore, *On Heidegger's Nazism and Philosophy* (Berkeley: University of California Press, 1992), especially chap. 6, "Nazism and Technology," pp. 204–243.

14. Jaspers addressed this topic several times in three book-length works and in numerous articles. The 1923 version was reinterpreted and expanded to nearly twice its original length in 1946, in light of the obviously dramatic political, social, and economic changes of the previous decades. This was the work that was translated into English (with some omissions) by H.A.T. Reiche and H. F. Vanderschmidt in 1959 under the title *The Idea of the University* (Boston: Beacon Press). Jaspers again addressed this topic, under the same title, with Kurt Rossmann, in 1961 (Berlin: Springer Verlag).

15. I say "now controversial" because many, including Jaspers, were full of praise at the time of its delivery. See the text of the rectorate together with his postwar reflections in Günther Neske and Emil Kettering, eds., *Martin Heidegger and National Socialism: Questions and Answers*, trans. Lisa Harries with an Introduction by Karsten Harries (New York: Paragon House, 1990), pp. 3–32, 237–238.

16. Even this was "not enough" for some members of the philosophical community—especially exiled surviving Jewish scholars such as Gershom Scholem. See my comments on Gershom Scholem's view of *Die Schuldfrage*, Jaspers's radio lectures preparatory to this treatise, and his condemnation of Jaspers's defense of Hannah Arendt's critique of Zionism during the Eichmann trial in *Transcendence and Hermeneutics* (The Hague: Martinus Nijhoff, 1979), pp. 138–141. One of the problems, of course, is that the German conception of *Schuld* is not directly equivalent to what English-speaking people understand as "guilt"—especially insofar as this term encompasses "shame." Heidegger, in fact, acknowledged this, as Karsten Harries points out in his essay.

17. The "spiritual" motif in Heidegger's rectorial address may, in fact, have been inspired, at least in part, by Jaspers's highly successful text on the same

topic. See also Jacques Derrida's reflections on Heidegger's use of *Geist* and *geistlich* in *Of Spirit: Heidegger and the Question*, trans. Geoffrey Bennington and Rachel Bowlby (Chicago: University of Chicago Press, 1989). Derrida sees the force of Hegel, and also Hölderlin, behind Heidegger's use of "spirit" in this instance; however, the themes developed by Jaspers in *Die geistige Situation der Zeit* (English translation by Eden Paul and Cedar Paul as *Man in the Modern Age* [1933]), are much closer, I think, to the immediate occasion of Heidegger's manifesto in 1933.

18. See "The Library of Living Philosophers" edition of *The Philosophy of Karl Jaspers*, ed. Paul Schilpp (LaSalle, Ill.: Open Court, 1957; augmented edition, 1981).

19. See my article "Jaspers, Heidegger, and the Phantom of Existentialism," in *Human Studies* 7 (1984):387–395.

20. See Hans-Georg Gadamer's essay on "The Phenomenological Movement" (1963), in *Philosophical Hermeneutics*, ed. and trans. David E. Linge (Berkeley: University of California Press, 1976), pp. 130–181.

21. See Hendrik Pos, "Reflections on Cassirer," in *The Philosophy of Ernst Cassirer*, ed. Paul Schilpp (LaSalle, Ill.: Open Court, 1949), pp. 63–72; see also Tillich's comments in this volume.

22. See Jaroslav Pelikan's sustained personal reflection on Newman in *The Idea of a University: A Reexamination* (New Haven: Yale University Press, 1992). While the German model of the university also plays a major role in Pelikan's assessment of Newman vis-à-vis the American university, he makes mention of Jaspers only in his bibliography, and of Heidegger not at all.

23. See Jaspers, "Philosophical Autobiography," in Schilpp, *The Philosophy of Karl Jaspers*, pp. 75/1–75/16.

24. Neske and Kettering, *Martin Heidegger and National Socialism*, p. 9.

25. See again Jaspers's *Man in the Modern Age*; and Heidegger's "The Question Concerning Technology," in *Basic Writings*, pp. 283–318.

26. See Alasdair MacIntyre, *Three Rival Versions of Moral Theory: Encyclopedia, Genealogy, and Tradition* (Notre Dame: University of Notre Dame Press, 1990). MacIntyre argues that only a tradition-based, actual "community of rational discourse" (as distinct from the largely theoretical community of Habermas) can overcome the dialectic of cancellation implicit in the largely privatized discourse of rationalism and irrationalism. The proposals of Margolis and Brinkmann, in order to be effective, need to meet the social/communal test, it would seem.

27. I am indebted to John McCumber on this point.

28. Karl Jaspers, *The Future of Mankind* (Chicago: University of Chicago Press, 1961), p. 209. See further development of this notion in my article "Glasnost and Enlightenment," in *Philosophy Today* (Summer 1990): pp. 99–110.

1   *Heidegger and Jaspers*

Paul Tillich

THE SUBJECT of my lecture tonight is Heidegger and Jaspers.[1] I believe that Heidegger is one of the great figures in the history of Western thought, and for this reason I have made him the primary subject of this lecture. Karl Jaspers, on the other hand, is one of the noblest figures in the history of contemporary thought, and I want to deal with him for a special purpose, namely, to clarify some of the confusion associated with existentialism—especially the matter of ethics.

Jaspers is driven by the question of humanity: What does it mean to be human? How shall man interpret himself? Jaspers does not come to these questions incidentally, for before he became a professor of philosophy at Heidelberg, he was a psychiatrist of major standing. In addition to his psychological interest in human identity, Jaspers is driven by ethics, and this ethical passion, whether individual ethics or social ethics, appears throughout his writings. This ethical interest is not merely theoretical; it arises out of his personal life. Jaspers demonstrated in practice what he affirmed in theory when he resisted spiritually the Hitler period from beginning to end, and under very difficult conditions and circumstances.

Heidegger, on the other hand, is driven by the question of Being: What does it mean when we say something *is*? What does Being mean? He attempts to penetrate into the ultimate structure of Being. Man, for Heidegger, is the doorway to the mystery of Being, and he enters into this path with all the powers of his great philosophical mind. But man is not himself the theme or the subject at the center of this inquiry. At the center is Being and nothing but Being. The world, according to Heidegger, is continuously veiling and unveiling, covering and uncovering, Being. The universe, therefore, is interesting to Heidegger, but not in and of itself. It is interesting rather as revealing and concealing Being. God also is a problem about which Heidegger expresses himself negatively, that is, always in terms of a question and never positively. To illustrate, I remember one evening, when we were colleagues in Marburg, Heidegger presented a paper. The next morning, I took a walk with him, and he asked me what I thought about it (incidentally, it was one of the best he ever gave). To his surprise I told him, "You gave a sermon last night, an atheistic sermon, but couched entirely in the phraseology of early German Pietism." He understood immediately what I meant and accepted it. This ambiguity in Heidegger's relationship to God persists throughout his work, for his interest is not theology but ontology, the question of Being and nothing other than Being.

We can thus generalize by saying that Heidegger wants to know what it means *to be* whereas Jaspers wants to know what it means *to be a person*. This means that the relationship between them is dialectical, for in order to know the answer to the question of Being, one must know what it means to be a person, and to know what it means to be a person, one must know what it means to be. The questions are not exclusive but different in emphasis. Moreover, when I now attempt to explain something about Heidegger's way of approaching the mystery of Being, it is necessary to remember how one must deal with any truly creative thinker. One does not merely restate his problems and proposed solutions, make a few comments and criticisms and, having done so, believe one has accomplished anything of significance. Certainly this is not the way one deals with the likes of Heidegger or any other great philosopher in the classical tradition. For such individuals are deemed great not only because of what has been judged, measured by our measure, to be correct about their thinking. Such thinkers are also great in terms of their errors. The error of a thinker like Nietzsche, for example, is more important than the small truths of hundreds of insignificant philosophers! For this reason I ask you *not* to dismiss the profundity, the difficulty, and the greatness of such thinkers by some trivial comment regarding their mistakes. This can always be done about everyone. The true task is to participate in the creative process of their thinking, for this is the only way to be fair to them and to their work.

Now I come to the basic question asked by Heidegger again and again, a question asked in many ways and asked differently by him in his different periods, but it is always the same question: *Why is there something and not nothing*? This question, to many, sounds absurd, but it is the question asked by philosophers from the beginning. And the question would indeed be absurd if one took the "why" in "why is there something and not nothing" literally. Such a question, of course, cannot be answered and perhaps would be even more absurd if it could be answered. The question therefore is not a logically answerable question so much as it is an *outcry*, the expression of [ontological] shock. And this shock is the birthplace of all philosophical thinking; it is the philosophical shock of the individual who, for the first time, has encountered the possibility that there might be nothing, or that there might have been nothing, and then asks the question: "What does it mean that there is something?" This is the sense of Heidegger's question, and it is a question that should not be rejected because of its logically impossible form but because it is a question that must be asked since it is the question that makes the philosopher a true philosopher. Those who have *never* experienced the shock implied by this question can never call themselves philosophers, even if they know the history of philosophy by heart.

What then is this Being in opposition to Nonbeing? Why is there something and not nothing? *Being* is to be understood in two ways. First, it can be understood as the highest genus of things. We can say that there are plants and there are individuals and that together they are living beings; and we can say that there are stones and that both living and nonliving beings are beings. Thus we have being as the highest possible abstraction, and, as the highest possible abstraction, this notion of being is also the emptiest, as Aristotle pointed out. This emptiness would mean that it is also meaningless to ask what this term is since it is simply empty abstraction. Nevertheless, this is not the question regarding Being which produces ontological shock. Being, when it produces philosophical shock, has to do with apprehending the *power* of Being, the power which means that there is something and not nothing, the power which resists Nonbeing, and it is a power present in all beings. I like to quote from Goethe when he says, "Have you ever noticed how *being* things are?" Now this cannot be understood easily in any language, whether German or English. What he means, however, has to do with the power of Being in things, for example, in a living being, be it plant or animal. That is what the question of Being points to—not as the emptiest of abstractions or the emptiest of concepts, but as something which produces astonishment even in children, who are, in fact, far more metaphysical than most adults: Why is there something and not nothing?

If this is the basic philosophical question, then we understand why it must be pursued as a matter of passionate thinking by everyone, since it is the most universal, the most fundamental, of all questions. As such, it must be distinguished from all other questions, for example, the question of what things are as particular species beings, whether stones or stars, plants or animals. Such things also exist, but this is not the philosophical question. The philosophical question is what gives all these beings the power of Being? Heidegger is of the opinion that very early in the history of philosophy these questions were confused. For the pre-Socratics, the question of Being was decisive; but by the time of Plato it was the different forms of being, the species of beings and their characteristics, their movement, matter, and form, which became decisive. Thus the question of Being is continuously being subverted, according to Heidegger, by the question of beings.

From this standpoint, Heidegger has a very interesting view of the history of Western thought. He notes that after the early Greek philosophers, such as Anaximander, Heraclitus, and especially Parmenides, after this archaic period, something happened which is akin to a *fall* from the creative origin, a fall in which the fundamental question of Being is lost and replaced by the question of beings and their characteristics. Thus the entire history of philosophy, for Heidegger, is the history of deterioration rather than progress in thinking—just the opposite of what progressivists hold to be the case.

Of course, Heidegger knows that history is not simply fall and deterioration. History is rather itself the witness to the self-concealment of Being. He has a beautiful image for this process when he says that man is the "shepherd of Being" and must "take care of Being," and that history, especially the history of thought, is witness to how well this is done. Man, therefore, gives Being a place to be, so to speak, a self-expression, a power to become actual in time and space. So human history, especially the history of thinking, which includes not only philosophy but also poetry (as, for example, in the case of Hölderlin, to whom he has dedicated so much thought and interpretation), is the decisive arena within which this revelation takes place. The history of thinking, therefore, is both a self-manifestation of the power of Being or the ground of Being, on the one hand, and the history of its deterioration, the arena of creation and failure, on the other. Because he believes that the original authentic question of Being has been lost, has gone into concealment, Heidegger dedicates himself to the continuous restatement of the question.

This leads to a consideration of another powerful Heideggerian metaphor, namely, his notion that "language is the house of Being." By this he means that Being habitates in language, in language Being finds its home, its dwelling. Heidegger's philosophy of language and world is one of the most interesting aspects of his thinking. He is a philosopher of the word. For him, as for the ancient Greeks, Being and the word which grasps Being belong together. He always feels that the miracle of Being and the miracle of language are somehow identical, that our language is able to grasp reality because Being gives itself to us through language, that language and Being are not asunder but belong to each other. In the word, the mystery of Being, the mystery that there is something and not nothing, finds its illumination like the clearing in the forest. Darkness becomes light in human language. Heidegger believes in the quest for the authentic word, since not every word has this power and one must search for the proper words.

Heidegger himself is very creative with language. When he published his first book, *Sein und Zeit*, his language seemed strange to many readers. When we told him so, he responded by saying, "But look at the language of Aristotle's *Metaphysics* and think about *his* language in contrast with the ordinary language of his time!—then you will see that the philosopher *needs* a language through which he is able to enter into the depths of reality." Obviously, one of the sad ramifications of this situation is that his great book, *Sein und Zeit*, remains [1954] untranslated—not because people are uninterested, but because no one is capable of doing so. For twenty years, people have been talking about the need for this translation; but it seems nearly impossible to do so. Indeed, it often seems impossible to translate him into understandable German!

The reason this is the case has to do with Heidegger's conviction (and I agree with him on this) that there are certain words for which there are no equivalents in translation. I remember a discussion I had with Martin Buber on what he called *Urwörter*, that is, original words which arise out of the depths of human experience and cannot be translated. For example, a word like *God* is such an *Urwört*, according to Buber, and Heidegger would agree. One of the unfortunate things about our civilization, with its instant public communication, is the deterioration of language, the loss of the dimension of depth in speaking, the loss of an understanding of the symbols and expressions in and through which one encounters reality, for every language is the product of the contact of mind and reality. Thus every language is already a prephilosophical philosophy, and no language, therefore, can be completely translated into another because it is *another* kind of encounter between mind and reality. From this point of view we must always understand *why* Heidegger always tries to go back to the original meaning of words. Critics object that this is very artificial, but it is, in fact, highly revealing if one tries to do it. Ask yourselves, for example, what the ordinary words you use on a daily basis mean in their original settings and their original conceptual condition, to the extent this can be known.

In order to say something about Being, in order to deal with the mystery of mysteries, one must have an entering door or a key to that door. That key is man himself, who experiences the structures of being through his humanity. But the statements about man in Heidegger are not meant to be a philosophical anthropology or doctrine of man. He is not interested in man *qua* man, as I've already pointed out. He is interested in that being who is able to ask the question of Being or, as he expresses it in another phrase, "Man is that being concerned about Being." For this reason and this reason alone, man is the key or the doorway to the question of Being or ultimate reality.

How then is it possible for man to raise the question of Being? The answer has to do with the fact that man has within himself both the existence he is and the possibility to ask the question about the nature of this existence. In order to show that Being is in us and for us, Heidegger enters into a discussion of what he calls *existentalia*, that is, those things which make humans exist the way they do. Now the first and most basic of these *existentalia*, for Heidegger, is time. Everything that exists, exists in time. Like some of his great predecessors, most notably Saint Augustine, the problem of time is central for Heidegger. The same is true of Kant, and so Heidegger attempts to interpret Kant from this point of view in *Kant and the Problem of Metaphysics*, one of his most profound books. But it is Heidegger speaking here and not Kant, and he admits this in the preface. Interpretation, if it is to be creative and successful, must be more than mere repetition. True interpretation is always the creation of something new, something which emerges between the text being interpreted and the interpreter. This, Heidegger knows very well indeed, and thus he goes back to Kant in order to show the significance of time for his own work.

There are other elements, other *existentalia*; most notably selfhood, the possibility of being oneself. Existence is always, as Heidegger insists, *my* existence or *your* existence—the existence of a particular subject. It is never just existence-in-general: I am the existent, it is *my* existence because I am not a mere thing, an object, but one who can become a self or lose oneself. Heidegger provides a lucid description of what it means to lose oneself. This he does by describing man's being with others in a world. But this being-in-a-world has the character of being with others and not being by oneself. He characterizes this condition with a word which does not exist in English, *das Man*, that is, the "general one" existing like everyone else—the *on* in French or the average existence. Thus man, who has the possibility of being himself and being authentic by himself, is also able to lose this possibility and usually does by being nonauthentic, content to be one-among-the-group, one amongst others. Existence, therefore, has above all to do with the possibility of becoming a self and, for this very reason, losing oneself. Heidegger's description of losing oneself has many aspects—one of which, for example, has to do with "idle talk," which is the kind of talk in which everything profound is reduced to everydayness, thus losing its profundity and true meaning. Another characteristic is ambiguity, since no concept can be exactly what it is but drifts into the various possibilities in which we find ourselves through everyday talk.

The question is "why" the idle talk and ambiguity of daily life? The answer is that we "flee into it," that is, we choose it. There is the flight from oneself into *das Man* and the average talk and the average form of being. And this flight arises from another aspect of our existence, namely, *Angst*, or anxiety in the sense of Kierkegaardian *dread*—the anxiety of being oneself drives us to flee to others, to idle talk, to the average existence, where the authentic self is hidden.

This anxiety is not fear. Fear is the fear *of something*, the somethings that occur in the average reality at every moment. Anxiety in the proper sense (*Angst*) has to do with the anxiety of being-in-a-world, of being finite, of being a mixture of Being and Nonbeing, of being threatened by death, by guilt, by care, by being anxious, and all the other characteristics of our being. This distinction between fear and anxiety is a fundamental distinction in existentialism and is very sharply elaborated by Heidegger. Anxiety is not anxiety of something but is the anxiety of being in the world, of being with others, of being thrown, as he says, into the world, of being thrown upon oneself and made responsible for oneself. This situation is the situation of anxiety in the proper existentialist sense; not the fear of something specific. If one has the fear of some specific thing, one can deal with it. But it is not this way with the anxiety of being in the situation of the lonely self thrown upon oneself and made responsible for oneself.

Now the most conspicuous form of existential anxiety is the anxiety of having to die. Heidegger's philosophy of death is one of the greatest sections in *Sein und Zeit* (§§46–53), his fundamental book. In this section he makes one basic distinction, and it is so central to existentialism that I want to develop it here briefly. In this section Heidegger asserts that we experience permanently the death of others as an event like any other event. We may not like to think so, but it is true. We read about death in the newspapers, in the obituaries. We hear about it everywhere, including the death of friends, of the people whom we love and to whom we are very dear. But it is always the other who dies. In contrast to the death of others, the anticipation of our *own* death is something absolutely different. If we look at the death of others, then it is simply the event of the life of someone else coming to an end, something that happens to everyone. But when we consider our own death, we experience the anxiety of our *own* finitude, of our being-for-death, of something that can and will happen to me.[2]

In contrast to all other beings, man is able to anticipate his own death through an act of reflection. He runs forward to it, and this has tremendous consequences. Only because we anticipate our death can we know ourselves as a whole, as a totality. This totality of our being and how we see ourselves as a totality can be perceived from only one point, the point at which I (the self) actually come to an end. And since we alone among all sentient beings can anticipate this point (everyone anticipates this end in one way or another), we can, in the anticipation of this point, look back at the totality of our being and how we see ourselves as a totality, as a whole. So to be human, to be a person, to be existing in this sense, to be thrown upon ourselves, is at the same time to look back from the anticipated moment of our death, the totality of our being, the point of my death and not the death of someone else.

Another characteristic connected with man's being thrown upon himself has to do with what we call *conscience*. Conscience, here, is not a tribunal which judges us. Conscience, for Heidegger, is a call, a summons to be what we are authentically: to be ourselves. This call which goes to you and to me to be ourselves and not something else, to be something which is not covered up by everydayness, idle talk, average behavior, and the conventional way of dealing with people. The call of conscience does not judge anything in particular. Conscience, for Heidegger, rather has to do with a fundamental phenomenon, more profound than any specific judgment about which one might have a so-called bad conscience. Conscience is the "silent call," as he says, "to be ourselves." It has no special contents or words; it is not the voice of God; it is the call to be what we are authentically. This silent call calls us out of the average talk of everydayness, its ambiguities and its shallowness.

Where there is conscience there is the consciousness of *guilt*. Here again it is not guilt about anything particular of which he speaks, but the guilt of losing oneself. Guilt is judged by conscience but not by conscience in the case of judging special things or events of which we might be guilty. Guilt is rather the inescapable situation of being the kind of being which we ourselves are, of being thrown into being and not being able to rely only upon ourselves. Our guilt is our nonauthentic being, and our conscience is our call to return to our authentic being, namely, to be a self. Thus Heidegger can say, "The call of the conscience is the call to have the courage to be guilty," because in the moment we take upon ourselves the need to be authentic, we also become guilty over-against the norms and rules by which we are living. Hence he calls for *resoluteness* to be oneself, to confront one's guilt, to heed the silent call of our conscience. This resoluteness is the courage to be oneself, to become guilty. It is obedience to the silent call of our conscience to be authentic and not only to be a part of the universal, general, average existence.

In *resoluteness* the authenticity of our being arises, a resoluteness which consists, according to Heidegger, in risking ourselves through the anticipation of our death. The problem is that this resoluteness has no specific criteria, and I am now at the point where I want to say something critical about Heidegger's *Daseinsanalytik*. I do not think that it is wrong; I think that Heidegger's analysis uncovers an abundance of profound insights into the human condition. But I also believe that one critical element is left out, namely, the normative element and criteria for judgment. Heidegger's resoluteness remains without direction—and this is what we find common to all existentialists insofar as they are existentialists and nothing more. Existentialists analyze the human situation, they analyze human finitude, temporality, death, anxiety, guilt, despair, *Sorge* or being anxious, and so forth. This they know and know better than entire generations of theological thinkers have known about such things. They have rediscovered dimensions of reality long-forgotten and long-overlooked, namely, *our* reality. But in the moment when they attempt to go beyond these insights, in the moment they attempt to transcend the realm of their analyses and try to provide answers, they necessarily fail. This is particularly obvious in Heidegger's conception of resoluteness. Courage, being-towards-death, resoluteness to be authentic—all these things are clear enough. But if you ask, "Now what?" there is no answer, because existing norms are dissolved in a concept of freedom which has no norms but is understood only as pure possibility—the situation radicalized by Sartre. Heidegger himself has made such a move in his later writings, a move, I believe, also present in his earlier writings, which amplifies this problem—even though some historians of philosophy think that the later Heidegger's mystical interpretation of Being is something new. But it is already present in his notions regarding the "shepherd of Being" and "language as the house of Being," which clearly have religious, mystical overtones. For Heidegger always goes beyond the mere analysis of human existence to Being-Itself, even though he never says *what* it is. Nevertheless, few formulations of Being are as profound as the manner in which he raises the question of Being. Thus, I like to compare his most recent period of thinking with that of a ship cruising around an island. The island is in a fog, he wants to approach it, to find out what it is, but he cannot go to it and he cannot see it. This is what Being is for Heidegger: it is mystery and nothing but mystery. But as mystery it is still the ultimate power.

Some of you might now ask the question: How does all this relate to Heidegger's personal life and to the fact that in the beginning of the Nazi period he became the Nazi rector of the University of Freiburg? To this question I want to say, first, something of a general nature: One should not judge the worth of a philosopher only in terms of the political shortcomings of one's life. We have, for example, the caricatures of the great ancient philosophers, Socrates and Aristotle, and knowledge of the fact that even Plato was foolish enough to become an advisor to the Hitler of his time, the Tyrant of Syracuse. In spite of these facts, one cannot identify the worth of a philosopher merely with the personal decisions of daily existence, the terms and circumstances of which are constantly changing.

Nevertheless one cannot avoid the connection between Heidegger's philosophy and the political decision he made when National Socialism came to power, namely, this idea of *resoluteness*. At that moment Heidegger found a lot of resolve, more than he had ever found before. But this resoluteness was, as *we* would say, demonic; that is, it was destructive, antiessential, and without moral justification. And it was this way precisely because Heidegger had no criterion by which to measure his resolve. Two years prior to Hitler's coming to power there was a very interesting discussion in Switzerland between Cassirer and Heidegger.[3] This discussion probably reveals as much about the situation as can be shown, namely, the conflict between one who, like Cassirer [and Jaspers], came from Kantian moral philosophy with rational criteria for thinking and acting, and one who, like Heidegger, defended himself on the notion that there are no such criteria. A year later Cassirer was in exile and Heidegger was the rector of Freiburg.

Now this illustration is philosophically, and not merely biographically, important, otherwise I would not mention it. It is philosophically important because it shows how pure existentialism cannot provide any answers in the area of moral philosophy and ethics. Sartre, for example, was not in the resistance movement because this was in accord with his moral maxim, as his novels clearly show. Sartre was in the resistance simply because it was an action, an action which liberated him from the dreadful freedom in which he could not find the basis for decision or direction.

Existentialism therefore needs something beyond the mere questioning and analysis of existence. It needs criteria, it needs a sense of ultimacy. And this brings me to a consideration of Karl Jaspers on one very basic problem—the problem which both Jaspers and Heidegger call *Transcendence*. Transcendence means "going beyond," reaching over, transcending something. In Heidegger this concept of Transcendence is highly temporalized and very futuristic as evidenced by the notion of "running ahead to one's own death." Transcendence for Jaspers, who comes from the classical humanistic tradition, is much more spatialized and vertical, having to do with the apprehension of what he calls the *embracing* or the *all-encompassing*—with the reality of something beyond the dichotomies and contradictions within the mundane world, especially the split between subject and object. Jaspers offers a humanistic description of the idea of God, and he asks the question as follows: If the all-comprehensive, all-encompassing, is beyond subject and object, and if we finite individuals are condemned to always live within the subject-object split, how can we say *anything* about the comprehensive Transcendence? Jaspers's answer is as follows: We know by way of *ciphers*, or *symbols* (he uses both terms), of Transcendence. In the symbol, he says, Being-Itself is present, and it is there and only there that you can find it. And Transcendence is present in its fullest power, in its highest power, just where it appears in sense perceptions. The visible symbol, therefore, is the place where the all-embracing Transcendence reveals itself to us. Thus the symbol, he says, opens itself up for Being and shows us the depths of Being; it opens our soul and opens us to the depth of reality. Every symbol, therefore, is infinite in meaning, and the symbolic cannot be replaced by the nonsymbolic. Artistic and religious symbols cannot be reduced to concepts. The symbol is rather the genuine form of Transcendence, and it is the only form through which we can approach ultimate reality. But in order to preserve the power of symbols, one must avoid deviations from their true meaning—and there are many such deviations. First, one cannot understand symbols such as God, Christ, or the Kingdom of God literally as objects. If you take them as objects, if you locate them in time and space, they lose their power and become absurd. Symbols must be understood very strictly as symbols. Neither must one think of symbols as allegories in order to substitute for the language of symbols another language which is not symbolic. What is expressed in symbols can only be expressed in symbols; there is no other way of doing it. Symbols cannot therefore be reduced to the language of concepts. Neither must one use symbols simply as occasions for aesthetic enjoyment, that is, perceive symbols for pleasure in order to be aesthetically *elevated* by them. Symbols reduced aesthetically lose their revelatory power with respect to ultimacy. Nor, finally, should symbols become simply the basis for dogma, as dogma becomes a substitute for the authentically revelatory that can only appear through the power of a cipher or symbol.

Because of their unique properties, ciphers or symbols, according to Jaspers, are able to point us beyond the world in which we live, are able to overcome in a partial or fragmentary way the subject-object dichotomy and the anxiety and ambiguity it produces. Jaspers therefore uses these existentialist terms and categories as much as Heidegger. But in contrast to Heidegger, Jaspers does not believe that philosophy can help us to overcome this limit. Philosophy has only the power to question, to analyze and diagnose, to show us the wrongness of human existence.

Philosophy also has the power to provide answers by pointing in the direction of what is right and good; but it does not, of itself, have the power to elevate us beyond the subject-object dichotomy of human existence.

And this leads me to my final point: When you deal with existentialists, don't go to them in order to find answers. The answers one finds in the later Heidegger, for example, do not come from existentialism but from the medieval Catholic mystical tradition within which he lived as a seminarian. The answers one finds in Jaspers come not from existentialism but from the classical humanist tradition or, more precisely, German Idealism; and the answers one finds in Gabriel Marcel come not from existentialism, but from classical Catholic orthodoxy. So also the answers one might find in Kierkegaard come from Pietistic Lutheranism, and in Nietzsche, from the philosophy of life with all of its romantic ambiguities and divine-demonic dimensions. Or if you take the early Marx and call him an existentialist, as I would do, then it is the classical tradition of the revolutionary sect going back to biblical propheticism which motivates him.

All of these answers are derived not from existentialism but from religious traditions. What, then, have the analyses of existentialism done for me, speaking now as a Protestant theologian, and what can they do for you? They have done something of great significance. They have opened up again the situation of what it means to be human, opened the entire realm of the question, and that man himself is *the question* whether he asks it or not. In this realm, the realm of the question, we see life in its questionable character, in its contradictions, in its anxiety and despair. And by opening up the question regarding the existential situation, existentialism has once again illumined the answers of the past— answers which cannot be understood if you take them only as traditional answers. Such answers can be understood only if one understands them as being embedded in our own existence. This is true in the entire educational realm: no answer is an answer if there is not a question for which it is, in fact, the answer.

Much education today is wrong precisely for this reason: Contents are thrown at students as answers for questions which have never been raised or explored. Now this situation is improved through existentialist analysis which has shown us again that we ourselves are the question—the question of existence and Being! Only having discovered this question can students began to understand that traditional symbols were the answers to just such questions, the question that we ourselves are. For this reason we should be grateful, whatever our stand on the answers, that the existentialists, and here not only philosophers but even more so dramatists, artists, and poets, have opened before us once again the human condition with all its problems, its anxiety, its guilt and despair, and everything that is connected with it. Only by dealing with the questionability of the human situation, therefore, can we rediscover not only what the answers of tradition originally meant, but also what they mean for us today as they put before us the task of deciding which answers speak to our question, the fundamental question in which we as individuals participate, the universal question of existence and Being.

EDITOR'S NOTES

1. This lecture was originally given at the Cooper Union Forum in New York City on March 25, 1954. It is published here for the first time with the kind permission of Paul Tillich's daughter, Dr. Mutie Tillich Farris. Words in brackets are the insertions of the editor.

2. This is why Jaspers called death the "ultimate boundary situation" since, as the "death of experience," it is the only thing we cannot experience. See *Philosophy*, Book 2, Part 3, Section 2 (Chicago: University of Chicago Press, 1971).

3. The encounter to which Tillich refers took place at Davos, Switzerland, in 1929, and is described in some detail by the Dutch philosopher Hendrik Pos in "Reflections on Cassirer." One could, in fact, substitute Jaspers for Cassirer in this description, since Pos presents Cassirer as the noble representative of northern European liberal culture, with Heidegger sarcastically portrayed as the representative "of *petit bourgeois* descent from southwest Germany"—a "gloomy somewhat whinning and apprehensive" man "who despised Goethe" and "who never lost his accent." After a heated debate on Kant's first critique, with Cassirer focusing on spiritual liberation by way of the moral law vis-à-vis Heidegger's obscure ruminations on a metaphysical comprehension of Being, "the magnanimous man [Cassirer] offered his hand to his opponent," according to Pos, "But it was not accepted." See *The Philosophy of Ernst Cassirer*, ed. Paul Schilpp (LaSalle, Ill.: Open Court, 1949), pp. 63–72.

It is also reported on the Tillich transcript that while returning to Union Theological Seminary following the lecture, Tillich told his students that political judgments regarding Heidegger's relationship to National Socialism are necessarily muddled owing to his wife's enthusiasm for the Nazis, namely, that Heidegger "did not have the courage to resist." Conversely, Jaspers's wife was Jewish, and this fact has raised doubts in the mind of some, for example, Gershom Scholem, regarding the nature and quality of his resistance. Commenting on the reception of Jaspers's *Die Schuldfrage* and in the wake of Jaspers's defense of Hannah Arendt's critique of the Eichmann trial, for example, Scholem said, "It was not enough." See my *Transcendence and Hermeneutics* (The Hague: Martinus Nijhoff, 1979), pp. 139–141, for more on Scholem's assessment of Jaspers and Heidegger.

2

Heidegger's Philosophy of Being from the Perspective of His Rectorate

Leonard H. Ehrlich

1

THE QUESTION raised by Heidegger's brief involvement with the Nazi regime has accompanied his spreading fame and influence worldwide. Sometimes the question lies dormant, sometimes it flares up. Yet curiously, before anyone gets to the bottom of the matter, the question recedes into dormancy, for reasons that have become typical.

For example, attention is drawn to Heidegger's *thinking*, which has been a movement from one thought to another, challenging the fascinated reader to follow, penetrate, absorb, assimilate, only to be faced with having to grasp the next newly published thought and trying to see its relation to what came before. And by drawing attention to Heidegger's thinking, the question raised by his Nazi involvement is deflected in one of a number of ways. Either one says that his thought is one thing, his personal actions another, having no bearing on the former; or else one trivializes his Nazi involvement, saying it was a misstep out of the innocence of one who was apolitical or politically naive, and hence has no bearing on his thought; or else one disregards Heidegger's political misstep by not exposing oneself to those who raise the issue or even by discrediting them, by sidestepping the issue when faced with it, or by urging the overriding importance of Heidegger, especially in regard to his clarification of the modernity that made Nazism possible in the first place. Some have also suggested that after his brief association with the Nazi regime Heidegger was the nucleus of an internal resistance to it.

The question raised by Heidegger's association with Nazism is serious. The way to take it seriously is to face it on Heidegger's own terms, that is, by taking his thinking, elusive though it is, seriously. Attempts to meet Heidegger on his own terms have so far not succeeded. Why? One who succeeds in the Herculean task of mastering Heidegger's thought can be expected to be so caught up in it that he loses a requisite measure of critical distance. Heidegger's sense of phenomenology in fact means to take thought beyond the sort of reflection that is needed for critical distance: Criticism is thought about thought, and thus doubly removed from Being; but, according to Heidegger, it is the calling of thought to be at the disposal of Being, simply and without any presuppositions. One cannot be expected to spend a major portion of one's lifetime mastering a way of thinking for no other reason than to expose the limits of its significance. But if it is daunting to attain an informed critical distance, it is much more unlikely that one can muster the capacity and the patience to see whether Heidegger's misstep might spell the bankruptcy of his thinking. And in the unlikely event that one would make any significant headway toward seeing this, one would run the risk of being dismissed as an unfair spirit, and there is little likelihood that one would convince anyone but oneself and the like-minded.

But Heidegger is too important a thinker. We cannot pursue our own thinking in distinction from his by leaving him aside. We have to permit him to challenge us, and, taking him seriously, we must clarify our opposition in terms of the questions and configurations that form the basis of his thinking.

Heidegger's thought is rightly regarded as one of the most decisive reorientations of philosophy in these times that are in dire need of such. Many who for this reason are influenced by Heidegger, are incredulous when faced with the fact of Heidegger's misstep.

One of the typical reactions was, What do these facts matter? With the Nazi assumption of power in 1933, Germans were swept up in the *Aufbruchstimmung*, the mood of national resurgence, and Heidegger was no exception.

We answer: But there were exceptions, and among leading academics these silent exceptions may have been the rule. Even if there had not been any such exceptions, the fact remains that it is Heidegger to whom being swept up by this Nazi-induced mood is attributed. But Heidegger's actions as rector of his university showed that he was not merely riding the wave of enthusiasm. Rather, he saw in the regime of the now-empowered Nazi movement the condition and the momentum for reawakening the German nation's spirit to a forgotten but merely slumbering openness to Being. To him Germany was the nation gifted with the language that is the abode of Being as no language had been since that of the Greeks before Socrates. As it happened, the regime Heidegger had meant to use was not at his disposal; in fact, it used him and was glad to be rid of him when he resigned, his extraordinary usefulness to the regime having come to an end. But it is the Nazis and no other political actuality that Heidegger saw as a fitting instrument for the realization of the German spirit's reversion to its special destiny in the history of Being. Therefore, as I see it, it is not a matter of *tu quoque*, the question as to whether Heidegger was any different from others in being caught up in the mood of resurgence. The question we must ask Heidegger is: why the Nazi movement as the clearly perceived vehicle for recalling the German mind to Being?

Various are the modes of *tu quoque* applied to the case of Heidegger in order to shield his philosophy of Being from the significance of his misstep. One is to attribute endorsements of Heidegger to persons whom the public would expect to be especially sensitive to what Heidegger's misstep implies, especially Jews. A prime example, though by no means the only one, is Hannah Arendt's address on the occasion of Heidegger's eightieth birthday, in 1969, a few months after Jaspers's death.[1] But Arendt's appraisal of Heidegger's involvement with Nazism can be discerned more clearly in Arendt's correspondence with Jaspers than in an uninformed reading of that address. Given the occasion, the address tends to be generous to Heidegger. (The last time I spoke with Jaspers, a half-year before his death, I touched upon his relation to Heidegger. In this connection I asked him how he would explain Arendt's postwar contact with Heidegger. He replied that one has to understand Arendt's sovereignty of mind.) Reading the Arendt/Jaspers correspondence provides a good antidote to the usual reading of the address. According to the way it is usually received, it is an exoneration of Heidegger's misstep, a reverse *tu quoque* in which Heidegger looks good compared to others, and a liberation of his thought from any questions raised by his misstep. And of course this imputed exoneration is invariably held out as most significant coming as it does from a Jew—again a variant of the *tu quoque* phenomenon.

But what Arendt actually does in that address is to draw a comparison between Heidegger and others who did not, even after the event, seek to recognize the nature of Nazism as a phenomenon of modernity. And who would not sense the irony in the following series of statements, an irony that is not contrived but lies in the nature of Arendt's assessment: "[Heidegger] was still young enough to learn from the shock of the collision, which after ten short months . . . drove him back to his abode, and to settle in his thinking what he had experienced.[2] Arendt then tells of Heidegger's discovery of the "will," and continues: "No one before Heidegger saw how much [the will] stands opposed to thinking and affects it destructively. To thinking there belongs 'Gelassenheit'—serenity, composure, release, . . . in brief, a disposition that 'lets be.' "[3] This

Eckhardian phenomenon of *Gelassenheit* is, of course, a highly important aspect of the later Heidegger's thinking about what calls for thinking. But after briefly considering this, Arendt says: "We who wish to honor thinkers, even if our own abode lies in the midst of the world, can hardly help finding it striking and perhaps exasperating that Plato and Heidegger, when they entered into human affairs, turned to tyrants and Führers."[4] What I wish to advert to in this passage is not that Heidegger's turning to Hitler should give us pause, and not the misleading parallel of Plato/Dion and Heidegger/Hitler. Rather it is, first, that the "thinkers" are being honored; it is, secondly, that the "thinkers" misstep when "they enter into human affairs," misstep because they are nothing other than thinkers to whom, as "thinkers," willing is destructive of thinking; and it is, thirdly, that unlike they who are the "thinkers," "we," the ones who wish to honor the "thinkers," have "our own abode . . . in the midst of the world." Therein lies the irony: Heidegger is vaunted as the thinker, Heidegger is charged with being merely thinker. And, honoring the "thinker" from her "abode . . . in the midst of the world," Arendt dismisses him, in her final words, to *his* abode: "[It] does not . . . matter where the storms of [his] century may have driven [him]. For the wind that blows through Heidegger's thinking . . . does not spring from the century he happens to live in. It comes from the primeval, and what it leaves behind is something perfect, something which, like everything perfect, falls back, in Rilke's words, to where it came from."[5]

We can recognize here the idea Arendt was developing at that time, the idea of "The Life of the Mind," the mind whose "abode lies in the midst of the world," and as such is not only "thinking," but also "willing," thinking and willing that are inextricably tied to one another as well as to "judging." And so the overall scheme of this work, worked out by Arendt in the few years following that address and left incomplete when Heidegger and she died within six months of each other, is also a commentary on the location of Heidegger's abode away from the abode that "lies in the midst of the world," a commentary that becomes explicit in Section 15 of the second part of the work, the part on "willing."

2

It should not surprise us to see the many variant applications of *tu quoque* to Jaspers. It is said, for example, that in his letter to Heidegger, dated August 23, 1933,[6] Jaspers "emphatically praises Heidegger's rectorial address,"[7] with all that this supposedly emphatic praise implies. What it implies could, for example, be heard at the final panel discussion of the Yale International Colloquium on Heidegger.[8] In his comments on

Heidegger's rectorate, Manfred Riedel, a leading editor of Heidegger's literary estate, referred to Jaspers's draft on the rejuvenation of the university, a draft written about a month before that letter and in part in response to Heidegger.[9] Riedel maintained that in his draft Jaspers presented a scheme of university reform much in the same spirit of the *Führerprinzip*, the Nazi authoritarian leadership principle, which was instituted for the first time at a German university under Heidegger's rectorship. By means of the absurd conflation of Jaspers's conception of the university as an "aristocracy of the spirit" and the Nazi leadership principle, Riedel meant to show that what Heidegger was instituting was no different from what Jaspers was endorsing. A discussion of relevant passages from the two documents should dispel such misconstruals.

Let us refer to a few telling passages from both Heidegger and Jaspers. Heidegger conceived a new constitution for the University of Freiburg. The Baden ministry of the land recognized it as the sort of scheme that served the Nazi purpose of politically aligning the universities with the new ideological regime, and it was consequently instituted for all universities in Baden and served as the model for the other nazified lands of Germany. Press coverage hailed the new constitution as being in accord with the *Führerprinzip*,[10] as was desired by the regime. Let us look at a few telling passages:[11]

> The Rector is the *Führer* of the University. All privileges previously held by the Senate devolve upon him.
> The Senate is the main support of the Rector.
> The Senate makes no decisions, hence it takes no votes.
> The business of the faculty is conducted by the Dean. Deans . . . are appointed by the Rector. In all matters pertaining to the Faculty the Dean has exclusive right of decision. Other members of the Faculty may be called upon for council. . . . The Faculty does not make decisions.

Here are parallel passages in Jaspers's draft:

> The Rector and the Deans are to be strengthened in their freedom vis-à-vis the Senate and the Faculty. They are to disclose their actions but are not to be dependent on majority decisions except in the case of certain limited vital questions (appointments, habilitations, changes in statutes and rules).[12]

The first sentence cited here from Jaspers's draft can be construed as a version of the *Führerprinzip*, but only if (disregarding that the relation of the administration's authority to the faculty is merely that of being "strengthened in their freedom") one construes that authority as being absolute. But the second sentence makes it clear that the administration's independence from faculty decision is limited in the case of appointments, habilitations, and changes in statutes and rules. And, of course, this includes everything that is vital for the faculty's academic freedom. It means, for example, that faculty cannot be dismissed for any but academic reasons, in particular not for political reasons, such as being Jewish. And in case the little phrase "They are to disclose their actions" is missed, Jaspers offers the following elaboration based on his "idea of the university," which is based, in turn, on the truth of critical inquiry, and excludes political considerations:

> Whenever this responsibility [of university administration] devolves on one individual there is need of a corrective in order to prevent a misuse of freedom. This is accomplished by putting internal pressure on the decision-maker so that he arrive at a maximum of earnestness, comprehensive knowledge and reasonableness. After certain periods of time still to be determined, the decision-maker has to justify his actions. Anyone from among the professions for which he has acted is free to criticize him relentlessly and to show up his mistakes. . . . He must be given the opportunity to reply, and there must be a disinterested authority which, out of genuine insight based on what it has heard, can mete out punishment.[13]

And Jaspers concludes this point with a remark about universitarian authority in its polar oppositeness to the authority underlying the *Führerprinzip*:

> This is our only hope that there will be men ready to take over leading positions, men who are certain of their abilities as well as of their earnestness to take risks. There is no achievement without a personally endangering risk.[14]

This contraposition of Jaspers and Heidegger on the question of academic authority deserves two comments. First, what is at play in the two statements? Ostensibly they are two versions of the relation of faculty to an administration that is concentrated in one person. But in the two versions there reverberate two divergent ideas of what legitimates and validates academic authority. Both versions are informed by their authors' shared deep concern over the fragmentation of the university into divergent fields, over the loss of any sense of what holds them together, and, especially in the case of Jaspers, over the dissipation of the enterprise of inquiry in the pursuit of trivia and inanities. The two statements diverge in the way they propose to restore a sense of the unity that would make the university again a university in its true meaning. It is this divergence that we have to discern.

First Heidegger. As early as 1929, in "What Is Metaphysics?" Heidegger says that the fragmentation of the university is artificially maintained by means of its technical organizational structure and is confirmed by "the practical usefulness" of the different disciplines.[15] What is the result of the artificially sustained reduction of disciplines to the fragmentation of practical usefulness? It spells "the demise of the rootedness of the disciplines in their *Wesensgrund*,"[16] which is inadequately translated as "essential ground."[17] These phrases are programmatic for his involvement in the rectorate under the aegis of the Nazi regime. This is borne out in his retrospective justification of 1945:

> I saw in the movement that had come to power the possibility of an inner self-collection and of a renewal of the people. . . . I believed that the university, renewing itself, might also be called to significantly participate in the inner self-collection of the people. . . . For that reason, I saw the rectorate as a possibility to lead all capable forces . . . toward this process of reflection and renewal, and to strengthen and secure the influence of these forces.[18]

What I have just quoted indicates the extent to which Heidegger saw the empowered Nazi movement as a suitable vehicle for what he was about, it shows how unperturbed he was by the slightest doubt that he possessed the key to what would redirect the nation to its "historical purpose," and it shows how sure he was of his capacity and calling to marshal and to "lead" the forces of self-renewal. What was the key to this great renewal that would go out from the university? This is what the rectorial address was meant to spell out. And Heidegger says so, also in retrospect, that is, in the same apology of 1945, where he states the four major points of his address. The first two of these points are significant for us:[19]

1. The grounding of the sciences in the experience of the essential area of their subject matter.
2. The essence of truth as the letting be of what is, as it is.

It should be noted that where the translation speaks of "essence," the original of both points refers to *Wesen* in the primordial sense in which Heidegger uses the word. *Wesen* in the primordial sense means the Being of a being insofar as it makes its presence felt; or alternatively the abiding of something insofar as it is noticeable.[20]

The German of the passage under consideration reads as follows: "1. Die Begründung der Wissenschaften in der Erfahrung des Wesensbereiches ihrer Sachgebiete."[21] This means that the various sciences represented at the university are to be retrieved from their scattering by leading each scientist—if leading he or she needs—to the experience of the grounding of the respective subject matters in the precinct of its *Wesen*. How do we experience the grounding of the subject matter of our scientific knowledge in its *Wesen*? The second point makes this clear: "2. Das Wesen der Wahrheit als Seinlassen des Seienden, wie es ist."[22] This point characterizes letting beings be in their Being as the essence of truth, as the *Wesen* of truth, as the way in which Being is disclosedly present to thought prior to, or perhaps better: beyond any interpretation on the part of man (the being that is there as a thinking being), in any case, with such predispositional interpretations bracketed out. What is the programmatic thrust of the second point as regards that to which the scientist is to be led? The thrust is that the researcher's experience of that grounding (of his subject matter in its *Wesen*) would come to realization in his letting it be in its Being. Even as the counterpart to Being is truth, so is disclosed Being to *aletheia*, and *Wesen* to letting be.

We do not know what the consequences would be of the scientist's experience of the grounding of his subject matter in its *Wesen*, what consequences for research, for the various academic disciplines, for the very meaning and actuality of the subject matter. We do not know how the disparate disciplines would again become a university through this experience. And, by its nature, this reversion to the ground of Being is beyond the ken of knowledge, for knowledge is a matter of reflection, testing, control, debate, and critique. Experience of the grounding in Being is, in Heidegger's vision, positively opposite to this sense of knowledge. We also do not know whether such a redirection of thinking being is possible: forgetfulness of Being is the condition of mankind.

3

But we do know that, according to Heidegger, what the age needed was a positive redirection toward this perhaps unlikely goal. We also know that he saw himself as thrust into the position of leadership in that direction, for example, in this passage of his rectorial address: "What is decisive in leading is not simply being out in front, but the strength of being able to go alone, not for reasons of caprice or desire for dominance, but by virtue of a most profound destiny and a comprehensive duty."[23] And he adds: "Such strength ties one to what is of the essence (literally: *das Wesentliche*), it effects selection of the best, and awakens authentic followership."[24] We know, thirdly, that Heidegger perceived the rectorate under the aegis of the empowered Nazi movement to be the vehicle for his leadership. Of the many indicators of this that can be gleaned from what has been published about this phase of Heidegger, I consider two to be particularly telling.

One is a usually disregarded minor incident reported by Jaspers about their last meeting on June 30, 1933: "At table [Heidegger] said in a somewhat furious tone, that it is mischief that there are so many professors of philosophy, in all of Germany only two or three should be retained. I asked: 'And which ones?' No answer."[25] In this case no answer is a most telling answer. We know what the answer would have been, had Heidegger been less modest.

Heidegger actually proceeded to exercise leadership in the sense under consideration. I am referring to the encampment of students and instructors that Heidegger convened at Mount Todtnau, near his home in the Black Forest, in preparation for the new university year beginning in the fall of 1933. To be sure, the Nazi authorities found ways of insinuating themselves. This is noteworthy but not of interest here.

What is of interest is that the Todtnauberg encampment was structured along the lines of the hierarchical paramilitary authoritarian leadership principle that was even then taking shape in the SS. The leader, so designated, of the encampment was Heidegger. The aim of the encampment combined two projects: On the one hand, Heidegger meant to promote the unity of the university by strengthening the relation of the "actual leadership" of faculty and the "true followership" of students in "knowledge-service." This aim was, on the other hand, to be informed by Heidegger's directing the "knowledge-service" of the coming semester to the experience of the grounding of all inquiries and their subject-matters in their *Wesen*.

Available sources for this characterization of Heidegger's aim in convening the encampment are sparse, but unmistakable. In his apology of 1945 he says the encampment had been meant "to prepare instructors and students for the authentic [*sic*] work of the semester, and to clarify my [*sic*] conception of the *Wesen* of science and of scientific work, and, at the same time, to present it for expatiation and articulation."[26] What did Heidegger say about the project in prospect? There is a memorandum that Heidegger directed to the instructors chosen to participate. Among other things it says:

> The period of the encampment must not be spent on an empty program.
> Instead it must be a matter of growth arising from actual leadership and in
> this way bestow on itself its own order. A few lectures presented before the
> plenum of the camp community are to effect the fundamental mood and the
> fundamental attitude. Decisive articulations [or discussions] among groups
> must facilitate and spark the communal articulations [or discussions].[27]

The lecturer before the plenum was Heidegger, and the camp, even though split up into groups, was most likely conducted in the manner of a Heidegger seminar.[28]

On the surface the instructions to the instructors are vaguely formulated. As a historian Hugo Ott does not know what to do with them, although he rightly notices that the memo is full of the rhetoric of the movement, especially the rhetoric of sacrifice, courage, and testing one's mettle. But there is no doubt about the projected program of the camp and its procedure. One of the students was the only avowed student of theology among them, and he did not understand much of what went on, or what Heidegger was about. And no wonder: In retrospect we know that Heidegger's philosophy of Being was even then only at the beginning stages of articulation, and far from ripe for the aim of the leadership he—we must say—blithely assumed. But that student understood that in one of the lectures Heidegger railed against Christianity in the following way:[29] It is not enough to attack Christianity with regard to the doctrine of the Christ; it is the doctrine of creation that has to be attacked, or as we would now say, deconstructed. For, according to this doctrine, *das Seiende* is nothing other than the product of an artisan, as if the consequent feeling of *Geborgenheit*, of being sheltered and at home in the world were not an untrue invention, and opposed to the knowledge, the noble knowledge, about the "Ungeborgenheit des Daseins," the insecurity of Dasein. We do not need to deconstruct these rough, uninformed notes of the young theologian in order to hear what reverberates in them.

Heidegger is, no doubt, correct in his retrospective report on what he tried to accomplish at Todtnauberg, even if he is less than ingenuous about many other aspects of his rectorate. He says that on the first day "I tried, by means of a lecture about university and knowledge, to clarify the core of my Rectorial Address. . . . Right away fruitful conversations ensued in the individual groups about knowledge and science, knowledge and faith, faith and *Weltanschauung*."[30] On the second day party big shots crashed the encampment and caused Heidegger's goal of gathering the disparate disciplines into a true university to come to naught.

What can we discern here? First, what reverberates in the programmatic core of Heidegger's rectorial address, and in his activity as the university's rectorial leader, and in the constitution that he devised for the university, is his philosophy of Being. Secondly, Heidegger perceived the ways and the substance of the empowered Nazi movement as the appropriate opportunity to marshal the forces for renewing the university in his sense, and ultimately as the right vehicle for the realization of his philosophical vision. Thirdly, we have had sufficient indication that Heidegger perceived the promotion of convictions prevailing in the Nazi regime as the means of promoting his own cause, his own vision.[31]

In realizing this vision within the structuring of human reality, whether political, universitarian, or any other, there is no place for what reverberates in the passages on university rejuvenation that we cited from Jaspers. There is no sense of the "need of a corrective in order to prevent misuse of freedom" when "responsibility of university leadership devolved on one individual";[32] there is no place for critical control over those in the seat of authority, or in Jaspers's words, for the "corrective" of "putting internal pressure on the decision-maker so that he arrives at a maximum of earnestness, comprehensive knowledge and reasonableness." There is no place for periodic accountability. There is no place for "anyone from among the professions for which he has acted [to be] free to criticise him relentlessly"—far from it, for in Heidegger's conception the leader leads the representatives of the professions to experience the grounding in their *Wesen* of their respective subject matters whatever they may be, without reference to their knowledge of, and their stature in, their respective fields. Hence there is also no place for "a disinterested authority" to "mete out punishment," that is, for an authority not determined by political or personal interests, and indeed by no other interest than that of upholding standards of inquiry and of teaching in the spirit of inquiry, and of recognizing the attainments of the human spirit; in short, by no other interest than that of humanly fallible, critical, arguable, debatable truth, truth gained, refined, upheld through deliberation as well as what Jaspers calls "communication," rather than through the declamation of a vision without the risk of exposure to those who are not like-minded. It is in this sense that I characterized what reverberates in the quoted passages from Jaspers's draft as standing in polar opposition to the *Führerprinzip*, whose espousal reverberates in Heidegger's utterances and actions. And at no place is this more evident than in the final passage I quoted earlier, where Jaspers says that the atmosphere of the university leader's accountability vis-à-vis recognized peers "is our only hope that there will be men ready to take over leading positions, men who are certain of their abilities as well as of their earnestness to take risks. There is no achievement without a personally endangering risk." Ultimately there is no place in Heidegger for this sense of personal risk. One might object and point to the fact that the sense of risk is precisely what is stressed in the rectorial address and in related documents, such as Heidegger's memo to the instructors of the encampment. In the rectorial address, for example, we read the following: "If we really will the *Wesen* of science, then the teaching faculty of the university must positively advance to the outermost positions of danger, the danger of the world's constant uncertainty. . . . There—in nearness to *Wesen*, there where all things press in."[33] Yes, there is risk in Dasein's being-in-the-world, and this risk is the ineluctable and very condition of the disclosure of truth in experiencing the grounding of all things in their *Wesen*. And yet, this is not what is at play in Jaspers's conception of *personal* risk, the personal risk of attaining to truth in the configuration and vicissitude of what is, in each case, one's own historicity. It is the risk of grappling with the otherness, or the recalcitrance, of what I direct my attention to, whether cognitively, vitally, or in human association, the risk of subjecting inquiry to the test and the standards of evidence, the risk of exposing one's thought to the challenge of the otherness of the fellow human being and of being the other for the other. We cannot discern any sense of such personal risks to be at play in Heidegger, much less to be the condition of the disclosure of the truth of Being, and hence even less as appropriate or possible in the atmosphere that Heidegger found suitable for his leadership in the recovery of Being.

I am led to the conclusion that it is no accident or misstep that Heidegger perceived the Nazi regime, at least as it at first seemed to him, to be the right vehicle for the realization of his philosophy of Being. But disclosing the ground, in his philosophy of Being, of his attempted use of the Nazi regime as a vehicle is a difficult task. Jaspers led the way in maintaining that this is what would have to be done. Jaspers's insight into Heidegger was anything but shallow, but he had neither patience nor time for an adequate mastery of Heidegger. Yet his "Notes on Heidegger"[34] and passages in other writings, whether they refer to Heidegger or not, give strong hints as to what would be involved.

4

What, after all, is the issue?

The issue is the question of Being, more precisely: the question of thought as the topos, the locus, the place of Being becoming truth. I am purposely stating the issue in Heidegger's terms. For the way of disclosing how Heidegger's perception of Nazism is grounded on his philosophy of Being is to counterpose it to a possible philosophy of Being that does not need and does not reach for a Nazism as the vehicle of its realization, and to do so in the terms in which Heidegger poses and takes up the question of Being.

What is the Nazism for which Heidegger reached as his appropriate vehicle? He deplored the regime's biological racism, its war of world conquest, and the sweeping way it mustered technology for its purposes instead of leading the nation back to the sources of Being latent in its language, its poets, its soil. The Nazism that Heidegger saw, and that he thought he had grasped as his vehicle—the Nazism that might have been but in practice wasn't—is, in short, Nazism as a regime of a disciplined, authoritarian, spiritually German-nationalistic and hence exclusionary, yet popularly participatory, totalitarianism. Heidegger deplored that the Nazi regime failed to be what he thought it ought to be, and he never gave up being a Nazi in *his* sense, and opposing other tendencies, such as those of political pluralism, or religious ecumenism, or dialogical culture.

Our problem then is to see what the treatment of the question of Being might be like that would have prevented Heidegger's association with Nazism, and to see this in Heidegger's terms.

What are the principal features of Heidegger's philosophy of thought as the place of Being becoming truth? It is the calling of thought to be at the disposal of Being. But under what circumstances would thought be fulfilling its calling? Negatively, if it divested itself of all concerns and pursuits that follow the interest of the one who thinks, if it questions all certitudes: that is, the cognitive certitudes concerning things, the ethical certitudes that determine willing and motives and interhuman relations, the convictional certitudes gained from tradition. Thought that is determined by interests and certitudes is thought that manipulates what there is, it places Being at the disposal of thought, and Being is forgotten. This has to be reversed. The reversion of thought to its calling would not apprehend beings in their determinations as such or such beings, or useful for this or that, but would think them in their Being, and would let them be in their Being.

To forestall misunderstandings, two things: First, reversion is not a matter of turning away from the life of the forgetfulness of Being and, so to say, waiting for Godot. Rather, the reversion is to be effected on the forgetfulness of Being. Hence Heidegger's endless, lifelong task of deconstructing the testimonies of forgetfulness in the long history of philosophy, a deconstruction not for the sake of destruction, but for the sake of finding the traces of thought experiencing the *Wesen* of Being behind the thickets of philosophical and theological constructions; hence also the project of turning to the beginnings of thought that follows its calling. He sought this beginning in pre-Socratic testimonies, prior to the forgetfulness constituted by metaphysical and scientific and technical thought, and in the unencumbered spiritual primordiality of language of a people grounded in its world. This world shows itself as nature, as the soil that the people work, as the elements that challenge them and that delight them, recalcitrant, implacable, awful, yet homelike and giving. This beginning in the language of a people thus grounded Heidegger recognizes in Greek—and the preeminent heirs to this beginning are the German people, if only they will turn to their legacy. Hence also Heidegger's trivialization of the significance of marshaling people for purposes of willing that distract from the calling of thought, whether in the form of ethical codes, or wars of aggression, or conformance of the "they," or religious beliefs, or technological achievements. Hence, finally, together with the dismissal of objectivism and subjectivism and formalism and the "they," Heidegger dismisses as distractive from the calling of thought all forms of transcendental human motives, so also the concern over being true to oneself. All such is dismissed under the pejorative of the "anthropologization" of Being.

Secondly, we ask, What would be the result of the reversion? Would the thinkers—and thought is always a matter of thinkers—be abandoned without guidance in their pursuits? Is the life of fallenness, the life of the forgetfulness of Being, the life of the "they" abandoned? Heidegger's answer: Not at all. For to be at the disposal of Being is not a matter of contemplation or of confrontation with the mystery of Being. Instead, it is a matter of letting thought be guided by Being, a matter of thought receiving "die Richte des Seins," the direction of Being.

In this sense followers of Heidegger say that, while his philosophy of Being renders ethics in the old sense impossible, it provides new possibilities of giving human action a right direction.[35]

Let me now attempt a preliminary approach to the question of Being that would afford protection from seeing Nazism as its appropriate vehicle of realization.

Let us start at the heart of the matter, the question of Being. In Heidegger, it is the question of what calls for thinking. It is historically the core question of all reflective thought. The question cannot be answered, otherwise Being would be treated as a being among beings, and not as the Being that is equally the Being of all beings. What this unique question of Being bespeaks is the thought-wise wonderment that Being is at all, and that thought seeks to fathom Being at its very source. Heidegger too speaks of Being as the source of Being.

How can one grasp thought as the place of the disclosure of Being? Thought, as we ordinarily practice it, is concerned with beings; it is reflective, critical, methodical, goal-directed, inferential, in short, discursive. The conclusion Heidegger draws from this is that ordinary thinking cannot be pious toward Being. Formally, this is correct. Hence Heidegger considers ordinary thinking, and the tradition that belongs to it, as the forgetfulness of Being. Formally, this is also correct. Furthermore, inasmuch as ordinary thinking is the activity of the concerns of human beings in their respective individualities, Heidegger's appeal to revert to Being can only be an appeal to thought as thought, not to thought as that of the individual thinking being. Formally, this too is correct. Hence the enterprise of reversion can commence, if at all, only by an appeal to human beings where their individuality is suspended, that is, in addressing human beings at a level where thought is suspended insofar as it is the thought of an individual. Why? Because individuals are the place where the kind of thinking prevails that can be convinced only by evidence, by argument, by communicative dialogue, by catering to interest and motivation, and so on. Now one can imagine that masses of human beings would suspend their individuality for this venture by their own choice, but it is not likely. Hence participatory totalitarianism may seem to be the ideal venue for motivating the onset of reversion—provided, ironically, that one is in the position of leadership over the "they." This is not an innocent irony; it is an instance of how "der Fall Heidegger" reveals itself as "der Fall Heideggers," that is, Heidegger the case as Heidegger's fall, "fall" in Heidegger's sense.

We cannot dispute that for Heidegger the life of the forgetfulness of Being is the domain where the reversion is to commence. In this he is touching chords that resound in many variations in thought about Being. It is the yearning for fathoming Being at its source and is expressed in a yearning for regaining what has been lost, usually through man's own fault. We are reminded of some myths that govern human realization: the story of the Fall; the Christian's expectation of the second coming of Christ, when the salvation effected by God in the past will be reestablished; the attainment of nirvana in stages and levels of Being, as for example in the Mandukiah Upanishad; the fact that when Jews return the direction given to man by the source of Being, the Torah, to the shrine, their liturgy has them say, "Turn us to you, and we shall return, renew our days as of old"; and Hegel has Being as Spirit labor away from its alienation toward its self-realization in the exertion of the Concept through the endless path of history.

Those who know Heidegger will quickly tell us that of course mankind or the individual cannot leave the life of the forgetfulness of Being behind and be open for the disclosure of Being. Heidegger characterizes his own significance by likening himself to John the Baptist pointing at Jesus and saying, "There comes one mightier than I." The point is that the forgetfulness of Being is actuality, our only actuality, and hence the only possible vehicle for *aletheia*, the unforgetfulness of Being. Heidegger would counter that other vehicles are nearby: Language as the repository of the beginning, and deconstruction as the labor through the tangle of forgetfulness to the source and the beginning. Heidegger goes so far as to regard language as the very abode of Being, a powerful thought, an unforgettable image.

Yet we must demur because, as Jaspers noted, though language may be *an*, it is not *the* abode of Being. A few points in brief: (1) It is said that language is testimony for the direction of Being given at the beginning. This statement is itself not a disclosure of Being. It is either a transcendental presupposition or the articulation of a fundamental faith. (2) By language Heidegger means mainly words in their primordial meaning-function. But families of meaning-functions are discernible only by the sort of sophisticated hermeneutic reflection that is precisely thought in its forgetfulness. It also shows the meaning-functions Heidegger often envisages to be arbitrary *because* they are not subjected to the give and take of hermeneutic reflection.[36] (3) What we are able to arrive at hermeneutically as the putative beginning is anything but the beginning: Either we fix on a point in time as the beginning, in which case we are not at the beginning and consequently there is none; or the beginning is *always* to be found—here and now. (4) Language is not confined to the meaning-function of words, but extends to various dimensions, thus also to those of syntax, attribution, imagery, symbol, story, myth, allusion, and others.

Let us dwell on the question of the beginning as related to language.

The meaning of words could be indicators of the direction of Being. But such meaning does not tell us whether it refers to the *beginning* of the direction of Being. No doubt the beginning can be thought as having been forgotten. And this thought can be the onset of a return to the beginning that may give us direction out of the ground of Being. In this sense directing our thought to the beginning can be a moment of thought that has in fact been expressed in many ways. It has been referred to as thinking and living out of the sources of Being; or as the pure, as in the critique of pure reason; or as fundamental knowledge; or as thinking and living out of the ground of faith. No matter how it is expressed, it is in any case a phenomenon of historicity. What does this mean? It means that whatever functions for any one thinker as the beginning, has to be made true temporally, it has to be temporalized into truth. And this is not possible for any thinking being in a pristine state, in a state prior to or outside of being already there as this historic person; it is not possible without a person risking himself or herself, without his or her commitment, without the original offering of his or her ownmost temporality, without proving oneself with respect to what counts as fundamental truth. All this is to say that the beginning is always tied to the historic originality of the individual thinking being. Hence it cannot be said that what is authentically the beginning is to be found at a point in time prior to a historic thinking being. And it certainly cannot be said that the beginning that counts as the source of truth can be brought into view by dismantling the historic configurations of thought. It is like the onion: Removing the layers does not lead to what is authentic but to nothing. The core of the onion is not at its core but in the layers around the core, and it is we in our respective being who are these layers. Isn't it ironic that Heidegger's labor of deconstruction, which was to have redeemed Being from its subjectivistic anthropologization, has become a strategy for having things mean anything the clever strategist wants them to mean?

If we would seek the authentic beginning in language, then not in the linguistic testimony at some alleged beginning, but in the language that is in each case our own, here and now.

5

The discussion of language and the beginning has a wider import. We ask, What is thought as the place of the truth of the beginning? We answer, It is the thought of the thinking being that exists only in its historicity. As this being and no other it is in each case the being that essentially participates in its own configuration through willing, thinking, striving, acting, failing. And when we recognize that the thinking being is a matter of historic configuration, then we have to recognize something further. The temporalization of its portion of truth takes place in the configuration of its historicity. If this is regarded as the anthropologization of Being, then note the following: There is no alternative to the anthropologization of Being, much less is there a choice between anthropologization and Being.

Instead the prevailing alternatives are, on the one side, a regard for the historicity of the thinking being, a regard that has the consequence of confining oneself to the limits indicated by it, and on the other side, an erroneous estimation of one's own historicity and blindness for the unbridgeable abyss between Being-for-the-being-that-thinks and Being-as-such, a misestimation that usually carries in its wake all the hubris and consequences that, beyond personal tragedy, are perilous to one's fellow thinking beings.

NOTES

1. Hannah Arendt, "Martin Heidegger at Eighty," in *Heidegger and Modern Philosophy*, ed. Michael Murray (New Haven: Yale University Press, 1978).

2. Ibid., 303.

3. Ibid.

4. Ibid.

5. Ibid.

6. A portion of the letter—misleadingly excerpted in this sense—was published in Günther Neske and Emil Kettering, eds., *Antwort: Martin Heidegger im Gespräch* (Pfullingen: Verlag Gineske 1988); English edition: *Martin Heidegger and National Socialism: Questions and Answers*, trans. Lisa Harries with an introduction by Karsten Harries (New York: Paragon House, 1990). The full text of the letter appears in Walter Biemel and Hans Saner, eds., *Martin Heidegger/Karl Jaspers: Briefwechsel 1920–1963* (Munich: Piper Verlag, 1990); English trans. by Edith Ehrlich, in Leonard H. Ehrlich and Richard Wisser, eds., *Karl Jaspers: Philosopher among*

Philosophers/Ein Philosoph unter Philosophen (Würzburg: Verlag Königshausen and Neumann, 1993).

7. Günther Neske and Emil Kettering, "Preface to the German Edition," in Neske and Kettering, *Martin Heidegger and National Socialism*, p. 37.

8. "Heidegger 1889–1989: An International Colloquium," Yale University, October 13–15, 1989. The papers of the colloquium were published in Germany: Christoph Jamme and Karsten Harries, eds., *Martin Heidegger: Kunst—Politik—Technik* (Munich: Wilhelm Fink Verlag, 1992). The book does not include an account of the discussion that took place at the colloquium, hence also not Riedel's remarks.

9. Riedel had access to the copy of Jaspers's draft that he had sent to Heidegger and hence is among Heidegger's papers. Jaspers's draft has been published in the meantime: Cf. Hans Saner, ed., "Karl Jaspers: Thesen zur Frage der Hochschulerneuerung," in *Jahrbuch der Österreichischen Karl-Jaspers-Gesellschaft*, ed. Elisabeth Salamun-Hybasek and Kurt Salamun, vol. 2 (Vienna: VWGÖ, 1989); English trans. by Edith Ehrlich and republication of the German is forthcoming in Ehrlich and Wisser, eds., *Karl Jaspers*. For a discussion of Jaspers's draft see Hans Saner, "Jaspers's 'Theses on the Question of University Renewal' (1933): A Critical Comparison with Heidegger's 'Rectorial Address,' " in Ehrlich and Wisser, *Karl Jaspers*.

10. See, e.g., Guido Schneeberger, *Nachlese zu Heidegger* (Bern: self-published, 1962), p. 115n.

11. Ibid., p. 114.

12. Saner, "Jaspers's "Theses," in Ehrlich and Wisser, *Karl Jaspers*, p. 33.

13. Ibid.

14. Ibid.

15. "Durch die praktische Zwecksetzung . . . erhalten." Martin Heidegger, *Was ist Metaphysik?* 5th ed. (Frankfurt am Main: Vittorio Klostermann, 1949), pp. 22–23.

16. Ibid., p. 23. "Dagegen ist die Verwurzelung der Wissenschaften in ihrem Wesensgrund abgestorben."

17. See Neske and Kettering, *Martin Heidegger and National Socialism*, p. 16.

18. Martin Heidegger, "The Rectorate 1933/34: Facts and Thoughts," in Neske and Kettering, *Martin Heidegger and National Socialism*, p. 17. Heidegger wrote this apologetic appraisal of his rectorate in 1945, when he was under investigation in the course of denazification; it was published posthumously, in 1983.

19. Ibid., p. 20.

20. It is hopeless to try to capture primordial meanings in the form of definitions. Historical linguists think that all these w- or v- words that are related to *Wesen* have their origin in the putative Indo-European word for dwelling. As to *Wesen*, the user of German speaks, for example, of *das Heereswesen*, which means the ostensible, or functioning, in any case discernible, presence of an army; or, there is a common old German expression in everyday transactions, "mach' kein Wesen," which does not mean what one would literally translate as "don't make an essence," but something like "don't make a fuss," "don't impose your feelings

about a matter on those around you." In English this sense of Wesen is present in "was," where, significantly, it is the indicative—never the subjunctive—of the imperfect of to be.

21. Martin Heidegger, Die Selbstbehauptung der deutschen Universität/ Das Rektorat 1933: Tatsachen und Gedanken (Frankfurt am Main: Vittorio Klostermann, 1983), p. 27.

22. Ibid.

23. Heidegger, Die Selbstbehauptung, p. 14. For the translation in the English edition see Neske and Kettering, Martin Heidegger and National Socialism, p. 9.

24. Ibid.

25. Karl Jaspers, Philosophische Autobiographie (Munich: Piper Verlag, 1977), p. 101.

26. ". . . das Dozenten und Studenten auf die eigentliche Semesterarbeit vorbereiten und meine Auffassung vom Wesen der Wissenschaft und der wissenschaftlichen Arbeit verdeutlichen und zugleich zur Erörterung und Aussprache stellen sollte." Heidegger, Die Selbstbehauptung, p. 35. My translation of the passage differs from Harries's, which renders it as follows: "to have prepared teachers and students for work during the actual semester and to have clarified my understanding of the essence of science and of scientific work and, at the same time, to have presented it for consideration and discussion." Neske and Kettering, Martin Heidegger and National Socialism, p. 27.

27. Cited in Hugo Ott, Martin Heidegger: Unterwegs zu seiner Biographie (Frankfurt am Main: Campus, 1988), p. 218.

28. Such seminars became familiar among Heidegger's followers after the war. At such meetings Heidegger would make a presentation of his thought, which was then expatiated in conversation with the participants and thereby articulated among them. Similar procedures are followed at meetings where, in the absence of Heidegger, the substance of the seminar is a topic or passage in Heidegger's writings. It would be amiss to think such a seminar to be a matter of posing a problem or taking up a problematic text for the sake of comprehension, interpretation, and criticism. Instead, a Heidegger seminar, whatever tack it follows, is, in effect, guided toward implanting Heidegger's thinking in the manner of seeds ("seminar") among the participants.

29. See Heinrich Buhr's contribution to Günther Neske, ed., Erinnerung an Martin Heidegger (Pfullingen: Verlag G. Neske, 1977), p. 53; cited in Ott, Martin Heidegger, p. 216.

30. Heidegger, Die Selbstbehauptung, p. 36; for Harries's translation see Neske and Kettering, Martin Heidegger and National Socialism, p. 27.

31. With the formulation of this last point I sidestep the question of whether Heidegger personally subscribed to the more odious features of Nazism, such as radical anti-Semitism and all that this entailed. My formulation is all that is required for supporting the thesis that Heidegger's misstep is a consequence of his developing philosophy of Being. Short of simply regarding him as a Nazi, this last point seems to be the most charitable interpretation of discrepancies between facts and claims about Heidegger's relation to Nazism. Let us recall, for example, the passage in Heidegger's negative recommendation of Eduard

Baumgarten: "Baumgarten comes from that liberal-democratic circle of Heidelberg intellectuals gathered around Max Weber. . . . After running aground with me he entertained close relations with the . . . Jew Fraenkel." The apparently unsolicited letter was written in December 1933, when Heidegger was still rector but after he had become disillusioned about his ability to effect his self-conceived mission as rector under the Nazi regime. The issue is not that Heidegger meant to damage Baumgarten but the manner in which he tried to do so by attributing to Baumgarten two associations that were anathema to the Nazis: liberal-democratic intellectuals and Jews. By the Heidelberg-Weber circle Heidegger was referring primarily to Jaspers, thus in effect and gratuitously denouncing him to the Nazis; and yet at that time he professed to maintain his friendship with Jaspers. As to "the Jew Fraenkel," associating someone with a Jew was at that time the kiss of death; and yet it is said that Heidegger was not anti-Semitic. Jaspers confronted Heidegger with the Baumgarten letter after the war, especially in regard to the phrase "the Jew Fraenkel," but Heidegger did not respond. No doubt those who—seeing a serious flaw in Heidegger in his capacity for denunciation and personal betrayal—are justified in regarding as mendacious the attempts at glossing over his reference to "the Jew Fraenkel" by pointing to Heidegger's friendship with Jews. I do not mean to distance myself from this appraisal by not making that fact a central issue. Rather, I see the way in which, through his philosophy of Being, Heidegger left himself open to such reprehensible choices, and I do this by focusing on the relation of that philosophy to his choice of the Nazi regime as a uniquely opportune vehicle to realizing it.

32. Responsibility of "leadership devolving on one individual" would accord with the "leadership principle" only if the authority of the leader is absolute vis-à-vis those who are being led.

33. "Wollen wir das Wesen der Wissenschaft, dann muss die Lehrerschaft der Universität wirklich vorrücken in den äussersten Posten der Gefahr der ständigen Weltungewissheit . . . in der wesentlichen Nähe der Bedrängnis aller Dinge." Heidegger, *Die Selbstbehauptung*, p. 14. My translation.

34. Karl Jaspers, *Notizen zu Martin Heidegger*, ed. Hans Saner (Munich: Piper Verlag, 1978). Excerpts in Edith Ehrlich, Leonard H. Ehrlich, and George B. Pepper, *Karl Jaspers: Basic Philosophical Writings: Selections*, (Athens: Ohio University Press, 1986).

35. For an approach to ethics in a Heideggerian sense, see Emil Kettering, *Nähe: Das Denken Martin Heideggers* (Pfullingen: Verlag G. Neske, 1987). For an example of Heideggerian ethics, see Werner Marx, *Gibt es auf Erden ein Mass?* (Hamburg: Felix Meiner, 1983); in English: *Is There a Measure on Earth?* trans. Thomas J. Nenon, Jr., and Reginald Lilly (Chicago: University of Chicago Press, 1987). For a critique of Heideggerian ethics, see Cheryl L. Hughes, "Heidegger and Levinas: The Problem of Ethics" (Ph.D. diss., University of Massachusetts at Amherst, 1992).

36. See my "Sein und Wahrheit bei Heidegger: Versuch einer periechontologischen Kritik," in *Martin Heidegger—Unterwegs im Denken*, ed. Richard Wisser (Freiburg and Munich: Verlag Karl Alber, 1987), where I tried to demonstrate this with respect to truth as *aletheia*. An English version of this article is forthcoming in Ehrlich and Wisser, *Karl Jaspers*.

3

Shame, Guilt, Responsibility

Karsten Harries

THE FOLLOWING REMARKS were prompted by my reading of the Heidegger–Jaspers correspondence,[1] a reading that left me disappointed, even a little sad, saddened not so much by the fact that these two thinkers show themselves to have been all too human, all too often petty and rancorous, but by lost opportunities for a genuine *Auseinandersetzung* as Heidegger understood that term: a "confrontation in which the essence of those who confront one another exposes itself to the other and thus shows itself and comes to appearance."[2] Essentially the same sadness surfaces in a number of Jaspers's letters, where Jaspers understands their failure to really confront one another as a betrayal of the kind of philosophizing he dreamed of, radical thinking grounded in genuine communication. For this betrayal he blames not only Heidegger, but himself: Too preoccupied with his own work and way, he "was not up to the meetings with Heidegger, as time was to tell."[3]

The correspondence invites us to illuminate philosophical discourse by leading it back *ad hominem*, to the thinkers' lives. Philosophers have generally considered such *ad hominem* considerations suspect. Should we not respect the autonomy of philosophical texts and allow them to speak for themselves? But just what does it mean to "allow a text to speak for itself"? To understand any text we have to know the place from which it is spoken. To understand a physics text, for example, we have to understand that the personal circumstances of the author do not matter. Scientific objectivity demands that these be left behind, just as the fact that an author wrote, say, in English rather than in German or French, should be recognized as irrelevant to the expressed meaning. The very style of such texts communicates such a demand.

What about philosophical texts, where we should ask whether philosophical texts are sufficiently alike to require all the same kind of

49

reading? Does "allowing a text to speak for itself" mean the same thing when reading Frege as when reading Heidegger or Jaspers? And if not, what does that say about philosophy? What is the proper context for reading Heidegger's *Being and Time*? Does it call for an examination of Heidegger's association with the Nazis, as Margolis and Rockmore suggest?[4] When reading a scientific paper, what does it matter whether its author was a hero or a scoundrel? What do the merits of a philosophical text have to do with the personal failings of its author?

But what understanding of philosophy is here being presupposed? As this correspondence shows, Heidegger and Jaspers shared the very different conviction that our understanding of philosophical texts remains hollow as long as such texts are not led back to life, *ad hominem*. Philosophy, Jaspers writes, seeks "in what is most personal the universal. For this reason the concrete person in his facticity is brought into philosophizing when there is the question of a critique";[5] and again: "Philosophy bears witness in the reality of life, judging, acting,—down to every ground in the soul,—to every corner of the house,—in all the ways of communication. Separating the matter from the person is appropriate in the sciences, not in philosophy."[6] In *Being and Time* we meet with a similar conviction. Heidegger there quite explicitly refuses to sever the philosopher from the concrete person's inevitably specific ethos. He asks: "Is there not, however, a definite ontical way of taking authentic existence, a factical ideal of Dasein, underlying our ontological interpretation of Dasein's existence?" In other words, does Heidegger's analysis of the essential structures of human being in the world and with others, of care and guilt, of authenticity and resolve, not presuppose this author's choice of a particular way of being in the world, which in *Being and Time* means also the choice of a particular hero? His unambiguous answer: "That is so indeed. But not only is this fact one which must not be denied and which we are forced to grant; it must also be conceived in its positive necessity, in terms of the objects which we have taken as the theme of our investigation."[7] This claims that unlike natural science, fundamental ontology can never be a disinterested, "objective" pursuit of the truth, but is inevitably grounded in the thinker's specific ethos, in his personal stance toward persons and things. Already Heidegger's letter of June 27, 1922, criticizes those who consider it inappropriate or indelicate (*unfein*) to ask a thinker for his basic position and who are content to criticize superficial details. In the days of Plato and Aristotle things are supposed to have been different. To ask a thinker for his basic position in this sense is to ask him to declare his understanding of philosophy and its place in the world. Such a declaration cannot finally be a matter of mere words. It has to express itself in the way one lives. Thus it was not just by his words, but by his example, by his personal style, that Heidegger sought to awaken his students to his understanding of what philosophy should be: "If we do not succeed in awakening such a consciousness in today's youth positively and concretely, all talk about a crisis of science and the like is just that—mere talk."[8] The teacher of philosophy must earn the right to his chosen profession, not by speaking of his vocation, but by providing his students with a living example of what it means to be a philosopher. The "fundamental transformation of philosophizing at the universities . . . will never be accomplished by the mere writing of books," Heidegger states in his letter of July 14, 1923. The genuine philosopher has to teach, as Socrates did, by example, by living his philosophy. In the letters from the twenties Heidegger presents himself as attempting to live such a paradigmatic life.

Jaspers shared this conviction. Philosophical questioning originates in radical reflection that surpasses established and accepted sense, calls us to another place, even as it leaves us groping for words and perhaps wondering whether we are bewitched by nothing at all. And just because Jaspers knew of the danger that the philosophical impulse, like Heidegger's call of conscience, might pull the individual out of the world, out of reality, he insisted that philosophy test itself in dialogue. Philosophy, as he understood it, becomes truly itself only when it risks its supposed insights in a confrontation without reserve. In 1930 Jaspers thus hoped that Heidegger would be able to join him as a colleague in Heidelberg precisely because "this would decide whether the two of us are able to communicate in the most radical philosophical discussion, or whether the old solipsistic way, that always prevailed in the universities, will continue: where there is polemics, but no realization, and where one 'did not get too close' " (May 24, 1930). Traditional philosophy is here linked to the subject thinking in isolation. That subject is to be replaced by partners in dialogue. Jaspers at least seems never to have wavered in his conviction concerning the importance of genuine *Auseinandersetzung*.

1

I opened the correspondence with high expectations, perhaps too high, too high because fed by what were also very personal concerns. For many years now I have myself been caught up in a continuing confrontation, or *Auseinandersetzung*, with Heidegger's work to whom my own owes so much, a confrontation that from the very beginning was burdened by my need to confront and appropriate what belongs to a past that I cannot disown without doing violence to the person I am today, and yet cannot simply affirm, bound up as that past is with an evil that demands even as it resists understanding. This confrontation was also burdened by the difficult relationship that separates and joins philosophy and politics. That twofold burden shadows the Heidegger–Jaspers correspondence from its very beginning, helps to shape its progress with its interruptions and new starts, their developing attitude to what philosophy should be, closely tied to changes in mood expressed in the letters' changing styles.

The rhetoric of *Kampf* and *Auseinandersetzung* is very much a part of the style of these letters, especially in the twenties. Thus in his letter of June 27, 1922, Heidegger knows himself joined to Jaspers "by a rare and self-sustaining battle community" (*Kampfgemeinschaft*) that he professes to find nowhere else. He is in a mood to fight. In this spirit he demands of the genuine thinker the readiness to place himself and his products into a "battle position of principled confrontation *bis aufs Messer*," down to the use of knives, suggesting bloody combat. To be sure, the arena remains first of all academic, an arena of thought, the knives only metaphorical knives—and there is quite a bit of metaphorical knifing of colleagues, in which both, Heidegger more than Jaspers, engage. The agon of thinking intertwines with the all-too-human concern to put down the competition for the few available professorships.

Jaspers thanks Heidegger for his sense of their being joined in a *Kampfgemeinschaft*, and proposes that they try out and strengthen this battle community by having Heidegger join him for a few days in his small, somewhat primitive apartment, while his wife is away. Aware of Heidegger's financial situation, he even includes money for the trip (September 6, 1922). The days spent together were no disappointment. Heidegger writes that their battle community had now been secured, praises also "the security of the 'style' of these days, which saw one day grow naturally into the next," even as he finds their new friendship *unheimlich*, uncanny "in that sense in which world and life are uncanny for the philosopher" (November 19, 1922). The ground on which they jointly stand is indeed *unheimlich*, a nameless ground that calls the friends beyond the academic world in which they are forced to seek their ways and make their homes toward the vague possibility of a more real, more genuinely alive, philosophizing.

When Heidegger finally receives the anxiously awaited call to Marburg, he proposes to keep up the good fight, and adds that he will not come alone, but accompanied by his personal band of sixteen loyal disciples, although Heidegger speaks not of disciples, but of a *Stosstrupp*, a shock troop of loyal followers (Heidegger calls some of them mere *Mitläufer*) who are supposed *die Hölle heiss machen*, literally to heat hell for his Marburg colleague, poor Nicolai Hartmann, who has been cast into the role of representative of the enemy, the philosophical establishment.[9]

Such bellicose talk calls for an analysis *ad hominem*, which suggests that it springs in good part from a quite different mood, the outsiders' spirit of revenge. Jaspers thus confesses to Heidegger that the academic philosophical establishment fills him with such a mood of rejection, hatred, and anger that it threatens to interfere with his own development (July 2, 1922). And Heidegger, too, presents himself as a lonely outsider, ready to fight, dreaming of genuine friendship: "I live a solitary life," Heidegger writes Jaspers (April 17, 1924), "living with my wife and the children is an altogether different positive possibility. But for a man— who at least attempts to fight, friendship is the highest possibility another can give him. I wrote my word of 'battle community' out of my loneliness." This mood of loneliness invites questioning: Does Heidegger's privileging of the sense of the uncanny in *Being and Time*, of a sense of not being at home over a sense of being at home (Bachelard was to insist on the priority of the latter), not rest on an all-too-human, all-too-ontic, personally and culturally conditioned homelessness? How are such disagreements to be settled?

The rhetoric of battle returns in a new key, when Heidegger congratulates Jaspers for his "great work," the three volumes of his *Philosophie* (December 20, 1931). Postponing certain reservations and objections, Heidegger heaps extraordinary, if vague, praise on his friend and his work. "What remains essential is that finally something has appeared in philosophy that *cannot be gotten around* and is *entire* [etwas *Unumgängliches und Ganzes*—favorite terms whose use and valorization by Heidegger demand questioning]. You speak from the clear and decisive stance of the conqueror and from the richness of the existentially tested." Heidegger goes on to suggest that now that this work has been completed, Jaspers should ready himself for the second and decisive step that would establish him as the " 'knowing leader' [*Führer*] and guardian" and lead him into what is genuinely public. Philosophy is to gain reality and substance by descending into the political arena.

Heidegger had no doubt long dreamed of just such a descent. But for himself he now claims much less and in a way that suggests a renunciation of hopes connected with the publication of *Being and Time*. For some time, he tells his friend, he has found himself surprised by the dubious success of that book, professes to know that he ventured too far, too soon, beyond his powers and without recognizing how narrow were the limits of what he was able to question. He compares himself to a watchman in a gallery, whose job it is to make sure that the curtains on the windows are drawn and opened properly, so that the great works on exhibit can be seen in the best possible light.[10] Philosophy appears here as something that belongs in a kind of museum.

Jaspers's mood is not at all that of the "conqueror." He rejects the label, which seems to him not just wrong—he understands himself as still standing before the door and, like Heidegger, claims only to be serving the great thinkers of the past—but, and more importantly, the label is an obstacle to the kind of dialogue he continues to seek: If each were only willing to really confront and criticize the other's main work, in a discussion with no holds barred, then beneath what such a critique might destroy, the deep, still unnamed, still elusive core, in which he continues to feel himself to be at one with Heidegger, would begin to radiate and open up those new possibilities beyond academic phenomenology, beyond monological thinking, of which he dreamed. The course of such a confrontation should then be presented to the public as a common effort, as an example of a new, genuinely dialogical, style of philosophizing.[11]

But such an effort, Jaspers knew, cannot be willed, it has to happen, and by then Jaspers seems to have had little hope that it would. The mood at the letter's end is sadness. Jaspers himself speaks of *Trauer*, mourning, even of *Schmerz*, pain. He considers himself condemned to monological thinking, condemned to work just with "paper and pen," speaks of "a deep pain, which only repeats what has been for my entire life," the pain "that I cannot get into the world, that I am not allowed to seize in living presence human beings by their heads, to allow myself thus to be seized." Heidegger, he feels, not without envy, is different. The future of philosophy, he predicts, will therefore lie in his friend's hands.

Jaspers wrote this letter only one and a half years before Heidegger assumed the rectorate of the university of Freiburg. The *Rektoratsrede* did indeed introduce a new tone into philosophy.

2

Heidegger was later to complain that his rectorial address was understood neither by the academic community, which was the intended audience, nor by the Nazis, who, as Heidegger knew, would take a keen interest in what the much-heralded philosopher-rector would have to say, nor by those later critics who would hear in it only what aligned him with the Nazis, not his opposition—misunderstood, because all missed the mood communicated by its very deliberate style. Pathos rules the style of the *Rektoratsrede*, which in the way it forces together classical Greek thought and concerns of the day invites comparison with the style of Nietzsche's *Birth of Tragedy*, as well as with the style of Nazi architecture. Heidegger's choice of words left no doubt in the audience about the timeliness of the speech, no doubt either that the fundamental mood of the *Rektoratsrede* was in some sense "oriented towards battle.'"[12] But what sort of battle? How many of those who listened to Heidegger could have been expected to understand "battle," as he later was to claim it should have been understood, as meaning first of all the Heraclitean *pólemos*, that is, as *Auseinandersetzung*, as confrontation that lets those who are confronting one another truly come into their own? Can this claim be reconciled with the invocation of Clausewitz or with what is said in support of *Wehrdienst*, military service? Heidegger's subsequent insistence that "that is the sense of *battle* as it is philosophically thought, and what is said in the address is only thought philosophically,"[13] his protestation that nothing was further from his mind than a celebration of the warlike covers up his responsibility for the speech's style and its reception.

Did his friend Jaspers understand the speech? In his remarkable letter of August 23, 1933, Jaspers praises the address's style and density, which is said to make it "the up to now only document of a contemporary academic will that will remain." "The great gesture of your beginning with the early Greeks touched me once again like a new and at the same time self-evident truth. In this you agree with Nietzsche, but there is the difference that one can hope that you, some day, will realize in philosophical interpretation what you now say." To be sure, such praise raises questions: Style and density are said to be expressions of a *will* that will remain, not necessarily of insight, and the comparison with Nietzsche could be read as a veiled critique. The contrast between "now say" and "some day realize in philosophical interpretation" suggests a peculiar emptiness in the present words, a discourse rather like a hollow shell, an emptiness on which Jaspers touches more explicitly when he tempers his praise by speaking of features of this speech that are all too timely, of "something in it, that seems to me a bit forced," of "sentences that seem to me to have a hollow ring." A superficial timely jargon floats over a suggestive and seductive depth that remains in need of careful interpretation.

Not surprisingly, Jaspers lacked the courage to risk a genuine response. In a note, written almost thirty years later, he suggests that, while he attempted to make the best of the speech, he had by then ceased to trust Heidegger, had come to understand him as the mouthpiece of a ruinous, destructive power.[14] In 1933, however, Jaspers would seem to have seen the situation in a rather different light. We cannot overlook the fact that he must have agreed with much of the speech's content. Jaspers shared Heidegger's profound dissatisfaction with what the German university had become: an assemblage of different interest groups that had lost sight of the whole. He, too, had become convinced of the need for radical renewal. He, too, was fascinated by the Führer principle, even as he recognized the enormous responsibilities such leadership should bring with it. And he, too, thought that the present situation had opened up an extraordinary possibility that would never return again, although he saw that opportunity shadowed by an equally extraordinary danger: "The possibility of a true renewal of German science is at the same time the danger of its definitive death."[15] Heidegger attempted to seize that possibility, and Jaspers, as his "Theses on the Question of the Renewal of the University" shows, would have liked to, but knew that "without being asked, I cannot do anything, since I am told that, since I do not belong to the Party and as the husband of a Jewish woman, I am only suffered and cannot be trusted."[16] Thirty years later Jaspers replaces the contrast between timely, but hollow, talk and words that touched him like a new, but self-evident, truth with the contrast between the person Heidegger, whom with his "speeches, action, and appearance" he had come to find ignoble and strange, and the spirit still animating his philosophizing (*Fluidum des Philosophierens*). In that spirit, now seen to dwell somewhere beyond the all too personal, Jaspers continues to sense a profound bond: a shared ideal of philosophy, even if that ideal remained little more than a vague promise.[17]

With this distinction between Heidegger's person and the spirit of his philosophizing we return to the question of the relationship between philosophy and life, which is also the question of the autonomy of philosophical thinking. Jaspers here accepts just that divorce of the concrete person from the spirit of his philosophizing to which both he and Heidegger had once objected. But if the height opened by Heidegger's ontologizing to those who come under its spell may seem to contrast with the petty superficiality and familiarity of much that is said, is the ascent to that height not an escape, a diversion that has to leave the person and his responsibilities behind, and that leaves no room for genuine community?

3

If Heidegger's descent into political reality had to profoundly separate the two friends, the collapse of the Nazi regime brought with it the possibility of a resumption of their never-quite-realized dialogue. But Heidegger remained silent. And only in 1948, when he was about to leave Heidelberg for Basel, did Jaspers make a half-hearted attempt to put an end to the silence that had risen between them. He drafted a letter in which he expresses his disappointment that Heidegger had not written: "When in 1945 the danger of National Socialist censorship had passed, I waited for a letter from you that would explain what I could not comprehend. Since in 1933, without explanation, you stopped meeting me and finally broke off all communication with me, I hoped that you would initiate a completely open exchange that had only now become possible." Jaspers speaks of good memories, of the pain of having been separated from someone to whom he felt very close, also of wanting to preserve the possibility that, despite all that had happened, they might once again exchange "serious words" (March 1, 1948). But never mailed, this letter remained part of a painful monologue weighed down by the burden of the past. Much later, in 1966, Jaspers added a comment, presumably addressed to posterity, that he no longer knew why he had failed to send that letter, but he conjectured that it was because Heidegger never "recanted *in public* his political position. Such publicness was necessary," he continues, "because in 1933 Heidegger had appeared in public with speeches and writings. What was unbearable, objectively and humanly, was that after 1945, like a coward, he simply absented himself [*kniff*]."[18] Public actions called for a public acknowledgment of responsibility and therefore of guilt.

Jaspers was, of course, not the only one to feel that Heidegger owed the world something like a public *peccavi*, a critical self-confrontation and admission of guilt. Many have found Heidegger's silence after 1945 more difficult to understand than his political engagement in 1933. Among them was his former disciple Herbert Marcuse, who in 1947 wrote to his once "venerated" teacher, imploring him to "declare his error." Without such a declaration, common sense would refuse to see in him a philosopher, "because it considers philosophy and Nazism irreconcilable. With this conviction it remains right."[19]

Does it? Heidegger, of course, did not acknowledge the authority of Marcuse's common sense. And does Heidegger's thinking not force us to call it into question? What sense can anyone who accepts the analysis of authenticity and resolve offered in *Being and Time* make of guilt and moral responsibility? To what does such responsibility respond? To the norms "they" have established? Is such a morality not inescapably inauthentic? Can we appeal then to timeless norms? To the categorical imperative? To the silent call of conscience? But that is not a call to a specific place; it is a call to "response-ability," perhaps, but not a call to what one usually means by guilt.

Did Heidegger understand himself as guilty? Gadamer raised this question: "Did he not feel in any way responsible for the horrible consequences of Hitler's seizure of power, the new barbarity, the Nürnberg Laws, the terror, the sacrifice of humanity's blood in two world wars—and finally for the indelible ignominy of the extermination camps? The answer is clearly no. That was the corrupted revolution, not the great renewal of the spiritual and moral strength of the people that he dreamed of and that he longed for as the preparation for a new religion of humankind."[20]

But if so, does Heidegger not bear responsibility for such blindness? Was Heidegger's chosen ontological eye not that one eye too many that rendered him ontically blind and let him stumble into guilt, repeating, much more tragically, Thales' fall into the well? And is the later Heidegger's much-discussed "yes" and "no" to the technological world, his preaching of a *Gelassenheit* that allows us to live in the technological world, enjoying the many ways in which it has made life easier, yet without losing our soul to it, as spiritual resident aliens, not an evasion of responsibility?

Although Jaspers did not mail this letter, eleven months later he did send a letter to Heidegger, addressing the "darkness" that had come between them (February 6, 1949). In this letter he recalls his profound shock when he saw a copy of Heidegger's negative evaluation of Eduard Baumgarten, with his remark on Baumgarten's association with the "Jew Fraenkel." Jaspers had referred to this evaluation already in December 1945, in his report to the commission considering Heidegger's future at the University of Freiburg, a report that, he requested, was to be made available to Heidegger. In that testimonial he had opposed Heidegger's return to teaching, at least for some years, but did recommend a pension and that Heidegger be allowed to write and publish as he wished. Jaspers must have felt that this matter had to be addressed and cleared up if there was to be any chance for the kind of communication of which he continued to dream.

In his reply Heidegger declares himself ready for the desired dialogue (July 5, 1949). He speaks of his inability after 1934 to find a way toward such a dialogue, of his increasing *Ratlosigkeit*, of feeling lost in the world, uncertain of where to go. Jaspers is touched and answers with a sad letter in which he likens his own public existence since 1945 to that of a puppet that really has little to do with him. Notwithstanding his many attempts to speak to his fellow Germans, he feels alone and at a distance. His *Grundbewusstsein*, his basic mood, is that of someone who still stands before the doors and fails to pass through them, coupled with hope that something of decisive importance might yet become clear to him or be brought to him by others, hope shadowed by the melancholy knowledge that he may not have much longer to live. He sends Heidegger some of his speeches (July 10, 1949), and Heidegger reciprocates, sending Jaspers three of his writings, including the "Letter on Humanism."

Fascinated and repelled, Jaspers finds the whole opaque; he wonders once again how philosophy is to go "beyond the monologue—and the passing along of the monologue by others." Jaspers considers it a matter of life and death for our present philosophizing. Instead of serving as a means of communication, Heidegger's discourse appears to him to block it. "Grasped in the immediacy of your sentences, the meaning material in which you philosophize is often unacceptable to me. I cannot understand some of your central words. Language as 'house of Being'—I resist: all language appears to me to be only a bridge. Shouldn't language cancel itself in communication, becoming reality, through action, presence, love? I could almost invert and say: where there is language, Being is not yet or no longer" (August 6, 1949).

4

Successful communication, as Jaspers understands it, requires us not to become too fascinated by the surface of the words. The particular discourse may not intrude itself; it must perish, vanish like coins spent to buy something, bring forth actions or thoughts. But such an understanding of communication, Heidegger could reply, reduces language to an instrument and places language at the service of the established and accepted. So understood, communication precludes genuinely radical thinking. Such thinking cannot in principle use language as a ready-made instrument. Heidegger therefore chose to write in a way that forces us to attend, not just to what is said, but to how it is said, to the music of the discourse. As a result of this breakdown the instrumental function is rendered questionable. We are forced to slow down, perhaps to a standstill. Jaspers remarks in his *Notizen* that he quickly got stuck reading Heidegger.[21] "One is always stumbling into the absurd."[22] But such stumbling invites the reader to attend to the text's style and to the mood it communicates, where Jaspers is right to remark that many of Heidegger's texts move us as aesthetic constructs do—Jaspers invokes Rilke[23]—and remarks in another place that for that reason they don't liberate the reader, but absorb his attention.[24]

Heidegger's experimentation with style cannot surprise the careful reader of *Being and Time*, where mood is said to disclose Dasein's stance in the world and is discussed as a presupposition of understanding and interpretation.[25] Adequate interpretation of a text thus presupposes that we have understood its ruling mood, even as we are aware of our own mood, also of the possible gap between the two moods. In *Being and Time* Heidegger does not develop the implications of the significance of mood. We are given no more than a hint when mood is said to communicate itself in what we can call the music of a discourse, in "intonation, modulation, and tempo,"[26] that is to say, in a text's distinctive style. This recognition of the ontological significance of style, which is taken to disclose something more fundamental than assertions, is a presupposition of Heidegger's attempt to take a step beyond an understanding of truth that seeks its primary locus in clear assertions, a step that in the end must render academic philosophy peripheral. The *Beiträge* attempt to realize what in *Being and Time* is barely hinted at. Heidegger's call for a radically different stance, for a step beyond the technological world, required not so much a new message as a new style, where, given the measures provided by that world and its discourse, this style has to appear as an irresponsible escape from reality.

With this turn to style the language of thinking moves into the neighborhood of poetic language. But does it not also move toward the kind of monological thinking that Jaspers thought philosophy had to leave behind? Heidegger agrees with what Jaspers has to say about monologues, but only to add to it, and the addition is very much in keeping with his understanding of authentic discourse: "Much, however, would have been gained if monologues were allowed to remain what they are. It almost seems to me that they are not yet [genuine monologues]. For that they are not as yet strong enough." Heidegger goes on to remind Jaspers of Nietzsche's word: "Together a hundred profound lonelinesses form the city of Venice—this is its magic. An image for the human beings of the future" (August 12, 1949).

Jaspers is prepared to grant Heidegger that we may not yet be strong enough for genuine monologues, that the "authentic, essential lies 'beyond' communication and non-communication, subject and object, thinking and Being," also that our thinking becomes groundless and scattered when it loses this relation, but Jaspers also calls it "a great seduction: to run away from the world and from human beings and from friends,—and to gain nothing in return—except for an infinite light, an abyss that cannot be filled," and he speaks of the need to tear oneself from such seductive magic by subjecting it to the discipline of thinking (August 17, 1949). Once again the idea of a public confrontation surfaces, a confrontation without polemics, but also without reserve, a confrontation that would penetrate beyond their different positions to their ground. Although Jaspers is no longer certain that there is indeed a common ground, he points out that even in the absence of such a ground something unusual might yet be achieved: the exchange would demonstrate that even where a common ground cannot be assumed, it is possible for philosophically thinking persons to confront one another. And in such confrontation something like a common ground announces itself after all, even if not yet named. In a subsequent letter Jaspers emphasizes once more that such confrontation would also have to make visible the personal dimension that could not be detached from the philosophical matters under discussion (January 14, 1950).

In his answer Heidegger does finally get personal and, coming back to what he had written much earlier about his *Ratlosigkeit*, offers Jaspers "a single sentence" to clarify what he meant: "I did not visit your house since 1933, not because a Jewish woman lived there, but because I *was simply ashamed* [*weil ich mich einfach schämte*]. Since that time I not only have not visited your house, but also not Heidelberg, to which only your friendship gave its special meaning" (March 7, 1950). Jaspers thanks Heidegger and suggests that with this declaration of his shame Heidegger had "entered into the community of all of us, who have lived and live in a situation for which 'shame' too is an appropriate word" (March 19, 1950). By acknowledging his shame (*Scham*), not his guilt (*Schuld*), Heidegger had established a bond between himself and his fellow Germans. Jaspers goes on to liken Heidegger to a dreaming boy who didn't know what he was doing, who replaced reality with wishful thinking and then faced a rubble heap and allowed himself to drift. Continuing to reflect on Heidegger's admission of shame, Jaspers sends him, a few days later, three of his recent publications, including *Die Schuldfrage*, remarking on how little his countrymen were interested in that little book (March 25, 1950).

In his reply (April 8, 1950) Heidegger eagerly picks up Jaspers's image of the dreaming boy and confesses that he failed to understand the true significance of his engagement in 1933. He now speaks of guilt, but in a way that evades his personal guilt. In *Die Schuldfrage* Jaspers had distinguished between four kinds of guilt—criminal, political, moral, and metaphysical[27]—and claimed that every German had reason to address the matter of his own political, moral, and metaphysical guilt. In his letter Heidegger addresses only the last, and that in a way that constitutes what Jaspers in his book had called an evasion of guilt by seeking refuge in the general.[28] Heidegger writes, "The guilt of the single individual remains and remains the more, the more single that individual," but then quickly shifts from the topic of guilt to his world-historical perspective: "But the matter of evil has not yet come to its end. It is only just now entering its proper epoch. Nineteen thirty-three and before, the Jews and the intellectuals on the left, as the ones who were immediately threatened, saw more clearly, more sharply, and further. Now it is our turn." Heidegger does not hesitate to include himself, together with the Jews and the intellectuals on the left, among the victims of the still-progressing rule of evil, among those who, precisely because they are outsiders, see more clearly and further. And what they see in their exile and homelessness is the hidden advent that heralds a future whose shape we moderns, caught up as we are in our technological world, cannot delineate.

It took Jaspers more than two years to answer. Heidegger's refusal to draw distinctions that must be drawn, a refusal masquerading as insight into the essential, his self-serving summary of his life made it difficult for Jaspers to answer. And that difficulty was compounded by Heidegger's talk of a hidden advent. Jaspers's fears that Heidegger had replaced traditional philosophy with prophetic fiction without content or authority seemed confirmed. "My horror grew when I read this. That is, as far as I can think, a pure dream, belonging with so many dreams—'timely in each case'—that have fooled us for this half century. Are you about to appear as prophet who, possessing hidden knowledge, shows the supersensible, as a philosopher who leads away from reality? Who trades the chance for what is possible for fiction? In such cases one has to ask for authority and proof" (July 24, 1952). Jaspers continued to hope for genuine communication. Its absence he construed also as a failure of his philosophizing. Heidegger failed to reply. It was to be the last letter of substance in the correspondence. Only a few birthday greetings follow.

5

A final reflection: At the center of philosophy lies an ethical concern, born of the demand that human beings assume responsibility for their thoughts and actions—Heidegger might have invoked the call of conscience—and the consequent refusal to rest content with maps and authorities that have come to be established, accepted, and taken for granted. Genuine philosophy, it seems to me, comes to an end either where a definitive map or at least a definitive method appears to be in hand—think of a religion certain of its truth—or where there is no longer any confidence that responsible thinking is capable of working toward such maps or methods. Philosophy remains alive only as long as the question: what is the right way, continues to be asked, because that way remains questionable even as we grope to find words for the unspoken that directs our search. So understood, philosophy remains alive only as long as it does not claim for itself the "general and binding validity claimed by science."[29] Because it has its ground in what lies beyond established and accepted sense, philosophy has to be content to cast its conjectures toward some possible future consensus. The philosopher speaks without authority. When he claims authority he betrays philosophy as he betrays his humanity. Philosophy so understood harbors within itself the temptation of the self-elevation of the lonely thinker into a demigod, a leader or prophet, a temptation to which Jaspers thought Heidegger had succumbed. And because of this temptation, philosophy must be willing to develop and test itself—in dialogue. Philosophy has genuine life only in a shared groping that seeks to delineate what someday may become a new common sense.

NOTES

1. Martin Heidegger/Karl Jaspers, *Briefwechsel* 1920–1963, ed. Walter Biemel and Hans Saner (Munich: Piper Verlag, 1990).

2. Martin Heidegger, "The Rectorate 1933/34: Facts and Thoughts," in *Martin Heidegger and National Socialism*, ed. Günther Neske and Emil Kettering, trans. Lisa Harries (New York: Paragon House, 1990), p. 21.

3. Karl Jaspers, *Notizen zu Martin Heidegger*, ed. Hans Saner (Munich: Piper Verlag, 1978), p. 233.

4. Victor Farías, *Heidegger and Nazism*, trans. Paul Burrell and Gabriel R. Ricci, ed. and with a Foreword by Joseph Margolis and Tom Rockmore (Philadelphia: Temple University Press, 1989), p. xvi.

5. Karl Jaspers, *Philosophische Autobiographie* (Munich: Piper Verlag, 1977), p. 109.

6. Jaspers, *Notizen*, p. 259.

7. Martin Heidegger, *Sein und Zeit*, 7th ed. (Tübingen: Niemeyer, 1953), p. 310; trans. John Macquarrie and Edward Robinson, *Being and Time* (New York: Harper and Row, 1962).

8. Letter of June 27, 1922, *Briefwechsel*, p. 28.

9. Letter of July 14, 1923, *Briefwechsel*, p. 41.

10. Letter of December 20, 1931, *Briefwechsel*, pp. 144 and 145.

11. Letter of December 24, 1931, *Briefwechsel*, p. 146.

12. Heidegger, "The Rectorate 1933/34," p. 20.

13. Ibid., p. 21.

14. Jaspers, *Notizen*, pp. 181–182; reprinted in *Briefwechsel*, p. 258.

15. *Briefwechsel*, p. 261. Footnote 4 to the letter of August 23, 1933, provides a summary and excerpts of Karl Jaspers, "Thesen zur Frage der Hochschulerneuerung," typescript, published in *Jahrbuch der Österreichischen Karl-Jaspers-Gesellschaft*, ed. Elisabeth Salamun-Hybasek and Kurt Salamun, vol. 2 (Vienna: VWGÖ, 1989), pp. 5–271.

16. From a comment on a never-mailed letter, presumably to the Ministerium des Kultus und Unterrichts in Karlsruhe that Jaspers had added to the "Theses." *Briefwechsel*, p. 260.

17. Jaspers, *Notizen*, p. 165; *Briefwechsel*, pp. 258 and 259.

18. Comment of October 30, 1966, added to the unmailed letter of March 1, 1948, *Briefwechsel*, p. 269.

19. Herbert Marcuse, letter of August 28, 1947; reprinted in *Pflasterstrand* 279/280 (1980).

20. Hans-Georg Gadamer, "Superficiality and Ignorance: On Victor Farías' Publication," in *Martin Heidegger and National Socialism*, p. 143.

21. Jaspers, *Notizen*, p. 164.

22. Ibid., p. 47.

23. Ibid., p. 49.

24. Ibid., p. 153. "Er erzeugt nicht das Selbstdenken, nicht die Freiheit,— sondern ästhetische Befangenheit."

25. Heidegger, *Sein und Zeit*, p, 134.

26. Ibid., p. 162.

27. Karl Jaspers, *Die Schuldfrage: Ein Beitrag zur deutschen Frage* (Zurich: Artemis, 1946).

28. Ibid., p. 89.

29. Jaspers, *Philosophische Autobiographie*, p. 36

4

The Psychological Dimension in Jaspers's Relationship with Heidegger

Harold H. Oliver

THERE ARE ENOUGH materials on hand to determine the nature of the personal and professional relationship between Heidegger and Jaspers. The three sources on which I shall rely most heavily are the posthumously published section of Jaspers's "Philosophical Autobiography" dealing with Heidegger, which we have in the second edition of Schilpp's volume on Jaspers,[1] Jaspers's *Notizen zu Martin Heidegger*,[2] and the recently published *Correspondence*.[3] The first is unique in containing Jaspers's sole public statement about their relationship—a record that he chose to withhold from the public until after Heidegger's death. It was, in fact, published after both had died: Jaspers in 1969 and Heidegger in 1976. It represents what Jaspers intended philosophers around the world to know about his version of their relationship up to the time it was written in 1953.[4] The second source, the *Notizen*, constitutes a kind of "anthology" of Jaspers's private reflections about Heidegger extending over many years. The third, the *Correspondence*, gives us access to the private exchanges between the two philosophers from 1920 to 1963.

The first may have been controlled by Jaspers with respect to the way in which he wanted the relationship to be remembered; the second and third are valuable because they lack any control either may have wanted to exert in determining the way they wished their relationship to be assessed.[5] The second and third have different values for us in terms of their difference in character. My intention is to consider them *seriatim* as a way of determining psychological aspects of the relationship between Jaspers and Heidegger.

65

Jaspers's "Philosophical Autobiography" and the Report on Heidegger

Any assessment of the Heidegger-Jaspers relationship has to take into account the fact that Jaspers entered into it with what he regarded as a disadvantage, namely, that—unlike Heidegger—he was not trained in philosophy, but came to it after a successful career as a "psychopathologist." His work *Psychopathology* appeared in 1913; even his first work in philosophy, published in 1919, carried in its title the word psychology: *Psychology of World Views.* It would be fourteen years before he would publish a work with philosophy in the title—his *Philosophie.* Meanwhile, in 1922 he became a full professor of philosophy at Heidelberg, a position for which—on his own admission—he was "not ready."[6] The long interval between his assuming the professorship in philosophy and the appearance of his first major work in the field led some to conclude that he was "done for"—to use his own expression.[7]

Extremely disaffected with the philosophical climate in Germany after the First World War, Jaspers had respect only for Heidegger, seven years his junior, whom he was anxious to meet. Their first meeting took place in Freiburg in the spring of 1920. Finding Husserl's manner *petit bourgeois* on that occasion, he was instantly attracted to Heidegger: "Only Heidegger struck me as different [from the others]. I visited him, sat alone with him in his study, noticed that he was studying Luther, observed the intensity of his work, was in sympathy with his penetrating, concise way of speaking."[8] Jaspers came to the early judgment that "Heidegger alone addressed himself to complexes of questions that appeared to me the most profound."[9]

Heidegger visited Jaspers in Heidelberg on many occasions as a guest in the Jaspers household. At first Jaspers found the conversations rewarding, although he noted that he did most of the talking. For a short time it seemed that they "were on the same road"; Jaspers even spoke of a "feeling of solidarity" between them, claiming that "we talked to each other with a beautiful ruthlessness that did not exclude outspokenness about our observations." In Heidegger, Jaspers "saw a contemporary who had something that otherwise existed only in the past and that was indispensable to philosophical thinking." He even credits Heidegger for introducing him to the richness of Christian thought.

Yet there was something unsettling in the relationship as Jaspers viewed it. There were, as he put it, defects: "Thanks to his frequent visits with us in Heidelberg, a lively intellectual exchange developed between us over the years. Nevertheless, it remained a strangely isolated relationship. I did not introduce Heidegger to my friends, and Heidegger did not introduce his to me. In neither case was this deliberate. Yet it was a sign of a defect, as if neither of us wanted the other to enter into his substantial world." Jaspers reports that it was a strange kind of relationship: "I already had feelings of astonishing aversion during the first year [of our meetings]. From the very beginning, our relationship was devoid of enthusiasm. It was not a friendship grounded in the depths of our nature. In behavior and language, something distancing seemed to be mixed into the atmosphere." Jaspers was impressed with Heidegger's "profundity but could not tolerate something else, something undefinable." He further laments: "Sometimes it was as if a demon had crept into him; consequently, out of a tendency to seek the essential in him, I told myself to disregard his *faux pas*. During the decade the tension increased between sympathy and alienation, between admiration for his abilities and rejection of his incomprehensible folly."[10]

The distance between them was especially evident in their failure to appreciate each other's major publications. The appearance of Jaspers's *Psychology of World Views* was the first sign of trouble between them; for while Heidegger told Jaspers that "it meant a new beginning for philosophy,"[11] he was quite critical of it in an unpublished review (the manuscript of which he shared with Jaspers). An element of dependency is evident in Jaspers's note: "I probably disappointed Heidegger." When Jaspers's *The Idea of the University* appeared in 1923, word came to him that Heidegger had said that his "booklet was the most irrelevant of all the irrelevancies of the time."[12] It was not the negativity of the remark that troubled Jaspers, but the sign that the "the mutual openness" their relationship "required" had been violated.

The publication of Heidegger's *Being and Time* in 1927, as Jaspers states, "led to no deepening of our relationship."[13] He further notes that he "reacted [to the book] by not being particularly interested, as I had years ago reacted to his criticism of my *Psychology of World Views*." He admitted that when he had read some pages of Heidegger's manuscript in 1922, "they were unintelligible to [him]." Admitting "some admiration for *Being and Time*," Jaspers added: "The book appeared unproductive for what I sought philosophically. I rejoiced in the achievement of a man with whom I was associated but did not have much desire to read it. I soon got stuck because the style, contents, and way of thinking did not appeal to me."[14] Jaspers believed that his failure to grant Heidegger "the service of a careful reading and criticism as he, my junior, had done for my *Psychology of World Views*" surely disappointed Heidegger—the second time this phrase appears in Jaspers's account!—and was responsible for Heidegger's lack of interest in his further publications.

The National Socialist party came to power in the March elections of

1933, after which their relationship would rapidly deteriorate. Heidegger's visit to Heidelberg in late March was not particularly different. Jaspers commented, "We conversed as we always had." When the subject of the rapid development of the National Socialist party arose, Jaspers reports his "surprise" when Heidegger responded, "One has to join in," but he did not question. In May Heidegger visited Jaspers briefly "for the last time" in connection with a lecture by Heidegger at the university. "*Kamerad* Heidegger"—as he was introduced—lectured on the National Socialist program for the "renewal of the universities" and was received with great enthusiasm. Jaspers reports that he responded by sitting still: "I did not budge."[15]

Before they said good-bye for what would be the last time, in May of 1933, they exchanged opinions on matters of great difference between them, namely, Hitler, the Jews, and German universities. According to the Schilpp account, Jaspers and Heidegger "ceased writing after [Jaspers] was removed from office in 1937."

Jaspers defends his seemingly ambivalent response to Heidegger in the revealing words: "I cannot say no when once I have said yes to a human being. But I also cannot gloss over something essential out of conventional friendliness toward fellow humans." Jaspers concludes: "What has happened since 1933 and what is happening today appear to me open as far as Heidegger and I are concerned. I cannot lock the door."[16]

There is an important clue to Jaspers's estimation of Heidegger in Jaspers's report that "we had become adversaries, not because of books but because of actions. *The philosophical thoughts had to be understood in relation to the behavior of the thinker*."[17] He amplifies this principle as follows: "As little as any human being as a whole can be understood and known, just as little can the philosophical thinker be understood by his work. One may be able to penetrate, but not understand."[18] With this hermeneutical clue we turn to the second source, the *Notizen*.

Jaspers's *Notizen zu Martin Heidegger*

One of the passions of Jaspers's life was the need to understand Heidegger. To him this meant, not to follow the train of his thought, not a *Nachdenken* in Heidegger's sense—though he admittedly experienced some difficulty in this regard—but to "make sense" of Heidegger as "philosophisches Phenomen"; in other words, to fathom the person— to effect, if possible, a *Mitdenken*. To the very end Heidegger remained a riddle to Jaspers, yet the passion to solve the riddle had permeated Jaspers's whole being. The reason for this lay in his inner sense that his own public fate was somehow inextricably linked to Heidegger's.

"To understand Heidegger" as a hermeneutical project would entail a thoroughgoing engagement with his writings; that is, it would proceed on the assumption that "to understand Heidegger" means "to understand his thought" through his writings. Such an assumption usually underlies the serious philosophical inspection of any particular philosopher. In the usual operationalizing of this assumption little or no attention need be given to the external events in the life of the philosopher in question.

Jaspers's approach to understanding Heidegger, on the contrary, would seem to proceed from an alternative assumption, namely, to understand Heidegger as a person. Accordingly, Jaspers reads Heidegger's writings in the light of the latter's personal life rather than the converse. No "fusion of horizons" occurs; rather Jaspers is driven to make a *judgment* upon Heidegger as a person. Accordingly, his copious *Notizen* on Heidegger disclose the habits of mind of a "psychopathologist" rather than of a critical thinker. Heidegger's writings are of interest to Jaspers primarily as illustrations of the enigmatic character of his person; for while Jaspers had a deep feeling for Heidegger as a person, he seems to exhibit no deep interest in his writings. What he knew of them simply confirmed what he suspected of the person. Furthermore, it was his negative judgment on Heidegger as a person that precluded his full access to Heidegger's thought.

Two excerpts from the *Notizen* will serve to illustrate my claim: "I have not been able to read *Sein und Zeit* because it did not interest me,—and today have read only very few parts".[19] Then Jaspers goes on to confess, "I probably would have read him in more depth if I had not known him personally."[20]

In Jaspers's view, Heidegger had abandoned the *philosophia perennis* in favor of a highly idiosyncratic, poetic *Zauberei*. In the final analysis, Heidegger's thinking of Being was not a rational insight, but a "great mystification" that concealed a "false absolutization of Being."[21] The deeper disappointment, however, was not cognitive. It was rather the collapse of their earlier relationship. Jaspers wrote in 1953 or 1954: "The worst of all is this: to have been bound to a person only to have that come to an end."[22] For "I believed," Jaspers continues, "that I needed the joy of his understanding."[23]

Jaspers's interest in Heidegger assumed the proportions of an obsession. I suggested earlier that the reason for this "love-hate" relationship to Heidegger may have been Jaspers's feeling that his own viability as a thinker was bound up with the judgment his contemporaries would place upon Heidegger. Jaspers desperately sought a public confrontation with Heidegger as a way of altering this state of affairs, though this event was never to be. In this regard, there is something almost pathetic about Jaspers's asymmetrical relationship with Heidegger. Jaspers's judgment that Heidegger's thought was *kommunikationslos* was more of a reaction to Jaspers's abortive attempts to communicate with Heidegger than a necessary interpretation of Heidegger's philosophical thinking. His frequent overtures to Heidegger were never requited. He notes with pathos: "I often think of you! [and] You do not read me.[24] Indeed, Jaspers seems to stage imaginary conversations with Heidegger in lieu of dialogues that would never occur.[25] Once he even wrote: "Heidegger could answer me . . ."[26]

Despite his negative judgment on both the person and thought of Heidegger, Jaspers reveals an uncanny need to be judged favorably as a philosopher by his younger colleague—or at least to be taken seriously. In that sense we may interpret his characterization of Heidegger as *Gegner*—as a foil, for he admits that, because of Heidegger's silence, he can only be a potential *Gegner*. He even justifies himself to Heidegger by recourse to Nietzsche's line: "I honor whom I attack."[27] This remark was "addressed" rhetorically to the very person of whom he wrote: "[Heidegger] possesses a magic like a dwarf who reveals himself in the depths of a mountain on a twisted network of roots, in a deceptive ground that appears to be a firm growth of moss and yet is a swamp."[28] In the absence of a response from Heidegger, Jaspers's *Bekämpfung* assumed quixotic proportions, as, for example, when he wrote: "If Heidegger is not himself here, I cannot discuss with him."[29]

Our understanding of their relationship is enriched if we add insights drawn from the copious correspondence between them made available by Saner and Biemel in 1990. To this we now turn.

Evidence of the Relationship in the *Briefwechsel*

The first document published in the *Correspondence* is a letter from Heidegger to Jaspers apparently written immediately following his first visit to Jaspers's home in Heidelberg in the spring of 1920. It confirms what we have learned from Jaspers about their mutual hope for a repristination of philosophy: "I am happy about the evening spent with you, and have the *feeling* above all that we are working out of the same basic situation toward the revival of philosophy" (Ep. 1). In January of 1921, Jaspers tells Heidegger that his review of the *Psychology of World Views* is the only one about which he is "anxious" (Ep. 4). In August of 1921, Jaspers writes: "None of the younger 'philosophers' interests me more than you. Your criticism is of great benefit to me" (Ep. 7). In these excerpts and the ones to follow, my procedure is to cite the major references to the personal, and indeed, psychological, aspects of their relationship.

In October of 1923, Heidegger confessed to Jaspers: "I need not say to you how much I enjoyed the visit with you. What is to be said is always imperfect in letters"(Ep. 18). On the sensitive issue of his estimation of Jaspers's Idea of the University, Heidegger writes: "I have not finished reading [it]. Somehow I should like to express 'solidarity' with it. But I haven't gotten far enough along" (Ep. 20). In October of 1926, Heidegger writes warmly of his association with Jaspers: "That I enjoyed my visit with you and still am, I need not continue to express. I have the certain feeling that we expressed ourselves this time better than ever before, and that we are coming closer. Not a day passes in which I do not think of you and am thankful that we found one another" (Ep. 35). In Heidegger's letter of December 2, 1926, the issue of the "Jewishness" of a potential appoint-ment surfaces for the first time—a sinister portent of things to come (Ep. 37). After reporting the receipt of a copy of Being and Time, Jaspers simply remarks: "I have still not been able to read it; I have only leaved through it and sailed through a dozen pages" (Ep. 44). Four months later Heidegger writes that he is "still quite anxious for the further development of Jaspers's works" (Ep. 48). In May of 1928, Heidegger reiterates his wish that Jaspers's work will move unimpeded to its culmination" (Ep. 60).

Throughout 1928 they expressed wishes to visit one another and to discuss matters of mutual interest. In 1929 Heidegger wrote, after receiving a long-awaited reply from Jaspers, that he was pleased to have a "Lebenzeichen" from him (Ep. 82); a few months later Jaspers expressed his "sadness" that they had not "spoken" (Ep. 83). In June of 1929, Heidegger made the unusual confession: "Indeed I always philosophize with you in silence" (Ep. 84). A month later Jaspers indicated some discontent over two pieces Heidegger had sent him, namely, his book on Kant and the Husserl address: "I have now only fleetingly surveyed the book and am pleased with the lectures. It is obviously a completely new interpretation, self-contained, strange to me and without relation to what Kantian philosophy is to me. . . . On the Husserl address I have some impertinent questions"(Ep. 29). Four months later Jaspers spoke hope-fully about the possibility of an imminent visit from Heidegger in words full of pathos: "It would be very painful if nothing should come of this!"(Ep. 89) As the time rapidly approached when their relationship would suffer the negative consequences of National Socialism, their correspondence and visits intensified. In May of 1929 we have this remarkable letter from Jaspers to Heidegger: "For an unthinkable time I have belonged to no one as I have to you. It was to me like being free in unceasing transcending. What is so mutually common to both of us I hear in your words, partly strange to me, but still identical. Let us philosophize further!" (Ep. 95). In May of 1930 Heidegger waxed eloquent about the "feeling of friendship" between them (Ep. 101).

Jaspers was enthusiastic when there was talk in 1930 of Heidegger's joining the faculty of Heidelberg. His words to the latter are memorable: "Of all the possibilities your coming to Heidelberg is the only one that means something to me. It would then be decided whether we are in a position to philosophize in the most radical discussion or whether the old solipsistic way which was always the case in the universities would continue: where there was only polemic but no realization." In the same letter he also ventures a complaint: "When I think of the possibility of your coming I have an impulse that augments the wish—if I think of your silence in our conversations, I long above all for the mutual, radical discussion which occurred earlier, but has for so long been inactive" (Ep. 102).

In response to a letter in which Heidegger wrote to Jaspers, "You speak out of the clear and decisive posture of a conqueror" (Ep. 109), the latter responds cautiously: "I do not feel myself to be a 'conqueror,' as your friendly, but dangerously distancing formula says, but only at the threshold" (Ep. 110). Having received the indirect comment of Heidegger that "we have no camaraderie," Jaspers adds: "In recent years a sadness has come over my relationship to you." A few months before Heidegger's famous address as rector of Heidelberg, Jaspers reiterated what had always seemed to be the case between them: "If the writings have the tendency to estrange [us from one another], all the more must the [spoken] word connect" (Ep. 112). The discrepancy between Heidegger's *writings* and his *person* became increasingly enigmatic to Jaspers; it in fact became the problematic that would deepen Jaspers's conviction that the writings should be read in terms of the person, and vice versa.

Jaspers thus begins to speak of their relationship in the past tense: "I like to think back to the days with you. I thank you that we were mutually respectful of one another. In quiet moments which I do not forget, you let me gaze into your origins, as was one time very important, but . . . has become more so now" (Ep. 115).

On May 27, 1933, Heidegger delivered his controversial address on "The Self-Assertion of the German University." Jaspers's initial reaction to the copy he was sent was mixed. He praises Heidegger's high estimation of the early Greeks, but shows no awareness of the ominous character signaled in the address. He expresses the hope that the two of them can share a visit soon. Heidegger's reply, dated two years later, speaks of their relationship in vague generalities, and of the rectorate as a "miscarriage" (Ep. 120). The last letter between them before Jaspers was deprived of his teaching office in 1937 was written on May 16, 1936. Jaspers still boasts of an affinity between them: "Your attitude toward philosophy in this time is the same as mine; the things you treasure—Nietzsche, Hölderlin—bring us near" (Ep. 123). It is clear, nevertheless, that Jaspers has deep misgivings about the times.

There was no exchange of letters between them from 1936 to 1948, although the Nachlass contains the text of a letter written to Heidegger by Jaspers, but not mailed, in which Jaspers complained that he had received no word in response to his removal from office or to copies of his books that he had sent to Heidegger. It appears that a letter Jaspers wrote in 1948 was also not mailed, but it is nevertheless instructive for our purposes. He expresses the regret that no letter had come to him from Heidegger after the demise of the Nazi government in 1945—a letter that might explain "what is still inconceivable" to him (Ep. 125).

After Jaspers relocated to Basel, he sent a letter to Heidegger, extending to him an offer to renew their relationship. The words are memorable: "There was once something between us which bound us together. I cannot believe that it has been extinguished. The time seems ripe, so I turn myself to you in the hope that you will join me in the wish to exchange a word" (Ep. 126). Four months later Heidegger wrote to Jaspers, thus breaking the silence of some thirteen years. Heidegger wrote: "*That* you have written, is to me a great joy." He assures Jaspers that despite the things that have happened, his relationship to the latter has remained "unaffected" (Ep. 127)—a claim that Jaspers welcomes, as he writes in response (Ep. 128). Since there were no further visits between them, their correspondence has to suffice as their principal communication—a fact that makes these documents richer in intellectual content.

In 1950, Heidegger made an effort to explain why he stopped his visits to the Jaspers household in 1933. It was not, as supposed, "because a Jewish wife lived there, but *because I was ashamed of myself.*" He further expressed concern for her well-being (Ep. 142). Upon receiving this letter, Jaspers hastily replied, assuring Heidegger of his thanks—as well as that of his wife's—for the "frank explanation." He continues, generously: "That you have expressed being 'ashamed' means much to me. With this you enter into a community of all of us who have lived and [now] live in a state for which even 'shame' is an inappropriate word" (Ep. 142). Jaspers then assures Heidegger that he and his wife never believed that her Jewishness was the basis for the extinction of their relationship. Jaspers then shares with Heidegger his own version of the latter's behavior in 1933: "You will pardon me if I say what I once thought: that you seemed to conduct yourself toward National Socialism like a child who dreams, not knowing what he is doing, who accedes blindly and forgetfully to an undertaking which appears to him so different from what it is in reality and suddenly stands before a heap of ruins and drives himself forward" (Ep. 143). Heidegger in reply admits that his wife also had said the same thing about his "shame." With Jaspers's version of Heidegger's behaving like a child he fully concurs, hastening to add details about his election to the rectorate at Freiburg and its immediate aftermath that would confirm that interpretation. Heidegger confesses: "The guilt of the individual remains, and it is all the more lasting, the more individual it is" (Ep. 144).

After Heidegger's "explanation" the correspondence between them begins to wane. It would be two years before Jaspers would respond to Heidegger, justifying the "delay" as follows: "This delay was not only [due to] negligence, and was not occasioned by the multitude of insistent questions . . . ; rather the essential reason for it was an embarrassment (*Befangenheit*) provoked by the content of your last letters, their discussions about 1933 and the following years with which my remembrances were not in complete agreement" (Ep. 149). That he now breaks his silence is in the interest of "good will," the "consciousness of an obligation which issues from the indelible distant past." He further complains about Heidegger's failure to respond critically to his writings—an old complaint—especially to Jaspers's *Schuldfrage*, a copy of which he had sent to Heidegger. Writing now under the spell of Hannah Arendt's book *The Origins of Totalitarianism* (1951), Jaspers challenges Heidegger's superficial—even foreboding—grasp of postwar political realities—a deficiency that recalls the posture of Heidegger in 1933.

Jaspers's aggressiveness in interpreting Heidegger's political statements probably accounts for the six-year interval of silence between them that ensued after 1963. The spell was broken—once again, at Jaspers's initiative—by a letter bringing seventieth-birthday greetings to Heidegger. He is motivated by "an old distant past" to seek to revive the exchange. He writes: "I respond to you with empty hands and can only wish that you may be granted a more fulfilling, reflective and productive evening of life" (Ep. 152). Heidegger does not reply to this greeting until Jaspers' eightieth birthday three years later. In Heidegger's quite *feierlich* (so Jaspers replied) letter and Jaspers's measured response, nostalgia is overtaken by a feeling that their relationship was virtually at an end. For a period of six years there is no further communication until Heidegger's telegram of condolence to Gertrude Jaspers on the occasion of Jaspers's death.

Conclusion

The impression one gains from this report is that the relationship between these giants of twentieth-century philosophy was—in Jaspers's own words—"one-sided."[30] Jaspers was always reaching out to Heidegger, who responded in puzzling ways that generated frustration in the former. This is why I conclude that Jaspers's career-long attempt to "understand Heidegger" was more of a psychological than a philosophical enterprise. The *Briefwechsel* confirms what the *Notizen* indicate, namely, that Jaspers's personal reservations about Heidegger the man blocked his full access to Heidegger the thinker. As he said in his autobiographical statement: "One may be able to penetrate the thinker through the writings, but not understand." In the matter of his relationship to Heidegger, it is finally Jaspers the psychologist who prevails over Jaspers the philosopher. His psychological hermeneutic admonishes: Don't read the person through the writings; read the writings through the person.

NOTES

1. Paul Arthur Schilpp, ed., *The Philosophy of Karl Jaspers*, augmented edition (LaSalle, Ill.: Open Court, 1957), pp. 75/1–75/16.

2. Karl Jaspers, *Notizen zu Martin Heidegger*, ed. Hans Saner (Munich: Piper Verlag, 1978).

3. *Martin Heidegger/Karl Jaspers, Briefwechsel, 1920–1963*, ed. Walter Biemel and Hans Saner (Munich: Piper Verlag, 1990).

4. Schilpp, *Philosophy of Karl Jaspers*, p. xv.

5. On the "character" of the *Notizen* in this respect, see Saner's statement in the "Vorwort": "Wir haben uns für eine Publikation entschlossen, aus der Überzeugung, dass in den *Notizen* wirklich das steht, was Jaspers über Heidegger gedacht hat, und das en in ihnen am rückhaltlosesten *so* steht, *wie* er es gedacht hat: nicht abgelöst von der ertraumten Hoffnung, nicht von den Enttäuschungen und nicht von der komplexen Person Heideggers. Aber auch nicht gefiltert durch Konvention und Formung. Die Spontaneität dieser Aufzeichnungen bürgt für eine Wahrheit, die zwar nicht die objecktive der Analyse, aber die subjecktive der Redlichtkeit ist" (p. 20).

6. Schilpp, *Philosophy of Karl Jaspers*, p. 34.

7. Ibid., p. 36.

8. Ibid., p. 75/2.

9. Ibid., p. 75/1. It is of some importance for the thesis of this essay that Jaspers's knowledge of Heidegger at this time was based "wholly on the person"—as Saner notes (p. 8)—rather than on any direct knowledge on Jaspers's part of Heidegger's dissertation or *Habilitationsschrift*.

10. Ibid., p. 75/6.

11. Ibid., p. 75/3.

12. Ibid., p. 75/5.

13. Ibid., p. 75/6.

14. Ibid.

15. Ibid., p. 75/8.

16. Ibid., p. 75/16.
17. Ibid., p. 75/10, emphasis mine.
18. Ibid., p. 75/15.
19. Jaspers, *Notizen*, paragraph 122 (p. 142).
20. Ibid, paragraph 147 (p. 163).
21. Ibid., paragraph 198.
22. Ibid., paragraph 91 (p. 106).
23. Ibid., paragraph 122 (p. 142).
24. Ibid., paragraph 95 (p. 115).
25. Ibid., cf. paragraph 176 (pp. 193–96).
26. Ibid., paragraph 122 (p. 141).
27. Ibid., paragraph 122 (p. 141).
28. Ibid., paragraph 12 (p. 50).
29. Ibid., paragraph 102 (p. 125).
30. Schilpp, *Philosophy of Karl Jaspers*, p. 75/16.

5

On the Responsibility of Intellectuals: Reflections on Heidegger and Jaspers

Joseph Margolis

ONE CANNOT now read Karl Jaspers's postwar public essays—those, for example, like Die Schuldfrage, The Idea of the University, Reason and Anti-Reason in Our Time, The Future of Germany, all published with a flood of other books tumbling out from 1946 on—without a sense of Jaspers's own sense of scrupulous devotion to the responsibility of intellectuals. The courage of the Schuldfrage and The Future of Germany is certainly not dimmed by the somewhat boring and rather old-fashioned instruction of the Idea of the University and the Reason and Anti-Reason volumes. And yet, even in books of the latter sort, as much as in the former, there is, finally, an element of tact and seriousness and of work to be done that cannot be ignored, that implicates Heidegger's doctrines. It is undoubtedly because we cannot now read these books without a sense of Heidegger's looming presence in all of them; for Heidegger is certainly their unmentioned opponent—the Heidegger who at times lets slip his own contempt for Jaspers's vision. In fact, as Jaspers himself records Heidegger's explicit observation that his first booklet on the university, also titled The Idea of the University (1923), "was the most irrelevant of all the irrelevancies of the time"[1]—the same Heidegger who authored the Rektoratsrede, to be sure.

Even in the autobiographical essay that appears in the Schilpp volume, the original discussion of Heidegger, written for the occasion, was suppressed, on the author's change of mind, until Heidegger's death in 1976. And in the Notizen zu Heidegger, posthumously published by Jaspers's editor, Hans Saner, the evidence shows incontrovertibly that Jaspers must have been largely occupied with the sense of his particular calling: that is, that his own intellectual obligations must take the form of answering, one by one, all of Heidegger's political and philosophical outrages—in his own quiet way and by his own lights, mixing (as was his habit) tact and kindness and, now, the knowledge that, having survived the Nazi storm *inside* the country without compromise, he must come forward to bear witness again to the redemptive themes of the German *Weltanschauung*.

1

Nothing that I say regarding the obligation of intellectuals could possibly deserve comparison or the right of critique under those circumstances: except of course for the fact that Jaspers's own total devotion to the theme of human freedom entails a right and an obligation imposed on all of us. In fact, troubling as it must be, the truth is that we American academics, working in the incomparably more favorable setting of our own university world, have hardly come to terms—with the possible single exception, in recent years, of the airing of the Vietnam War—with the less arduous crises of our own history. There is a *Schuldfrage* there that we have yet to address that we cannot possibly answer as well as Jaspers. But that, frankly, is not my principal concern today.

Heidegger also had Jaspers on his mind, perhaps more as a consequence of their peculiar personal association than of any strenuous philosophical challenge—in particular, perhaps because of the deep uneasiness Heidegger must have experienced in his treatment of Jaspers, and in his sense that Jaspers was too honorable, too persistent in his friendship, too perceptive to be ultimately discounted. Even so, Jaspers figures explicitly in Heidegger's careful and detailed distinction between "scientific philosophy" and philosophy as *Weltanschauung* ("worldview philosophy") which appears early in the Marburg lectures of the summer of 1927, translated as *The Basic Problems of Phenomenology*. Heidegger had already reviewed Jaspers's *Psychologie der Weltanschauungen*, which appeared in its third edition in 1925, several years before the Marburg lectures. There is certainly no sense that Heidegger was preoccupied with Jaspers's detailed writings and statements in any sense matching that in which Jaspers must have been obsessively occupied with Heidegger. And yet, the conception of *Weltanschauung* is certainly pivotal for both thinkers. More than that, the entire question of intellectual responsibility—its very task and objective—depends on it.

The strange thing is that, regarding *Weltanschauung*, both begin from very nearly the same intuition; each moves in what is nearly the direction most opposed to the other's; and each is captivated by an inherently untenable position. Furthermore, each offers pronouncements about the responsibility of intellectuals that are conceptually inseparable from his own reading of *Weltanschauung*. Part of the story is a piece of fascinating gossip that the importance of Nazism renders unavoidable. Part is bound up with the dialectic of the more-than-implicit opposition between the two, which helps to define the options available to *us*. And part rests with the unspoken corrective that *we* may still usefully draw from the same intuition from which they jointly begin. For, on any reasonable review, that intuition is one that is almost universally shared by late-twentieth-century Western philosophy. So it may even be that the vagaries of academic history have their own instructive cunning.

Here is Heidegger's summary of Jaspers's position, which—let it be said again—Heidegger utterly condemns:

> In his *Psychologie der Weltanschauungen*, Jaspers says that "when we speak of world-views we mean Ideas, what is ultimate and total in man, both subjectively, as life-experience and power and character, and objectively, as a world having objective shape." For our purpose of distinguishing between philosophy as world-view and scientific philosophy, it is above all important to see that the world-view, in its meaning, always arises out of the particular factical existence of the human being in accordance with his factical possibilities of thoughtful reflection and attitude-formation, and it arises thus *for* this factical Dasein. The world-view is something that in each case exists historically from, with, and for the factical Dasein. A philosophical world-view is one that expressly and explicitly or at any rate preponderantly has to be worked out and brought about by philosophy, that is to say, by theoretical speculation, to the exclusion of artistic and religious interpretations of the world and the Dasein. This world-view is not a by-product of philosophy; its cultivation, rather, is the proper goal and nature of philosophy itself. In its very concept philosophy is world-view philosophy, philosophy as world-view. If philosophy in the form of theoretical knowledge of the world aims at what is universal in the world and ultimate for the Dasein—the whence, the whither, and the wherefore of the world and life—then this differentiates it from the particular sciences, which always consider only a particular region of the world and the Dasein, as well as from the artistic and religious attitudes, which are not based primarily on the theoretical attitude. . . . Philosophy, it appears, is . . . essentially world-view philosophy |and| naturally ought to be scientific.[2]

Heidegger draws here on Kant's authority, which he appears quite happy to accept, in assessing Jaspers's conception. That is, he reminds us of the convergence of Kant's notions of the "scholastic" and "cosmic" (or "cosmopolitan") views of philosophy—that philosophy "is indeed the science of the relation of every use of knowledge and reason to the final purpose of human reason, under which, as the supreme end, all other ends are subordinated and must come together in unity in it"; and that, accordingly, Kant's famous three questions regarding knowledge, action, and hope are, as Heidegger puts it, "concentrated in the fourth |question,] 'What is man?' For the determination of the final ends of human reason results from the explanation of what man is. It is to these ends that philosophy in the academic [or scholastic] sense also must relate."[3] In short, Heidegger shares the Kantian strategy for uniting the theoretical and the practical.

Now, Heidegger plays with the possibility that Jaspers had got philosophy's objective right: "Being is the proper and sole theme of philosophy," he affirms. He is careful to relate this pronouncement to the Greek sense of ontology, and he is also careful to observe that there is no equivalent in Greek thought for Weltanschauung ("kosmo-theoria")—the term is purely German, he says.[4] He goes on, in fact, to affirm that "the notion of a world-view philosophy is simply inconceivable . . . an absurdity."[5]

The conceptual fiddling, here, is not unimportant. We need to have Heidegger's formula before us:

> Philosophy is the theoretical conceptual interpretation of being, of being's structure and its possibilities. Philosophy is ontological. In contrast, a world-view is a positing knowledge of beings and a positing attitude toward beings; it is not ontological but ontical. The formation of a world-view falls outside the range of philosophy's tasks, but not because philosophy is in an incomplete condition and does not yet suffice to give a unanimous and universally cogent answer to the questions pertinent to world-views; rather, the formation of a world-view falls outside the range of philosophy's tasks because philosophy in principle does not relate to beings. it is not because of a defect that philosophy renounces the task of forming a world-view but because of a distinctive priority: it deals with what every positing of beings, even the positing done by a world-view, must already *presuppose* essentially. . . . Philosophy must legitimate by its own resources its claim to be universal ontology.[6]

It is plain enough that Heidegger construes his own version of phenomenology as he does by way of joining—and thereby correcting—the convergent functions of Aristotle's, Kant's, and Husserl's enterprises: for he characterizes it as pursuing the universal structures of being as opposed to the apparent structures of beings.

The curious thing is that, in a fair sense, Heidegger has completely misrepresented Jaspers's intention, in reporting, accurately enough, the project of Jaspers's *Psychologie der* Weltanschauungen; and that, as a result, what he correctly grasps as the limitation of Jaspers's project is—he fails to see—quite ironically, just what is also the essential limitation of his own project. Consequently, we, observing the stalemate (that is not perceived, of course, as a stalemate by either Jaspers or Heidegger) must redefine the philosophical undertaking *if* we mean to think along with

Jaspers and Heidegger; and, as a result of doing that, we must redefine the obligation of intellectuals in a fresh way. For the tradition that includes both of these thinkers insists on a *metaphysical* connection between what a rigorous philosophy could possibly discover—that bears at once on man's practical and theoretical concerns—and his intellectual obligations. This, of course, is simply the same point Kant had collected at the end of the First Critique. Surely Jaspers and Heidegger are in agreement here.

The trouble is that Jaspers thinks that we must pursue *Weltanschauung* both because each of us *is* a historical or factical *Dasein* and because there is no possibility, *granting that*, of ever reaching invariant or timeless universals of being; and that Heidegger, though he concedes factical Dasein, believes that we must (and apparently can) somehow extricate ourselves from that "phenomenal" limitation—to rise, not (it is true) to the universal invariances of plural beings (the "ontical" project Heidegger thinks Jaspers is committed to), but to the true "ontological" invariances of Being itself. Jaspers's sense of intellectual obligation is keyed to *his* sense that we cannot rise beyond *Weltanschauung* and that that is never enough for universal practical (or theoretical) principles; and Heidegger's sense of obligation is keyed to *his* conviction that we would indeed be directionless if we were confined to mere *Weltanschauungen* and that (fortunately) we are not so deprived because we may call on the saving possibilities of "scientific philosophy." When, therefore, Heidegger argues that "a world-view . . . springs in every case from a factical Dasein in accordance with its factical possibilities, and it is what it is always for this particular Dasein [and, further, that] this in no way asserts a relativism of world-views,"[7] he correctly grasps the relativistic consequence of *Jaspers's* option—*which Jaspers does not entirely grasp*; but he also wrongly supposes that *he* can escape the same fate by way of the phenomenological exercise he recommends in the Marburg lectures and in *Being and Time*.

To see matters thus is to grasp in the most stunningly clear way that *both* existential phenomenology and philosophy as *Weltanschauung* cannot escape a profound relativism (which need not, of course, be incoherent, despite ancient and modern rumors to the contrary) *and* that the attempt to ground the responsibility of intellectuals in metaphysics entails therefore a radical change of conception from both the Jasperian and Heideggerian options. In this important sense, the answer to the question of the responsibility of intellectuals is inseparable from our best interpretation of the tradition (as in a way both Heidegger and Jaspers saw) linking Aristotle, Saint Thomas, Descartes, and Kant.

The answer need not be a pessimistic one; but, on the argument being mounted, it cannot be an optimistic one in either of the senses favored by Jaspers and Heidegger. That is the strenuous truth that lies behind the indictment of Heidegger's Nazism and Jaspers's oversimple postwar progressivism.

Surprising as it may seem, it is the same conceptual incoherence that informs both views. Each of our philosophers pulls the same abstract rabbit out of the same historical hat: Jaspers, by a humanity we cannot decry; Heidegger by a privileged revelation no one else can espy. In this regard, Jaspers is perhaps closest to the view advanced by Karl Popper; and Heidegger may be judged to have betrayed, ultimately, as Kant and Husserl had before him, the inherent constraint those last worthies frankly concede before they press on in their inimitable way (which Heidegger criticizes but never escapes) toward transcendental invariances.

The important conclusion we mean to broach here is simply that the convergent failure of both Heidegger's and Jaspers's projects signifies that the obligation of intellectuals cannot be made to depend in any way on the universal structures of being: *there are none*; and that, therefore, we must retrace our steps with the greatest care *if* we mean to repudiate Heidegger's general line of practical instruction or to redeem anything like Jaspers's humanism.

We must remember that, in *Being and Time*, Heidegger specifically sets ontology the "task of destroying the history of ontology": "The specific kind of Being of ontology hitherto [analyzed, he remarks], its findings, *and its failures*, have been necessitated in the very character of Dasein."[8] "All research [he adds]—and not least that which operates within the range of the central question of Being—is an *ontical* possibility of Dasein. Dasein's Being finds its meaning in temporality. But temporality is also the condition which makes historicality possible as a temporal kind of Being which Dasein itself possesses, regardless of whether or how Dasein is an entity 'in time.' Historicality, as a determinate character, is prior to what is called 'history' (world-historical historicizing [*welgeschichtliches Geschehen*])."[9]

What Heidegger means by this gymnastic utterance is that, although Dasein *is* an entity, that is, has number, is individuatable, is therefore "ontical"—in fact, is thus encountered in its *Alltäglichkeit*—it is, as it turns out, also "ontico-ontologically distinctive," prior to all other entities, precisely in that "*fundamental ontology*, from which alone all other ontologies can take their rise, must be sought in the *existential analysis of Dasein*." For, "Dasein *has* a pre-ontological Being *as* its ontically constitutive state": it is literally such "as to be something which understands something like Being."[10]

But, of course, *if* Heidegger concedes this much, then, since the saving ontology he means to pursue—the ontology of the universal structures of Being (*Sein*) as opposed to the failed ontologies restricted to plural beings (*Seiende*) is, first of all, governed *by* our reflection on the privileged ontology *of* a particular being (*Dasein*), and, secondly, cannot be fundamentally different therefore (regardless of what Heidegger says) from the Aristotelian and Kantian options he means to supersede. He cannot have "destroyed" the history of ontology if the ontology of Being is itself recovered only by a rigorous analysis of the "ontological" import of the "ontic" nature of *Dasein*. Q.E.D.

Nothing that Heidegger accomplished thereafter, neither the oracular revelations of the metaphysical destiny of the German people (of the *Rektoratsrede*) nor the late inverted Platonism of the self-disclosing power of Being itself (of the "Letter of Humanism"), could possibly obscure (or alter, for that matter) the elementary sense in which *our* ontological discoveries (however much they may surpass any propositionally formulable findings about essences, in the old canonical sense) *are* grounded in *our* "factical" (*faktisch*) existence.[11] Hence, *if* Heidegger is right—and he is, of course—in exposing the incapacity of Jaspers's "worldview" philosophy to recover the invariant structures of Being or of beings, then that very argument demonstrates that his own undertaking must fail as well: for it begins with the same historically contingent existential reflection. The curious irony is that Jaspers seems to have grasped this essential point— less complicatedly, of course—at the very beginning of his own much less complicated career *and* without ever wavering thereafter.

The illuminating paradox is this: Once you begin with the resources of *Weltanschauung*—once you admit that you are confined to such resources initially—you can never claim to make discoveries that exceed them; otherwise, you must cheat conceptually. So Jaspers was right after all; and Heidegger must have been his unwilling and self-deceiving ally, who of course chose to repudiate, by that very connection, the liberal and democratic and humanistic themes Jaspers so obviously embodied. So much, therefore, for any *essential* (as opposed to any merely necessary) connection between scientific ontology and moral instruction: in particular, affecting the responsibility of intellectuals. Still, what defeats Heidegger defeats Jaspers as well.

Jaspers's mistake is a simpler one, but it is also remarkably closely linked to the initial intuition of Heidegger's very different undertaking. One certainly cannot now read the following, from *The Idea of the University*, without juxtaposing Heidegger's notion of scientific philosophy and Jaspers's vision (which, of course, goes unmentioned):

> Because science is limited to the cogent and universally valid, scientific research and discovery is limited to the study not of Being itself, but of its

appearance. Opposed to the narrower concept of science there is a broader one [of philosophical and existential thought]. Science can acknowledge this broader concept as complementary and perhaps even basic to itself, provided confusions are avoided. The type of thinking which illumines by flashes of insight [and is not essentially discursive] is not part of science but has its own independent roots. Science in this wider sense [wider than Greek science] includes any clear understanding obtained through rational and conceptual means. [It] is identical with the area of lucid self-knowledge.[12]

Jaspers's essential point, put negatively, is that "the universality of the 'new [modern] science' does not reside in an all-inclusive world-system, but in open-minded readiness to subject everything to scientific investigation."[13] So the universality of the new science—a fortiori, the universality of any philosophy that follows the new science, follows the appearances of things: philosophy as *Weltanschauung*—is not rightly universal in its propositional claims but only in its *openness to the impossibility of universal scientific and philosophical claims*. It is committed to the ideal of universal scientific and philosophical validity all right; but it cannot achieve that objective, and wisdom lies in understanding why—and how—rational science and philosophy may be "completed." To this end, Jaspers mentions, in the same context, that kind of thought ("speculative philosophy," for instance) "which requires our personal commitment in order to achieve the status of truth"; and "though [that] may function [only] as a cipher of code, simultaneously disclosing and concealing reality." All such forms of thought are evidently symbiotically connected with the wholeness of life.[14]

Jaspers is both careful and careless, however, in applying his vision to the question of German guilt. For one thing, in countering the evil that the *Schuldfrage* addresses, he says quite straightforwardly that "wherever men become aware of their humanity and recognize man as man, they grasp human rights and base themselves on a natural law to which both victor and vanquished may appeal . . . a universally human natural law." But he also remarks, more carefully, that this notion of "right," "the sublime idea of men who derive their existence from an origin which is secured by force alone, but not determined by force," "can apply only to guilt in the sense of crime [legal guilt] and in the sense of political liability, not to moral and metaphysical guilt." So right is not really universal: "All human norms," Jaspers affirms, "are full of flaws and injustice in their consequences."[15]

There is much that hangs on this distinction, both regarding metaphysics and the metaphysics of guilt and responsibility, in particular the responsibility of intellectuals. For, first of all, *what* could possibly be Jaspers's source of confidence in the "natural law" of legal and political life—in effect, of the "positive" or "factical," or *sittlich* in the merely descriptive sense? And, secondly, *what* could the deeper moral and metaphysical redemption he has in mind implicate? He himself considers that the "right" established by victors and holding "between victor and vanquished," may be "decided by acts of political will." Such events, he says, "become the fundament of a positive factual law which is not justified through right."[16]

Heidegger would have condemned such a natural law as one that merely catered to appearances. He would have appealed to a higher revelation that captured the existential essence of the German nation. Of course, Heidegger's claim is worse than nonsense, and Jaspers effectively counters its conceptual pretension (at least implicitly) by characterizing "moral guilt [as] insight, which involves *penance and renewal* . . . an inner development then also taking effect in the world of reality"; and "metaphysical guilt [as resulting] in a *transformation of human self-consciousness before God* . . . [that is, where (such an) arrogance as Heidegger's, may we say?] becomes impossible."[17]

But it looks as if Jaspers *cannot* justify the positive codes and norms of actual life: they are merely *sittlich* in the prejudicial sense of self-vindication, or else they appeal to a higher revelation beyond the play of appearances. On the latter option, Jaspers cannot really oppose Heidegger's conceptual strategy, he can only oppose his moral taste. Is that a fair conclusion? It is, if we but acknowledge that Jaspers is an exceedingly naive or optimistic theorist who believes that the scrupulous discursive probing of the very play of appearances (*Weltanschauung*) can truly progress (somehow) toward a deeper penetration of the ultimately impenetrable, endless truth of being—what, through the "ciphers" and "codes" of interpretation is endlessly revealed and concealed. The point is that Jaspers's trust in the validity of the "universally human natural law" *entails* a progressivism *of some sort*. It is curiously like Karl Popper's notion of "verisimilitude," which Popper ultimately repudiated—without, however, fully grasping that, in doing just that, he had utterly subverted the linchpin doctrine of his entire philosophical optimism.[18] Jaspers, more than Popper, of course, *requires* such a progressivism; for otherwise what could he offer to vindicate his analysis of German guilt? *It would not be enough to acknowledge merely that reality is ultimately unfathomable or, contingently, unreliable regarding any would-be universality.* Here, for instance is a passage that could have been written by the Popper that still advocated verisimilitude:

It is impossible to prove scientifically that there should be such a thing as science. . . . The choice of an object of science that is made from an infinite number of existing objects on the basis of this object itself, is a choice that cannot be justified scientifically. . . . The ideas that guide us are tested in the systematic process of investigation, but they themselves do not become an object of direct investigation.[19]

It fails for the same reason Popper's program does: it cannot rely on grounds internal to *Weltanschauung* and it cannot *discursively* extract any reliable criterion from Existenz or God or transcendence. And yet it needs *some* basis for its historical function.

Science and moral and political seriousness require what Jaspers calls "the second language," which develops and depends upon effective generalization and communication with one another via such generalization.[20] But, of this, Jaspers himself says: "We experience being in the ciphers of existence [that is, in the languages by which alone (human) Existenz can treat of transcendence, not transcendence itself]; it takes reality to reveal transcendence. About transcendence [being] we can know nothing in general; we can hear it only historically, in reality. Experience is the font of transcendent ascertainment as it is the font of empirical knowledge."[21]

If we take these concessions seriously, we are led to see that Jaspers *cannot* escape mere *Sittlichkeit* or an illicit progressivism, on the one hand; and cannot, on the other, effectively extricate himself to disallow Heidegger's pretensions, except in the completely vacuous sense that *no* presumptive law or norm *can be* transcendently vindicated:

> The cipher [says Jaspers] is what brings transcendence to mind without obliging transcendence to become an objective being, and without obliging Existenz to become a subjective being. It is a decline from the original genuine presence into the sphere of consciousness at large when exegesis of a cipher makes of transcendence an object, something we know, or when subjective modes of conduct are conceived and bred as organs for the perception and production of the metaphysical experience. . . . The original present reading of the cipher script is without method, not volitive, not to be produced according to plan. It is like a gift from the source of being. As a mundane ascertainment of transcendence, it seeks out the light from the root of possible Existenz, and its content is not an advancement of knowledge but the historic truth of transparent existence.[22]

Any retreat from this austere position—which Jaspers requires for the argument of the *Schuldfrage* and *The Idea of the University*—entails the illicit progressivism already noted.

Between them, therefore, between Heidegger and Jaspers, *we*, also advocates of radical history, must confess that we lack a *principled* foundation on which to applaud or condemn either Jaspers or Heidegger.

To say this is not to advocate irresponsibility or conceptual anarchy: it is only to oblige us to present our own prejudices in an honest way. Heidegger escapes beyond the *phainomena* of history; and Jaspers claims to find a sign of transcendent contact within blind history. Neither option is convincing.

The question of the obligation of intellectuals rests in this *aporia*. Jaspers has the advantage over his countryman, at least in the space of present history. For he is the champion of open and unlimited communication—the theme of the freedom, after all, of the *Schuldfrage* and *The Idea of the University*. But even freedom ("existential freedom"), Jaspers says, "is downright incomprehensible. . . . It will not fit any concept—and there alone is the sense of freedom *fulfilled*. . . . [It] *cannot be known*, . . . there is no way in which it might be objectively conceived. I am sure of it *for myself*, not in thought but in Existenz, not in musing and asking about it, but in action. Whatever I say about freedom is a means of communication, invariably open to misunderstanding and only indirectly indicative."[23]

2

The disorder of both theories is clear enough: In spite of criticizing Kant, they are, or they are analogues of, the Kantian intrusion of noumena into the rational ordering of the phenomenal world, or of the flight to noumena themselves. Between them, they exhaust the aporetical possibilities and turn us back, therefore, to the profound contingencies of history: in which, in a symbiotized world of a Kantian-like sort—shorn now of all pretense of universality, invariance, systematic closure, totalization, apodicticity, privilege, and the like—we are obliged to reconsider the genuinely risked (perhaps existential) nature of both science and morality within the limits of discernible existence. The obligation of intellectuals, therefore, is the very nerve of that deeper question.

Our finding may be put more powerfully. In a sense, the curious dispute between Jaspers and Heidegger ranging over more than half a century, between colleagues drawn together in a relationship at once more and less than that of friendship, is very nearly the central thought-experiment of the cunning of philosophical history bent on demonstrating once and for all, in the twentieth century, the end of a certain strand of thought. Between them, Heidegger and Jaspers confirm that *there cannot be a noumenal constraint or directive to theoretical and practical life that could be rationally vindicated or trusted*. They exhaust the principal options of any such Kantian-like enthusiasm; and they fail—as Kant fails, despite his own great care in attempting to limit his conceptual researches to what is clearly licit.

We may put things this way: Heidegger and Jaspers begin with the Kantian intuition that the phenomenal world cannot be self-legitimating, although its cognitive claims must (rationally) be legitimated. That is, speaking in an idiom that is certainly not theirs but not, for that reason, unfriendly to their own conceptual question, first-order judgment and action implicate a second-order query regarding the limits, validity, cognitive source, universal scope, and the like of all such judgment and action. Heidegger and Jaspers agree, in effect, in holding that no attempt at legitimation confined to what is internal to *Weltanschauungen* (Jaspers) or to *Seiende* (Heidegger) could possibly escape the historical contingency of such phenomena. That, of course, is precisely what (on Heidegger's view) Kant and Husserl failed to perceive.

Jaspers believed that wisdom lay in grasping just how the discursively ineffable reality of transcendence and Existenz constrains, *in a legitimatively pertinent sense*, the cognitive pretensions of first-order thought and action. Heidegger believed that wisdom lay in grasping just how the illumination provided by an ontological disclosure of Being (as opposed to any would-be ontic discoveries among plural beings) presumptively orients German destiny *with regard to ontic choices*. Jaspers's thesis seems the more modest and more reasonable of the two; Heidegger's, the more sinister. Fair enough. But the bare impression hardly counts philosophically: their respective maneuvers are ultimately the same (applied, of course, in absolutely opposed ways), based on noumenal resources that, on the Kantian grounds they share, must be cognitively quite inaccessible.

The fatal equivocation they exploit is already present in Kant. The *opposition* between phenomena and noumena, *joined* to the discovery of synthetic a priori constraints (applied to phenomena), is really beyond Kant's conceptual resources: the idea that a rational agent (that is, a reflexively numbered self that could not possibly know itself as such, noumenally) must proceed by supposing it may act as a noumenon (among others) and that doing that entails acting under suitably universalizable maxims is already a mark of Kant's failure to escape certain conceptually illicit pretensions. Heidegger's supposition that the noumenal disclosures of *Sein* are either vouchsafed by *Dasein* (which *is* ontical) or by the mysterious workings of *Gelassenheit* functioning (somehow) independently of the *initial* activity of *Dasein* is similarly made to yield (illicitly) a legitimated constraint on the theory and practice of the ontic world.

Jaspers's related option takes a dual form: along one line of thought (resembling Popper's), theory and practice within the space of *Weltanschauung* are able to be directed in a progressive way with respect to the ineffabilities of transcendence and Existenz; along the other line of thought (the inverse of Heidegger's), we are able to know, within the space of the former, that we have not plumbed the reality of the latter, which is precisely what saves us. In both instances, questions of grounding, revelation, relevance, critique, validity and lack of validity, legitimation, limits of discourse and reason and the like are answered by reference to our secret knowledge of what, on the hypothesis, cannot possibly be known.

The upshot of Heidegger's and Jaspers's maneuvers, particularly with respect to practice, morality, political responsibility, and intellectual work in the service of political responsibility, is either *arbitrariness or privilege*. Both start with the admission of a need to legitimate what cannot be self-legitimating: the *weltanschaulich* or *sittlich* or phenomenal world is the begin-all of responsible thought and action; but it cannot certify itself in any normative way. Heidegger and Jaspers manage, nevertheless, to find a noumenal source of validation to meet the obvious need: Heidegger pretends that there is a higher determinate destiny ontologically revealed within the ontic vagaries of history itself; Jaspers pretends that awareness of the deeper ineffability of reality reclaims whatever is valid in our determinate inquiries and commitments regardless of their content, or else (even worse) that certain determinate forms of liberal humanity are actually favored by that ineffability. Of course, there is not the slightest chance of making either argument stick; hence, there is an insurmountable conceptual lacuna in the systematic efforts of each—the same one, in fact, however much we are ourselves attracted to Jaspers's obviously decent values and repelled by Heidegger's turn to Nazism (even the more exalted version the *Rektoratsrede* so ingeniously introduces).

It is in this sense that the cunning of historical reason provides the tableau of the strange contest between Jaspers and Heidegger, focused by the indirection of Jaspers's *Notizen* and by Heidegger's final appeal to his colleague after Germany's defeat, by which we ourselves are led to grasp the conceptual hopelessness of ever constructing a legitimative strategy by noumenal privilege.

There you have a genuine philosophical discovery—and an advance. If only we could hold to it, if only we could restrict ourselves to *phainomena*: not in the self-defeating noumenalized sense Kant and Husserl had already betrayed (before Heidegger and Jaspers), the sense in which the noumenal (the real) is disjunctively opposed to the phenomenal and constrains or informs it; but only in the philosophically bland sense in which *we* do whatever we do, without pretending to mount any ladders of cognitive or existential progress, risked in the open, experienced, epistemically one-dimensional world we inhabit.

That we are likely to fail again and again is suggested by the recent but fashionable versions of Heidegger's and Jaspers's incoherent experiments: that is, those for instance concerning the privileged ineffabilities of Emmanuel Levinas and Jean-François Lyotard.[24] And yet, to mention these recent thinkers may have its heartening lesson as well. For, we are clearly blind, now, to their conceptual disorder, and we see that no reason has been given (or can be given) for supposing that the legitimation of inquiry and commitment—in particular, the legitimation of intellectual responsibility—can proceed only in the noumenal way. That way is permanently closed. We must seek another.

NOTES

1. Karl Jaspers, "Philosophical Autobiography," in The Philosophy of Karl Jaspers, ed. Paul Arthur Schilpp, 2nd ed. aug. (La Salle, Ill.: Open Court, 1981), p. 75/5.

2. Martin Heidegger, The Basic Problems of Phenomenology, trans. Albert Hofstadter (Bloomington: Indiana University Press, 1982), pp. 6–7.

3. The passage cited in Heidegger, Basic Problems of Phenomenology, p. 8, is closely linked to the discussion of "the canon of pure reason" in the Critique of Pure Reason, B833.

4. Heidegger, Basic Problems of Phenomenology, pp. 4, 11.

5. Ibid., p. 12.

6. Ibid., p. 11–12.

7. Ibid., p. 9.

8. Martin Heidegger, Being and Time, trans. from 7th ed. by John Macquarrie and Edward Robinson (New York: Harper and Row, 1962), p. 19 (German edition); p. 40 (English edition); italics added.

9. Ibid., italics added.

10. Ibid., pp. 12–19 passim (German edition); pp. 33–41 passim (English edition); italics added in the last sentence.

11. Ibid., pp. 7–8 (German edition); pp. 26–28 (English edition). Cf. pp. 3–6 (German edition); pp. 22–26 (English edition).

12. Karl Jaspers, The Idea of the University, trans. H.A.T. Reiche and H. F. Vanderschmidt (with some omissions) (London: Peter Owen, 1960), pp. 28–29. Cf. Victor Farías, Heidegger and Nazism, ed. Joseph Margolis and Tom Rockmore, trans. Paul Burrell and Gabriel R. Ricci (Philadelphia: Temple University Press, 1989), chap. 9.

13. Jaspers, The Idea of the University, p. 28.

14. Ibid., p. 29.

15. Karl Jaspers, The Question of German Guilt, trans. E. B. Ashton (with omissions) (Westport, Conn.: Greenwood Press, 1978), pp. 37–38.

16. Ibid., pp. 38–39.

17. Ibid., p. 29.

18. See Karl R. Popper, Realism and the Aim of Science (from Postscript to the Logic of Scientific Discovery), ed. W. W. Bartley III (Lanham, Md.: Rowman and Littlefield, 1983), pp. xxxv–xxxvii, 57–58.

19. Karl Jaspers, "Philosophy and Science," trans. Ralph Manheim, *Partisan Review*, 16 (1949): 879. The point of the analogy is perhaps most clearly confirmed in Jaspers's notion of *das Umgreifende* ("the Encompassing"), which appears to be inexhaustible but in some sense constant—beyond discursible structures. See, for instance, Karl Jaspers, *Reason and Existence*, trans. William Earle (London: Routledge and Kegan Paul, 1956).

20. Karl Jaspers, *Philosophy*, vol. 3, trans. E. B. Ashton (Chicago: University of Chicago Press, 1970), pp. 115–117.

21. Ibid., p. 114. See also pp. 142–144.

22. Ibid., p. 120.

23. Karl Jaspers, *Philosophy*, vol. 2, trans. E. B. Ashton (Chicago: University of Chicago Press, 1970), p. 162.

24. See Emmanuel Levinas, *Totality and Infinity: An Essay on Exteriority*, trans. Alphonso Lingis (Pittsburgh: Duquesne University Press, 1969); and Jean-François Lyotard, *The Differend: Phrases in Dispute*, trans. Georges Van den Abeele (Minneapolis: University of Minnesota Press, 1988).

6

Jaspers and Heidegger: Philosophy and Politics

Tom Rockmore

WHEN IMPORTANT PHILOSOPHERS interact, the results are often interesting and sometimes decisive for the philosophical debate. The association between Jaspers and Heidegger is an important instance of the interaction between important philosophers, with consequences for understanding the link between philosophy and politics. What was initially intended, at least from Jaspers's side, as a friendship between two significant thinkers, was transformed, for contingent reasons, into a complex confrontation between philosophy and politics.

1

We can begin our discussion of the association between Jaspers and Heidegger with a remark about the interaction between important philosophers. Philosophy is obviously a solitary enterprise. Professional meetings, such as colloquia and symposia, which are mainly intended for the display of "results," only rarely produce new ideas. A true philosophical partnership, a genuine meeting of the minds in which two or more thinkers interact on the same plane, is exceedingly rare. Putnam has recently pointed to the supposedly joint theory of Apel and Habermas, although this is a position that appears to exist more in his own imagination than in reality.[1] Marxists often point to the philosophical position of Marx and Engels. But what Marxists view as a single joint view on inspection is merely the conflation, mainly for political reasons, of two very different, in fact incompatible, theories.[2] What appears to be an exception only confirms the rule that important thinkers usually work in isolation, spinning out theories that shape and reshape the philosophical discussion. When they cross, the results are often important, sometimes spectacular.

Obviously, the encounters between philosophers do not need to require actual physical presence. They also occur when one body of thought intersects with another one, when theories collide, when a large body in the philosophical universe enters into the orbit of another large body and distorts the surrounding gravitational field, so to speak. It is possible to regard the history of philosophy as a series of clashes between opposing thinkers, an ongoing battle in the strife of systems.[3] When competing systems come into contact, when they conflict, the result, which is never unimportant, sometimes produces a realignment of orbits around the philosophical sun, in effect, a new and different philosophical universe.

In the history of philosophy, the infrequent encounters between important thinkers have sometimes shaped the ensuing discussion for decades and even centuries. It is well known that Plato's position took shape in the encounter with Parmenides and Heraclitus. The interaction between Aristotle and Plato led to the basic alternative between empiricism and idealism that has continued to echo through the centuries. Aquinas's assimilation of Aristotle from a Christian perspective defined later scholasticism. Kant's confrontation with Hume and Leibniz gave rise to modern German philosophy. Hegel's reaction to Kant and Marx's to Hegel are well known. Fichte's interaction with Kant determined the course of later German Idealism, including the positions of Schelling, Hegel, and Marx. Russell's initial acceptance and later rejection of British Hegelianism was a basic source of Anglo-American analytic philosophy.

2

For contingent reasons, above all the rise of National Socialism, the encounter between Jaspers and Heidegger is framed by the relation between philosophy and politics. This theme continues to haunt the philosophical discussion, particularly the discussion of Heidegger's thought. The claim that philosophy is not political, that it is no more than the disinterested pursuit of truth itself, wherever the discussion may lead, is a by-product of the old idea that philosophy is the final source of truth, and truth occurs in, but is not of, time. The view that philosophy is a neutral source of truth is widely represented, for instance, in Husserl's conviction that the condition of knowledge is the transcendental reduction, which Merleau-Ponty justly regarded as impossible. Another instance is Habermas's reinstatement of the Husserlian claim through his call for undistorted communication, that is, a form of ideal communication that never occurs but that could take place only in isolation from the social context.

The venerable conception of philosophy as a neutral enterprise has recently been raised again in the defense of Heidegger in two ways. His thought, so the story goes, is not political. Further, his political actions have nothing to do with his philosophy, since Heidegger the man and Heidegger the thinker have nothing in common. Unfortunately for Heidegger's defenders, this particular defense clearly fails. On the one hand, it denies Heidegger's own basic claim that all thought, including his own, is only the abstract conceptual tip of the iceberg largely constituted by more ordinary everyday activities, themselves preconceptual and hence prephilosophical, such as wishing, dreaming, acting with an end in view, and so on. Heidegger's own position forbids in this instance the particular strategy that his students have invoked to protect him and his thought against the consequences of his political turning to Nazism. Second, Heidegger's thought, including *Being and Time*, is intrinsically political in a profound sense. In the *Nicomachean Ethics*, Aristotle did not propose a mere handbook of ethical principles, but a work intended to induce moral behavior in the Greek city-state. Analogously, fundamental ontology does not intend merely to comprehend authenticity for human being, but to bring it about, to promote an authentic gathering of the German people—initially through a real, then later ideal, form of Nazism, in order to advance the grasp of Being. The political aim, identified as the realization of the Germans as German, remains an explicit theme throughout all of Heidegger's later writing.

If Heidegger's ontology is political, it does not follow that all philosophy is linked to politics. Yet no one who teaches philosophy for a living can be unaware of the political dimensions of the discipline, of the occasional need to mute certain opinions, to incline thought before power, as it were. It is not by accident that Kant, who advocated acting on principles of universal validity, delayed publication for prudential reasons, or that Hegel was accused, unfairly so, of transforming his thought, something Fichte actually did, for reasons of political expediency. It is significant that Aristotle withdrew from Athens to avoid a second occasion to sin against philosophy; and it is further significant that Spinoza, in difficult straits, preferred not to accept a position in order to avoid restraints on his thought.

The practical politics of philosophy, which we all face, is not the same as philosophy's theoretical relation to politics. The many philosophical analyses of politics can all be collected in two main views: the venerable idea that philosophy founds or grounds politics; and the more recent idea that philosophy provides the standard or criterion to evaluate the political realm. The view that philosophy founds politics is linked to a foundationalist view of knowledge that goes back in the tradition at least to Plato's conception of philosophy as the science of sciences. Plato's idea of the relation of philosophy to politics derives from a significant displacement of the original Socratic claim for the need to examine our lives. Plato's recognition that finally only a philosopher can provide the political discourse that Socrates exhibited in practice was certainly one of the factors that induced him to make philosophy the minimum necessary condition for the just state. Plato's view that philosophy founds or grounds politics was an application of his insight that pure theory was practically relevant to the social situation. It was precisely this view that was countered by Aristotle, who denied that pure theory is socially useful and saw no role for pure philosophy in the political arena.

There was an intrinsic ambiguity in the Platonic view that has long echoed through the later discussion of the political role of philosophy. Either Plato understood philosophy to be the real ground of the really existing state, and hence intended to bring about a just state in practice, or he merely envisaged an ideal state as defined from a philosophical perspective. The texts do not permit us to provide an unequivocal reading. It is not impossible that he may have intended both to describe an ideal state and to found the state in practice, since merely to raise the possibility in some manner is to bring it about, to help it come into being. On this reading of the Platonic view, theory is understood as continuous with practice, which it not only grasps but also transforms.

Both ways of reading Plato's idea that philosophy founds the state have been influential in the later discussion. In modern times, any number of revolutionary movements have been based on the conception of the ruler as a kind of philosopher-king with direct insight into reality, uniquely qualified to lead his or her subjects toward the promised political land of freedom and justice. Every reader will have a favorite example of this quasi-Platonic conception of the ruler as political genius. A related idea is still current among philosophers, recently in Heidegger's effort to found Nazism in fundamental ontology and, as has been said, to lead the leaders of the Nazi state, as well as in Lukács's effort to ground Marxism-Leninism in his position. The history of philosophy records many efforts to imagine an ideal state, which Hegel regarded as Plato's aim,[4] including writings by Machiavelli, Bloch, and others. All forms of socialism, whether reformist, revolutionary, scientific, or other, follow Plato's lead in this respect.

The Socratic notion that the unexamined life is not worth living already invites the philosopher to pass political judgment. It is only if the political last word is philosophical, if philosophy is the locus of the conception of an adequate political ideal, that it can represent itself as an adequate political judge. The main historical event that engaged the reflection of philosophy is the great French Revolution. One cannot understand later German Idealism without taking this event into account. The French Revolution attracted the interest of Kant, who, from the perspective of a theory already in place before it occurred, sought vainly to find a place for revolution within his theory. Fichte's Jacobinism, his early defense of freedom of speech as the means for legitimate expression of dissent, his political theory describing a closed commercial state seeming to anticipate Maoist practice, and his energetic reaction in talks to the Germans against Napoleon, are all attributable to his reaction to the French Revolution. Hegel's own analysis of revolutionary excesses, which he regarded as reason run amok, in the *Phenomenology of Mind* is even better known. Marx's theory is a philosophy of the modern industrial society that presupposes the second and final stage of the French Revolution for the transition to human history.

3

The political aspect of philosophy influences the relation between Jaspers and Heidegger. Their association, which apparently began, at least from Jaspers's side, in the hope of a rare philosophical friendship, was finally transformed by the National Socialist revolution. The differences in their reaction to that event, and the way in which Jaspers, through the force of circumstances, intervened at Heidegger's request to thwart Heidegger's hopes, raises some interesting questions about the ability of philosophy, or certain philosophers, to accommodate politics within their views.

Jaspers and Heidegger were roughly of the same generation. Jaspers, who was six years older than Heidegger, studied medicine and became a psychiatrist before turning to philosophy. Hence, Jaspers and Heidegger forged their philosophical arms at almost the same moment. Their positions, which are very different, are forever linked in the literature as proponents of the "philosophy of existence," a term popularly but inexactly grouping Sartre and Marcel as well. As two important thinkers of approximately the same age, whose interests in part overlapped, it was likely that Jaspers and Heidegger would enter into contact. It was further likely, since each was an original thinker, that the relation would ultimately come apart. It was, then, merely a trick of fate that Nazism played a crucial role in their relationship.

The association of Jaspers and Heidegger was meant to be philosophical, but in fact turned out to be highly political. We can distinguish at least the following levels:

(a) Their friendship, which was cordial and marked, at least on

Jaspers's part, by the hope of real dialogue. Jaspers was aware of the infrequency with which important thinkers achieve a real philosophical friendship, although he seems to have hoped to do so with Heidegger. In the *Spiegel* interview, Heidegger denies the influence of Jaspers's Jewish wife on their relationship with the remark that between 1934 and 1938 Jaspers continued to send his publications to Heidegger.[5] Heidegger's aim in doing so was to deflect from himself the suspicion of anti-Semitism. But we now know that he was indeed anti-Semitic, as were many other German academics of his generation. In fact, even the claim to have maintained friendly relations with Jaspers was fictitious since, if Jaspers is to be believed, starting in 1937 Heidegger no longer even acknowledged the writings Jaspers sent to him.[6]

(b) Their loose association, at least in the public eye, as philosophers of existence. This association, which is described even in serious academic studies,[7] is scarcely reflected in the texts beyond a certain general impact of Kierkegaard and Nietzsche in their respective positions.

(c) As philosophical rivals, even antagonists, for instance, through their deep concern with Nietzsche and their mutual suspicion about the other's work in this area. Heidegger's repeated criticisms of *Weltanschauungsphilosophie* are in part aimed at Jaspers, as well as at Dilthey and Husserl. After Heidegger broke with real National Socialism and turned to Nietzsche, he treated Baeumler, the Nazi Nietzsche specialist, with genuine respect, but was particularly harsh on Jaspers. In his Nietzsche lectures, in a passage removed from the version he published, Heidegger remarks that Jaspers's study of Nietzsche is the worst. Jaspers reports several times that although he was familiar with parts of *Being and Time*, and produced a series of notes for a fundamental critique of Heidegger's thought, he was unable to read the entire book, much less to study it in detail.[8]

(d) The link to Hannah Arendt, Jaspers's student, but for a time Heidegger's mistress. This link, which has been studied in detail, is interesting but not apparently important philosophically.

(e) Heidegger's reliance on Jaspers's help in a moment of existential need, when he was under investigation at the end of the Second World War for collaboration with the Nazi regime he had faithfully served as rector, in practice as the philosophical *Führer*, of the University of Freiburg im Breisgau.

(f) Jaspers's reaction to the rectorial address. In a letter to Heidegger, he praised not only the style and conceptual density of the speech. He added that both Heidegger and Nietzsche were concerned with the link between truth and ancient Greece, but that Heidegger differed from Nietzsche in that, in Jaspers's stiff academic prose, "one could hope for a realization of his philosophical interpretation. Your talk has for this reason a trustworthiness."[9]

(g) Through Jaspers's decisive report on Heidegger, which was the basis for the decision to remove Heidegger from the university. In response to a request from Friedrich Oehlkers, a member of the commission charged with the examination of the role of various members of the academy during the Nazi period, Jaspers provided a report that proved devastating to his friend Heidegger, who had turned to Jaspers and to Archbishop Conrad Gröber in his moment of need.

(h) Jaspers's later efforts to prepare a study on Heidegger's thought in order to come to grips with Heidegger's philosophy and the significance of Heidegger's Nazi turning. This work, which was never completed, has been published. It represents, even in its incomplete state, a useful attempt by one significant thinker to analyze the thought of another.[10]

(i) Jaspers's own effort to confront the problem of German guilt. His forthright study of this theme contrasts usefully with Heidegger's complicated attempt to deny what could be denied, and to minimize the importance of what could not reasonably be denied, in short, to fabricate a legend to preserve his person and above all his thought.

4

From the vantage point of the link between philosophy and politics, the three most interesting elements of the Jaspers-Heidegger relationship are Jaspers's report on Heidegger, Jaspers's later effort to criticize Heidegger's thought from the perspective of Heidegger's Nazism, and Jaspers's examination of the problem of German guilt for the analysis of Heidegger's Nazism and philosophy. Each of these aspects merits separate treatment.

The report, which is contained in a letter of three pages, is divided into six points.[11] Jaspers begins by stating that in their last meeting in 1933, Heidegger was evasive, particularly with respect to the Jewish problem. This remark is significant, since Heidegger's defenders have always claimed that he was not an anti-Semite, but, as a recently discovered letter proves, he in fact was. The significance of this discovery is less the confirmation that Heidegger shared the usual racial prejudice of the period than the way in which it pierces the wall surrounding Heidegger erected by certain of his defenders, those who desire to concede absolutely nothing.[12]

Jaspers continues with comments on Heidegger's denunciation of Heidegger's assistant Baumgarten, a gentile, for consorting with Jews, and his somewhat better treatment of Werner Brock, who was Jewish. He concludes that Heidegger was merely practicing self-control. He then turns to Heidegger's thought and its relation to National Socialism. For Jaspers, although Heidegger's thought combined a certain verbal magic with nihilism, in comparison to other thinkers he had a rare talent. On this basis, in his report Jaspers maintained that it was important for Heidegger to be able to continue to work and to write.

This assessment is realistic, even generous, since Jaspers's private assessment of Heidegger's thought was more critical. In private, Jaspers correctly stigmatized Heidegger's indifference to science, as well as Heidegger's entirely unself-critical perspective. Jaspers's remark about the rare combination of verbal magic and nihilism in Heidegger's thought is almost a definitive description of the famous rectorial address, as well as the recently published *Beiträge zur Philosophie*. Jaspers notes Heidegger's denunciation of Baumgarten, although at the time he was unaware of Heidegger's further covert denunciation of Hermann Staudinger—a professor of chemistry at the University of Freiburg who was later awarded a Nobel Prize—on the grounds that he had been a pacifist during the First World War. Jaspers seems further to have been unaware that as rector Heidegger fired Max Müller, a student leader and anti-Nazi, later a respected Catholic intellectual, on the grounds of political unreliability and that he later blocked Müller's efforts to gain an academic appointment.

With respect to National Socialism, Jaspers correctly notes that with Krieck and Schmitt Heidegger was one of the few German professors to help bring Nazism to power. He remarks that the political aggressivity of Heidegger's rhetoric is less important than its capacity for thought, and suggests, incorrectly as it turns out, that the political commitment might quickly change. In retrospect, this is a major error, since Heidegger's commitment to real Nazism, which may never have been deep, was quickly abandoned; but his commitment to ideal Nazism was a permanent component in his later thought. Heidegger's later position cannot be understood without an awareness that it was elaborated in the difficult circumstances due to his continued commitment to ideal Nazism.

Jaspers, who accepts the excuse, often raised, that Heidegger was basically apolitical, notes that a change from Nazism to anti-Nazism must be evaluated according to the circumstances. For Jaspers, a change is worthless after 1941, and of little import when it was not radically carried through after June 30, 1934, namely after the assassination of Ernst Krieck. According to Jaspers, Heidegger was basically apolitical. Yet one of the points that emerges from the publication of Heidegger's lecture courses is his profound immersion in the day-to-day conduct of the Second World War, hardly what one would expect from someone without political inclinations. Jaspers's failure to differentiate between real and ideal versions of Nazism, perhaps because it didn't occur to him that anyone would be concerned with the ideal form of an existing phenomenon, undermines the importance of when Heidegger withdrew from existing National Socialism.

The letter ends with a recommendation that Heidegger be allowed to continue to publish, that he be suspended from teaching for some years, and that he be reinstated only on the basis of the intervening publications and the newly obtaining academic situation. It is a matter of record that Heidegger lost his position, but that as early as winter semester 1950–51, he was again allowed to teach. Had Jaspers's recommendation been followed with regard to the scrutiny of Heidegger's writings in the intervening period, it would have been clear that Heidegger had not changed his political opinions. If we bracket the infamous passage on the misunderstood truth and greatness of National Socialism, which appeared only in 1953, at least two passages from this period would have cast doubt on Heidegger's change of heart. One passage is from a letter to Marcuse, his former student: "To the severe and justified reproach that you express 'over a regime that has exterminated millions of Jews, that has made terror a norm and that transformed everything connected to the concepts of spirit, freedom, and truth into its opposite,' I can only add that instead of the 'Jews' one should put the 'East Germans,' and that is even more the case for one of the Allied Powers, with the difference that everything that happened since 1945 is known to all the world, while the bloody terror of the Nazis in reality was kept secret from the German people."[13]

The other passage, which was excised from the published version, occurs in a lecture on technology given in Bremen in December 1949: "Agriculture is now a motorized food-industry—in essence, the same as the manufacturing of corpses in gas chambers and extermination camps, the same as the blockading of nations, the same as the manufacture of hydrogen bombs."[14]

5

Clearly, Jaspers's report on Heidegger represents the informed judgment of a philosopher on politics. In Jaspers's unfinished work on Heidegger's thought, he further sought *inter alia* to evaluate the political element in Heidegger's position. Although his notes on Heidegger go back until 1928, in 1933, when Heidegger's collaboration with National Socialism was clear, Jaspers began a critical consideration of Heidegger's thought.[15] Jaspers's notes, which are not systematically developed, cover a wide variety of themes, such as Jaspers's reactions to Heidegger's person, his treatment of Jaspers and Jaspers's wife, the confusions concerning the relation of Jaspers's own view and Heidegger's, Jaspers's reactions to various writings by Heidegger, Jaspers's reporting on others' views of Heidegger, and so on. The volume, whose notes stretch up until 1964, reveals an ever greater disappointment of Jaspers's hopes for his philosophical friendship with Heidegger and an ever deeper awareness of the extent to which Heidegger's thought was compromised forever by Heidegger's turning toward Nazism. The result is a fascinating document in which, as Jaspers comes to grips with his own relation to Heidegger, Jaspers confronts on an increasingly deeper level the link between Heidegger's thought and Heidegger's Nazism. If this work is an indication, Jaspers only gradually realized that Heidegger's link to Nazism was not a momentary aberration corrected after the rectorate but was linked—even permanently linked—to Heidegger's philosophical thought.

The image of Heidegger's life and thought that emerges from Jaspers's study is disturbing. For Jaspers, Heidegger's life and thought form a whole reflecting Heidegger's personal and philosophical irresponsibility, and of Heidegger's turning toward Nazism as founded in Heidegger's philosophy. Yet Jaspers's discussion of the relation between Heidegger's life and thought remains fragmentary since he limits his discussion to a series of observations that he never brings together in a systematic framework. We can best understand Jaspers's contribution to a grasp of Heidegger's Nazism by isolating a number of themes that recur in his discussion.

(a) Jaspers points out that although in 1933 when Heidegger turned to Nazism the later development of National Socialism was unknown, Heidegger, like everyone else, already knew that Nazism was linked to illegality, the hurting of the Jews, the robbing of positions, and so on.[16] It is important to stress this point, since some of Heidegger's defenders have argued that since in 1933 the future evolution of Nazism was unknown Heidegger is guilty of nothing more than a certain political naïveté.[17] The fact that, as Jaspers notes, Heidegger frequently went further than the Nazi party demanded, only deepens Heidegger's political complicity.[18]

(b) Jaspers insists throughout, in various ways, on Heidegger's personal irresponsibility. Heidegger, he states, was the only one of his friends to betray his trust in 1933, and unwilling as well publicly to assume his philosophical responsibility.[19] Heidegger's personal inability to accept responsibility is widely apparent: in his denunciation of others, in his silence after the rectorate, in his efforts to fabricate a legend to explain away his personal and philosophical failures, and so on. But

Jaspers goes even further in his description of Heidegger as possibly a kind of confidence man[20] and in his comparison of Heidegger's perversion of philosophy to Hitler's perversion of Max Weber's idea of the charisma of a leader.[21]

(c) From a philosophical perspective, Jaspers's critique of Heidegger's conception of resoluteness as " 'Resoluteness', but with respect to what?"[22] is significant. This theme is introduced late in *Being and Time* as part of Heidegger's analysis of authenticity as the choice of one's ownmost way of being.[23] For Heidegger, the understanding of Being demanded an analysis of Dasein that in turn required a notion of resoluteness. But Heidegger's conception of resoluteness lacks, as Jaspers now points out, any criteria at all. Since the idea of resoluteness had no content whatsoever, Heidegger could literally apply it in any way he desired, for instance, in a turning toward Nazism.

(d) Jaspers notes that as a philosopher Heidegger wanted to lead the leaders.[24] This is an important point that reflects a correct grasp of the opening paragraph of the rectorial address. Here, Heidegger raises a closely Platonic claim to ground politics through philosophy, more precisely to found National Socialism in fundamental ontology. Unfortunately, Jaspers, who perceives the import of Heidegger's claim, fails to develop the obvious analogy between Heidegger's practice and the Platonic view of the relation of philosophy to politics.

(e) Although Jaspers correctly states that Heidegger has not the slightest idea of true politics,[25] again he fails to elaborate an important point. In my view, Heidegger's understanding of the political dimension combines in approximately equal portions deductions from his fundamental ontology, a Platonic view of politics as grounded in theory, and the ideology of the German people, or *Volksideologie*.[26] Heidegger seemed literally incapable of understanding either political practice or the reasons for the failure of his own effort to found politics in philosophy. Heidegger offers an outstanding example of the frequent philosophical tendency to substitute theory, namely a theory of the way things ought to be, for the analysis of practice. One reason for his later concern with an ideal form of National Socialism is his inability to understand politics in any way other than through his own philosophical lens.

(f) Jaspers correctly states that Heidegger's turning to Nazism followed from Heidegger's thought,[27] but the analysis that justifies this conclusion is nowhere found in Jaspers's discussion. It appears there as an ungrounded assertion that can be justified only through a detailed analysis of Heidegger's texts. Among the first generation of Heidegger critics, to the best of my knowledge only Löwith offers the kind of reading of Heidegger's thought that can support this inference.[28]

(g) Jaspers finally points to, but does not analyze, the crucial link between Heidegger's thought and Heidegger's Nazism. Jaspers notes that it is normal to expect an inner change, but that if one considers Heidegger as philosophically important one cannot expect that Heidegger would understand his activity in 1933 as an error and, hence, as overcome.[29] If Heidegger was in fact attracted to Nazism through his thought, then one cannot expect Heidegger to free himself from Nazism without a fundamental transformation of his position, namely, the same position that led him in that direction. Once again, Jaspers fails to provide an analysis of Heidegger's thought to reveal why fundamental ontology could only lead Heidegger to Nazism, or something like Nazism, and why Heidegger's later thought is heavily dependent on the same elements that initially led him toward Nazism.

In sum, Jaspers's notes on Heidegger's thought usefully provide a number of crucial, but undeveloped insights into the link between Heidegger's thought and Nazism. Jaspers's discussion is, however, doubly insufficient. On the one hand, it simply overlooks Heidegger's strong attraction to conservative ideology, in particular the conception of the authentic gathering of the Germans as German, a persistent theme in his writings beginning with the rectorial address. Jaspers's insensitivity to this theme is not surprising, since he also failed to detect it in his initial letter of congratulations to Heidegger; for his congratulations were tendered for the very speech in which Heidegger announced his intention to lead the leaders. On the other hand, Jaspers does not link the bits and pieces of his discussion to a wider analysis of the relation of Heidegger's thought and National Socialism.

6

Jaspers never situates the insights composing his discussion of Heidegger's thought in an adequate conceptual framework, such as his own important study of the problem of German guilt.[30] His study is important as a framework for the analysis of the wider German problem as well as the specific problem concerning Heidegger's position. In his book *Die Schuldfrage*, Jaspers distinguishes four kinds of guilt: criminal guilt, concerning infractions of law; political guilt, which relates to the consequences of the actions of statesmen and states and which must be assumed by any citizen; moral guilt for any actions performed by an individual; and, finally, metaphysical guilt, relating to the solidarity between human beings as human being in which each is co-responsible for all wrongs and wrongfulness.[31] He further qualifies his conception of "metaphysical guilt" in the suggestion that one can perhaps come to grips with this problem in works of poetry and philosophy but not on a personal level.[32]

Jaspers' fourfold distinction is helpful toward understanding the relation of philosophy and politics in Heidegger's life and work. There is not, so far as I know, any reason to suggest that Heidegger is criminally guilty for any act performed because of his interest in National Socialism. Undoubtedly, he, like other Germans of his generation, must bear a share of the political guilt. Morally, he is personally guilty for a series of actions that have only recently come to light, including his denunciations of his student Baumgarten and the chemist Staudinger. It is possible, as we gain further access to the Heidegger Archives, that other instances of Heidegger's moral failings will be made known.

Heidegger's moral guilt is, by definition, an individual affair. It is the responsibility that he, as an individual, must bear for his individual actions. Metaphysical guilt refers to the corresponding responsibility that he should assume with respect to other people. In principle, each of us is responsible for everyone else. But the degree of responsibility each person incurs is a function of who he or she is. It is reasonable to expect that a philosopher be held to a higher standard than the average person, for virtually since the inception of the ancient Greek philosophical tradition, philosophers have maintained that philosophy offers a deeper, in fact incomparable, insight into the nature of reality. In theory, all of us are equal; but in practice, it makes eminent sense to distinguish degrees of metaphysical responsibility as a function of the relative degree of insight, for instance, through the relative grasp of the principles on which solidarity is based.

Obviously, we do not all grasp the principles of morality on the same plane. As Plato already points out, a shoemaker, or even an engineer, can be expected to know how to carry out a given trade or profession, to know how to do whatever it is that one, say, as a shoemaker or an engineer, ought to do, namely, repairing shoes or building bridges. Yet the philosopher claims to have another kind of knowledge, in one formulation to understand all other forms of knowledge as well as one's own, to grasp ultimate reasons and final causes, to strive for and to attain absolute knowledge, even wisdom. But the claim to achieve such knowledge carries with it a corresponding responsibility, since the philosopher, for this reason differs from all others, from shoemakers and engineers, in Husserl's apt phrase, as the functionary of mankind.

Heidegger's moral guilt, which he shared with many other Germans, is obvious. His metaphysical guilt, which is less obvious, and was not obvious to Jaspers, is more disturbing. Heidegger invoked the conception of the turning [Kehre] to describe the evolution of his thought. The relation of his philosophy to Nazism can be characterized as a triple turning: an initial turning out of the ivory tower to Hitler's National Socialism, in Heidegger's role as *Führer* of the University of Freiburg, in his effort to found Nazism in his philosophical thought; a second turning, this time away from real Nazism, in his resignation as rector and his turn inward to his philosophical thought; and, finally, a third turning toward an ideal form of Nazism, a Nazism yet to be realized, dimly discerned, on the basis of Heidegger's later thought, the so-called new beginning, in the poetry of Hölderlin.

The thread, which runs throughout and links together the three turnings, includes Heidegger's concern to realize the Germanity of the Germans, what he described as bringing about an authentic gathering of the German people, those heirs to Greek metaphysics; it further includes his concern to advance his lifelong concern with the problem initially raised as the meaning of Being. For Heidegger, the question of Being and authentic human being are interrelated and each calls forth the other. There is, I submit, a certain perverse courage in Heidegger's quite mad effort to found Nazism and to lead the leaders, to take on philosophy, on his own philosophy, ultimately on himself the final responsibility for the conservative revolution initiated by Hitler. One can say that through a crazy form of Platonism Heidegger here assumes the responsibility that philosophers have always demanded for the just life. The problem with this phase is not that he refused his responsibility but that he is grievously wrong in his perception of the opportunity for German authenticity that he discerns in the Nazi rise to power.

There is, on the contrary, a grievous lack of responsibility, an utter metaphysical guilt, visible in Heidegger's later effort, against the lesson of experience, to transfer his allegiance from real Nazism to an unreal, ideal form, to revise his position in order to transfer the responsibility from human being to Being in order to explain, in fact to explain away, the impotence of mere Dasein, in fact Heidegger's own Dasein, to shirk his responsibility for the failure of his political turn to real Nazism. In the period after the rectorate, Heidegger's later writing is marked by a decisive revision of his thought that comforts its author in the conviction that he could not be responsible for his turn from theory to practice, by a failure to comment on Nazism in his famous and persistent silence [*Schweigen*], by a renewal of his faith in Nazism, by insensitive statements about Jews and others, by the crafty fabrication of a system of explanation, what we can call the official view, intended to deny what could still be denied and to minimize the damage to himself and his thought.

Heidegger must bear an enormous metaphysical guilt for his failure to confront the results of Nazism, through his effort to evade responsibility. On one view, the role of philosophy is to name reality. If philosophy is the court of final epistemic resort, if pure reason is or is to be socially useful, then philosophers must accept their responsibility to reason as the condition of their responsibility, in fact their solidarity with others. In this century, intellectuals have not always been responsible. Others who can be singled out include Paul de Man and Lukács. Each of them in his own way fails the metaphysical test that Jaspers proposes, since each of them betrayed the cause of reason, and, as a result, betrayed his responsibility to other human beings.

7

I come now to the conclusion. I've discussed the relation of two important thinkers, Jaspers and Heidegger, from the angle of vision provided by their respective approaches to Nazism. Philosophy, which sometimes understands itself as removed from the social context, has a more than passing link to politics. Heidegger's position, which presents itself as an inquiry into Being, as pure ontology, even as deeper than theory and practice, is also intrinsically political. Heidegger's theory of Being, which gives rise to a conception of human authenticity, literally demands that this conception be realized in practice. Heidegger's turn to practice, his descent into the political arena, was not contingent, since it was required by his own theory. Like Aristotle's view of ethics, Heidegger's view of Being is also and necessarily political.

The distinction between philosophy as the ground and as the standard of politics offers a framework to grasp the difference between Jaspers's and Heidegger's understanding of the political realm. Jaspers eschewed the view of philosophy as the ground of politics in favor of a philosophical evaluation of political reality. He had the good sense not to enlist in the ranks of National Socialism, and the philosophical courage to come to grips with Nazism as a phenomenon with respect to the German people and his colleague, Heidegger. On the contrary, Heidegger failed to discern political evil, to which he gave the full support and prestige of his philosophical thought; and Heidegger later altered his choice of the means but not the end that drew him to Nazism even as he sought to conceal his allegiance to National Socialism.

Jaspers initially failed to be sufficiently sensitive to Heidegger's Nazi turning. Yet Jaspers later acted responsibly in his effort to understand the phenomenon of Nazism. One could have wished for greater insight into Heidegger's actions, for a greater understanding of the link between Heidegger's thought and Heidegger's politics. In his deep and abiding commitment to real and ideal forms of Nazism, Heidegger acted irresponsibly by betraying reason. There is something intrinsically perverse about Heidegger's behavior, which surpasses not only the deficiencies of his character, in order finally to dishonor his own thought, despite its brilliance, and philosophy as such. One of philosophy's proudest claims has always been the effort to name reality. But if Nazism is evil, in fact the main example of absolute evil in our time, then in his turn toward Nazism Heidegger failed to recognize reality, and in his continued allegiance to National Socialism, albeit by other means, he remained steadfast in his adherence to evil.

There is an old philosophical adage concerning the link between knowing and doing, knowing the good and acting to bring it about. If this idea was ever true, it is refuted by Heidegger's actions. In respect to Nazism, Heidegger's thought failed him and us, for he was unable to recognize Nazism as evil; and if Nazism is evil, he did not act to bring about the good. If philosophy is a means to truth, then only some philosophy is true, and only sometimes does the perception of the truth lead to the good.

Following Heidegger's hints, Heidegger's students like to maintain that Heidegger later confronted National Socialism. But Heidegger never did so except in a tangential, unessential manner; and Heidegger's thought apparently lacks the resources to comprehend Nazism, which he merely assimilated to modernity. Unlike Heidegger, Jaspers, who was concerned with limiting situations, had a framework able to comprehend and to confront National Socialism. Yet his application of that framework to Heidegger's position was only partially successful.

The closest Jaspers ever came to confronting the problem directly can be seen in an exchange of letters that has recently been made known through publication of the Heidegger-Jaspers correspondence. Here, Heidegger admits that in 1933 and earlier the Jews and the left-wing politicians, those who were directly menaced by events, saw further than he did; and he further privately accepts the existentialist conception of blame for the acts of the individual. In a passage on Stalin that illustrates the frequent link between an adherence to Nazism and the fear of Bolshevism, Heidegger writes: "Stalin does not need to declare war any more. He wins a battle every day. But 'one' does not see it. For us there is no possible evasion. And every word and every text is in itself a counterattack, if all this does not play itself out in the sphere of the 'political,' which is itself long since outwitted through other relations of Being and leads [only] a false existence."[33]

And he continues: "Despite all, dear Jaspers, despite death and tears, despite suffering and horror, despite need and torment, despite landlessness and exile, in this lack of a homeland it is not that nothing occurs;

here is hidden an Advent, whose most distant hint we can perhaps experience and must take up in [the form of] a mild [wind] blowing, in order to preserve it for a future, which no historical construction, above all not the contemporary one, most certainly not one which thinks in technical ways, will decipher."[34]

Jaspers's response, written by a fellow philosopher, by someone who unfortunately greeted the rectorial address as a conceptual breakthrough surpassing Nietzsche, is important. After quoting the passage about Stalin, Jaspers writes: "To read something like this frightens me. If you were in front of me, as decades ago so today you would experience my flood of words in anger and plea for reason. I find the questions urgent: Is [not] such a view of things through their imprecision the promotion of ruin? Isn't the possibility of doing whatever is possible spoiled by the appearance of the greatness of such visions? . . . Isn't the power of evil in Germany not also what has steadily grown and in fact prepared the victory of Stalin: the covering up and the forgetting of what has occurred, the new so-called nationalism, the return to the old ways of thought and all the ghosts, which, although null and void, ruin us? Is not this power the imprecision in all thought (imprecise because it accompanies the life and activity of the thinker)? Is not a philosophy, which one perceives and composes in such propositions in your letter, that which brings about the vision of the monstrous, again the preparation of the victory of the totalitarian in that it separates itself from reality?"[35]

And Jaspers continues, after citing Heidegger's passage on the Advent, as follows: "My fright grew as I read this. It is, so far as I can think, pure fantasy, in line with so many other fantasies, which, each 'in its own time'—has made fools of us during this half century. Do you mean to come forward as a prophet, who shows the transcendent from hidden knowledge, as a philosopher, who was misled through reality? Who neglects the possible for fictions? The same questions can be put to your views of full power and preservation."[36]

To my mind, Jaspers's alarmed reaction to Heidegger's troubling view of social reality is essentially correct. There is something irrational, fantastic, and frightening, not only about Heidegger's initial conviction that the future of the German people could be attained through National Socialism, but in his later insistence on an ideal form of Nazism after he broke with its Hitlerian form. There is Heidegger's evident psychological inability to confront his mistake, present even in his continued insistence on what Jaspers correctly diagnoses as Heidegger's self-characterization of himself as a prophet of Being, whose errors are due to reality itself; then there is Heidegger's obvious inability to provide the concrete analysis of experience, especially social experience, for which he increasingly substituted a complex mythology. At this late date, in order to salvage what is living in Heidegger's thought from his Nazism, it must be constantly kept in mind that his philosophical position and his Nazism are tightly, not loosely, conjoined, and perhaps finally inseparable.

Jaspers's indication of the mythological character of Heidegger's understanding of the historical process is correct, yet finally insufficient. For by virtue of the fact that neither Jaspers nor Heidegger was ever able to read the other's writings, Jaspers was finally much better acquainted with Heidegger the man than Heidegger the thinker. Although useful, important, in some ways ground-breaking, Jaspers's discussion of Heidegger's position is incomplete; for he never develops an analysis of what it was about Heidegger's thought of Being that led to the abandonment of human being. Unlike Löwith, for instance, Jaspers seems never to have understood that Heidegger's mythological understanding of Nazism is not merely a contingent fact, an accident of history, but essentially rooted in Heidegger's comprehension of Being itself.

NOTES

1. See Hilary Putnam, *The Many Faces of Realism* (LaSalle, Ill.: Open Court, 1987), p. 53.

2. For only the most recent discussion of this point, see Michel Henry, *Du communisme au capitalisme: Théorie d'une catastrophe* (Paris: Editions Odile Jacob, 1990).

3. See Nicholas Rescher, *The Strife of Systems* (Pittsburgh: University of Pittsburgh Press, 1979).

4. See Hegel's *Philosophy of Right*, trans. T. M. Knox (London: Oxford University Press, 1967), p. 10.

5. See "Only a God Can Save Us: *Der Spiegel* Interview with Heidegger," *Philosophy Today* (Winter 1976): 272.

6. On this point see Hugo Ott, *Martin Heidegger: Unterwegs zu seiner Biographie* (Frankfurt am Main: Campus, 1988), p. 315.

7. See, e.g., I. M. Bochenski, *Contemporary European Philosophy*, trans. Donald Nicholl and Karl Aschenbrenner (Los Angeles: University of California Press, 1961).

8. See Hans Saner's *Vorwort* to Karl Jaspers, *Notizen zu Martin Heidegger* (Munich: Piper Verlag, 1989), p. 1.

9. Letter from Jaspers to Heidegger of August 23, 1933 cited in Ott, *Unterwegs*, pp. 192–193.

10. For a summary, see Jaspers's *Notizen*, pp. 21–25.

11. For the text, see Ott, *Unterwegs*, pp. 315–317.

12. At this writing, the effort to defend Heidegger against any and all criticism is still under way. Examples include the fact that the edition of his complete writings will not include his letters, the fact that the Heidegger Archives

in Marbach are still closed to scholars, the occasional appearance of books, most recently Ernst Nolte, *Heidegger: Politik und Geschichte im Leben und Denken* (Berlin: Propyläen, 1992), that explain everything away, the unwillingness of such important bodies as the Society for Phenomenology and Existential Philosophy to present more than a single, carefully managed discussion of the series of problems following from Heidegger's Nazism, and so on. For discussion about the effort to turn away from Heidegger's Nazism in the Heidegger discussion, see my *On Heidegger's Nazism and Philosophy* (Berkeley: University of California Press, 1992), chap. 1.

13. Heidegger's letter of January 20, 1948, to Marcuse, cited in Victor Farías, *Heidegger and Nazism*, trans. Paul Burrell and Gabriel R. Ricci, ed. Joseph Margolis and Tom Rockmore (Philadelphia: Temple University Press, 1989), p. 285.

14. Cited in Thomas Sheehan, "Heidegger and the Nazis," *New York Review of Books*, vol. 35, number 10 (1988): pp. 41–42.

15. See Jaspers, *Notizen*, §115, p. 140.

16. Ibid., §164, p. 184.

17. See François Fédier, *Heidegger: anatomie d'un scandale* (Paris: Robert Laffont, 1988).

18. Jaspers, *Notizen*, §166, p. 187.

19. Ibid., §68, pp. 96–97.

20. Ibid., §55, p. 87.

21. Ibid., §235, p. 256.

22. Ibid., §157, p. 176.

23. See Martin Heidegger, *Being and Time*, ed. John Macquarrie and Edward Robinson (New York: Harper and Row, 1962), §74.

24. Jaspers, *Notizen*, §166, p. 187.

25. Ibid.

26. For this way of reading the rectorial address, see chapter 2 of my book *On Heidegger's Nazism and Philosophy* (Berkeley: University of California Press, 1992).

27. See Jaspers, *Notizen*, §167, p. 188.

28. See Karl Löwith, *Mein Leben in Deutschland vor and nach 1933: Ein Bericht* (Frankfurt am Main: Fischer, 1989).

29. See Jaspers, *Notizen*, §202, p. 222.

30. See Jaspers, *Die Schuldfrage: Zur politischen Haftung Deutschlands* (Munich: Piper Verlag, 1987).

31. Ibid., pp. 17–20.

32. Ibid., p. 18.

33. Martin Heidegger to Karl Jaspers on April 8, 1950, *Briefwechsel*, p. 200.

34. Ibid., p. 202.

35. Karl Jaspers to Martin Heidegger, July 24, 1950, *Briefwechsel*, pp. 209–210.

36. Ibid., pp. 210–211.

7

Heidegger and Jaspers on Plato's Idea of the Good

Klaus Brinkmann

PLATO'S IDEA of the Good continues to be an enigmatic concept. As far as I am aware, Plato scholarship has been unable to offer a satisfactory explication of it.[1] The aspect that seems to resist interpretation most stubbornly is the character of transcendence attributed to it by Plato in the well-known phrase that the Good, although itself a Platonic Form, is beyond being (*epekeina tes ousias*) and supersedes it in dignity and power (*presbeia kai dynamei hypechontos, Rep.* 509 B). At the same time, however, Plato insists that the Good constitutes the ultimate ground of all intelligibility. How could something barely intelligible be the principle of intelligibility? Could it be the case that conceptual determinateness— something the Forms are meant to provide—is possible only against the background of indeterminateness? But then again, Plato's idea of the Good seems to represent the ultimate principle of guidance for both knowledge and action. That seems to suggest that the Good functions as an *idée fixe*, that is, as a determinate and determinable Form. How are we to understand the claim, then, that the ultimate foundation of theoretical, as well as practical, knowledge is supposed to be both determinate and indeterminable?

In this situation of perplexity, it seems promising to turn toward the writings of two thinkers of this century who have commented on Plato's idea of the Good and who as philosophers in their own right might be able to suggest a solution to this Platonic paradox. In his essay "Plato's Doctrine of Truth"[2]—where doctrine is meant to refer to the unspoken doctrine, rather than the manifest teachings, of the dialogues[3]—Heidegger claims that the *Republic*'s simile of the Cave reflects a historical turning point in the understanding of the notion of truth. The emphasis on the visibility and the determinateness of the Forms, the idea of the Good included, indicates a shift in Western thought from the conception

111

of truth as unconcealedness to that of truth as correspondence or agreement. With this shift, the notion of truth in its supposedly germane sense of unconcealment (*a-letheia*) is being abandoned in favor of truth as correctness of perception and agreement of statement and fact (*orthotes*).[4] To underscore his point, Heidegger uses the rather dramatic expression that with the *Republic*'s interpretation of the Forms, *aletheia* comes to be under the yoke of the idea.[5] In other words, that which can be grasped clearly and distinctly now determines the nature of truth. At the same time, the attentiveness of thought to Being gives way to a preoccupation of the knowing subject with itself. Epistemology replaces ontology in the genuine sense, and subjectivity begins to outshine Being. I shall later return to the question of whether we should accept this reading as a satisfactory interpretation both of the Platonic conception of truth and the subsequent development of philosophical thought.

In Jaspers's interpretation of Plato's philosophy in *Die Grossen Philosophen*, first published in 1957, the Platonic idea of the Good is viewed very much as a precursor of the idea of Being as transcendence that was so central to Jaspers's own thinking. Consequently, Jaspers emphasized the Good's indeterminateness or, rather, its indeterminability. The idea of the Good represents a limit for thought, something unsayable in itself and which can only be touched, not grasped.[6] I shall argue that both Jaspers's and Heidegger's readings are justifiable to a certain extent and that this result affords an interesting insight not only into the Platonic Good but also an opportunity to uncover a fundamental Heideggerian dilemma.

The two philosophers' contribution to understanding the idea of the Good, however, does not constitute the only concern of this essay. Both Jaspers and Heidegger advocate a paradigm of philosophical reflection that is at odds with the traditional mainstream paradigm of philosophical rationality. Both philosophers, that is, value transcendence of Being more highly than either the speculative identity of thought and being or a Kantian-like restriction of philosophical cognition to transcendental knowledge, which is knowledge of the conditions of the possibility of empirical knowledge only, as distinct from knowledge of being as such and in itself. In this, they apparently satisfy the anti-idealist and antispeculative groundswell in nineteenth- and twentieth-century philosophy. But while Heidegger views Plato as a precursor of idealism and speculative philosophy to be overcome, Jaspers sees in him the founder of all genuine philosophical thinking. The broader question, however, remains, whether or not Heideggerian antiphilosophy and Jaspersian metaphysics represent the legitimate heirs to our philosophical tradition, or whether there are still grounds for favoring positions of the old-fashioned transcendental persuasion. It is this latter question that gives expression to the wider concerns of this paper.

To begin, I shall first summarize and briefly evaluate Heidegger's understanding of the Platonic idea of the Good, comment on the particular Heideggerian explication of the Platonic theory of Forms and his treatment of the Good, and propose an explanation of its idiosyncratic character. Next, I shall contrast the Heideggerian account of the Good with Jaspers's reading of it. Finally, I shall come back to the issue of how to resolve the conflict between traditional and post-traditional paradigms of philosophical rationality. There remains the problem, however, of whether Heidegger, despite his attempt to position himself outside of that tradition, can nevertheless be brought back into the fold. I shall argue that to accept the idea of a total discontinuity of thought in which Heidegger wants us to believe would lead to unacceptable consequences.

Heidegger on Plato's Doctrine of Truth

Heidegger regards the theory of Forms in the *Republic* as the key to understanding Plato's conception of truth. More specifically, it is the way in which the ideas or Forms become objects of cognition that determines Plato's hidden doctrine of truth according to Heidegger. And the closest we can come to an elucidation of these epistemological preconditions and requirements for grasping the Forms is arguably Plato's dramatic description of the ascent to truth in the simile of the Cave.

The most salient feature of Heidegger's reading of this ascent is his tendency to treat the Forms as that which displays the essential being of a being in its full *visibility*. Expressions of visualization abound in Heidegger's idiosyncratic translation from the Greek original. The Forms grant things their unmistakable *look* (Anblick) in letting shine forth what they are paradigmatically or typically. The essential determinateness of a being, its *eidos* or *idea*, is thus translated into its sensibly or intellectually intuitable image. It assumes the character of the authentic representation of a being's being. And, as Heidegger indicates, it requires only one more step to arrive at the Cartesian or Lockean *idea*, where the nature of a being becomes equated, if not identified, with its perceived representation (*perceptio*). With this, thought has already locked itself into the position of adopting a subjective perspective on being that quite naturally leads on to the conception of truth as an agreement or correspondence between a subjective representation and its allegedly objective correlate. On this occasion Heidegger does not elaborate on the details of the subsequent unfolding of the problems inherent in the subjective attitude of thought. It can, however, easily be seen that the circularity problem implicit in the idea of truth as correspondence must ultimately provoke the solutions we are familiar with under the titles of rationalism, empiricism, and transcendental and speculative philosophy. In any case, it is with Plato's ascent to the Good in the Cave simile that *a-letheia* has come under the yoke of *idea*.

Is Heidegger's strategy to lean heavily on the metaphors of visibility ultimately in unison with Plato's intentions? Initially, one might believe this to be the case. In particular, the simile of the Sun, which precedes that of the Cave and on which Heidegger implicitly relies, is indeed built around the idea of an illumination of being through an ultimate source of light. On the other hand, it is equally obvious that Plato's metaphors of visibility are just that, namely, metaphors. To be more precise, the simile of the Sun shows quite clearly that Plato wishes to establish not an equivalency between perceiving and thinking, but an *analogy* between the two. As the light of the sun is to the perceivability of sensory things, so the idea of the Good is to the *knowability* and *thinkability* of the Forms. It may be argued that in using the metaphors of visibility so purposefully, Plato set a prejudice for understanding the relationship between thinking and the object of thought in terms of perceiving and the object perceived. However, it would be more correct to say that this would transform the analogy into an equivalency, and thereby conflate perceiving and thinking rather than bring out their difference. After all, Plato makes Socrates use metaphorical language here precisely in order to mark the difference between what can be said and what can only be hinted at.

It is the neglect of the other two similes, those of the Sun and the Line, that gives Heidegger's reading of the Cave parable an air of decontextualization. This is even more striking with regard to his interpretation of the idea of the Good. Indeed, there is little in the simile of the Cave itself to suggest that the sun, insofar as it represents the idea of the Good, is nothing but the visible analogue of a Platonic idea, albeit the highest of them all. Going back to the simile of the Sun, however, we learn that the idea of the Good, despite its congeniality with the Forms, is also something more than that and quite different from the Forms in nature and function. In being described as that which is beyond being and superior in dignity and power to the Forms, the idea of the Good is precisely not the quintessential epitome of the Forms that Heidegger makes it out to be. According to the simile of the Sun, the idea of the Good constitutes the ultimate condition of the possibility of both pure thought and its objects, the Forms, and thus also of that which for its being depends on the Forms, namely, the world of phenomena. The idea of the Good, as I see it, represents Being pure and simple, without negation. As such, it is pure positivity. Consequently, it can never be captured by any one single determinate Form, because determination involves difference, and hence negation. To use Kantian terminology, the idea of the Good is a regulative idea. This would explain why the definition of the idea of justice, which constitutes the central theme of the *Republic* and its primary goal, should require an even more fundamental grounding than the one it receives in Book IV. Assuming that the Good grounds all the other ideas, the idea of justice, too, must ultimately be dependent on the Good, both for its essential nature and for the adequacy of our knowledge of it.

The most surprising fact in Heidegger's interpretation of Plato's doctrine of truth is, however, that the crucial determination of the idea of the Good, namely, that it is *beyond being* (*epekeina tes ousias*), is never mentioned. Nor has this determination, which admittedly occurs prior to the simile of the Cave, left any trace in Heidegger's characterization of the Good. The Good is, according to Heidegger, continuous with the Forms, it is the highest Form. The fact that it is also said by Plato to be beyond being makes it, however, discontinuous with the Forms. Heidegger ignores the discontinuity and instead highlights the continuity. The Good, for him, is something visible in the sense that it can be made out by sight and hence is something knowable (*ein Sichtiges und daher Kennbares*). This reading, which finds some justification in the text of the Cave simile—the future philosopher king does eventually get a glimpse of the sun, after all—is at odds with the Sun simile. In the latter, the Good functions as a condition for the intelligibility of the Forms, as a backdrop or horizon for conceptual determinacy, as the not-A that provides the foil against which to determine the boundaries of any definite A, and thus constitutes that which lies beyond the confines of determinacy and is simultaneously presupposed by it.

If this interpretation of the Platonic Good has any plausibility, then it should also be obvious that Plato's idea of the Good comes very close to being a genuine precursor of Heidegger's own notion of Being as the "lighting" that grants beings their unconcealedness or truth. But if this is so, then Heidegger's interpretation of Plato's theory of Forms reveals itself to be a conscious strategy to obscure this parallel. Indeed, how could Heidegger have acknowledged the fact that philosophical thought, from the moment of its self-conscious inception with Plato, remained alert to the idea of a Being beyond beings? It seems that Plato's threefold distinction between sensible things, the Forms, and the idea of the Good would constitute a perfect match for Heidegger's equally threefold distinction between beings, the being of beings, and Being as the condition of the unconcealedness of beings in their being. In particular, the insistence in the Sun simile on the transcendent character of the Good vis-à-vis the Forms makes it hard to avoid the conclusion that Plato preempted Heidegger's discovery of the so-called ontological difference between the being of beings and Being, or between essence and that which is beyond essence. To recognize this fact, however, would have endangered Heidegger's project of rewriting the history of philosophical thought in terms of a progression toward the oblivion of Being. But once we have become skeptical of this Heideggerian idiosyncrasy, we are free to acknowledge that the Platonic idea of Being as the ever-receding horizon of our knowledge of the being of beings has produced a rich progeny in the philosophies of Descartes, Spinoza, Leibniz, Kant, Fichte, and Schelling, to name but a few. One might even venture to surmise that the early Wittgenstein's boundary between that which can be formulated, or if not formulated at least shown, and that about which we must "remain silent" represents a distant—or perhaps not so distant—echo of Plato's original insight in the simile of the Sun.

Since it may not at first seem totally obvious that Plato's suggestion of a transcendent ground of the Forms is the precursor of similar conceptions in later philosophies, I would like to briefly substantiate this claim. Let me point out first of all that the God of Descartes's *Third Meditation* as an infinite thinking substance literally transcends the limits of the finite thinking self and is regarded not only as the author of the *cogito*'s innate ideas, but also as the creator of all finite reality and as the ground of its continued existence. Moreover, Descartes insists that the idea of an infinite thinking substance could not have been generated by merely negating the idea of a finite thinking substance, because God's infinity must be regarded as a positive reality and not just as the empty beyond of all limitations.[7] Ironically, this argument removes the possibility for the *Third Meditation* proof of the existence of God to be successful, because Descartes is now forced to concede that it is impossible to *comprehend* the idea of an infinite thinking substance, although we are still capable of *understanding* it. To understand, however, would be equivalent to touching, rather than embracing, an idea, as Descartes explains in a letter to Mersenne of May 26, 1630, which again translates into perceiving an idea clearly, but not distinctly. To understand, or perceive clearly but not distinctly, however, is less than would be required for establishing absolute certainty. However that may be, Descartes's God represents both an ultimate ground of all reality and of intelligibility, insofar as it is only through God's existence that the mind can be assured of an objective correlate of its intentionality. In this respect, Descartes's concept of God seems close enough to Plato's idea of the Good to maintain a resemblance between them.

It will not be necessary to discuss explicitly the references to a Being beyond being in either the late Fichte or the late Schelling; a parallel between Fichte's idea of "light" as ultimate transcending and transcendental ground and Plato's idea of the Good has been drawn by Ferber,[8] and Schelling's *Überseyende* recognizably echoes the characterization of the Good as being *epekeina tes ousias*. But I am tempted to include Kant's concept of an *omnitudo realitis* or *ens realissimum* among the descendants of Plato's idea of the Good as well. The *ens realissimum* is the indeterminable unconditioned totality of the real, which includes within itself the conditioned totality of the sum total of determinable reality. As such, the *ens realissimum* represents a transcendental ideal of reason that grounds the concept of the totality of empirical reality, where the latter concept has itself the status of a regulative idea only (cf. KrV, B 604). Through the *ens realissimum* (also called *ens originarium*, *ens summun*, and *ens entium*, cf. KrV, B606) reason thinks the *ground* of all determinability of the real (cf. KrV, B607). In this way, reason presupposes—and necessarily so, as Kant tries to argue (cf. KrV, B599–604)—a "supreme reality" (KrV, B607) beyond the totality of all that exists, and which serves as the "transcendental substrate" of the latter (KrV, B603). Like the Platonic idea of the Good, this 'most real being' is of "outstanding preeminence" (KrV, B607) and surpasses the totality of determinable reality.

Jaspers's Interpretation of the Idea of the Good

The result of our discussion so far is that Heidegger's reading of the simile of the Cave helps us to understand the significance of the idea of the Good in a rather unexpected way, that is, by taking into account the things that Heidegger so openly passes over in silence, rather than following his overt leads. With Jaspers, the case is quite different. The fundamental trait in Plato's thinking, according to Jaspers, is Plato's tendency to transcend the limitations of all determinate thought, and of all definite doctrine, so as to arrive at the ultimate source of thinking itself, the unconditioned that is beyond all determinability and thus remains essentially unsayable. Plato searches for a language in which the unsayable may be not so much expressed as hinted at.[9] In short, Plato's thinking is a quest for what Jaspers himself called the Encompassing. The best evidence for this is the dialectic of the dialogues, that is, their rejection of definitive solutions, the theory of the Forms, and the idea of the Good itself.[10] Despite some reservations about Plato's political philosophy in particular, Jaspers recognizes in Plato the creator of the notion of transcendence and the encompassing truth (*umgreifende Wahrheit*) that can be known only indirectly.[11] This primordial reality, although beyond all determinacy, nevertheless represents the ultimate guiding principle for knowledge and action.[12]

It is not surprising, then, that Jaspers should explicitly quote the notorious passage from the simile of the Sun, which places the Good in the beyond of being.[13] Quite in contrast to Heidegger, he even warns against taking too seriously the seeming continuity between the Forms and the Good. He finds it potentially misleading to make too much of the fact that the Good is also said to be an idea, because as a creative power (*schöpferische Macht*)[14] that grants the Forms their being, the Good must differ from those restful, inactive paradigmatic patterns that allow us to identify types of being.[15] Relying on the Sun simile more heavily than on that of the Cave, Jaspers even goes so far as to assert that "the Good is not an object of thought, just as we do not see the sun itself."[16] Socrates's recourse to the metaphor of the sun as an analogue for the principle of intelligibility that transcends intelligibility would appear to be the paradigmatic formulation of a Jaspersian cipher for the nonobjectifiable transcendence of the Encompassing.

In their views of the Platonic Good, Jaspers and Heidegger are clearly at opposite ends. While Jaspers emphasizes the transcendence of the Good, Heidegger completely ignores it and thus sees in the Good no more than the highest of the Forms. These differences are not differences of degree merely, but an expression of fundamentally different modes of appreciation. For Jaspers, Plato's discovery of the transcendent character of the highest truth in the form of the Good marks the appearance in philosophy of the idea of a metaphysical grounding of all determinate truth and thus the beginning of philosophy proper. For Heidegger, on the other hand, Plato's understanding of truth implicit in the Cave simile reveals a decisive shift away from the genuine conception of truth as an unconcealedness granted by Being toward a narrow, self-centered, subjectivist, and, in its consequences, ultimately tyrannical conception of truth as correctness of propositions or statements. And while Heidegger sees in the Platonic Good the attempt to define an ultimate standard of correctness, Jaspers explicitly claims the opposite to be true.[17] There can be little doubt, however, that Jaspers's reading of the Good appears to be more congenial to the Platonic spirit, while Heidegger's, despite all its genuine perceptiveness, clearly constitutes a *tour de force* that results in a misrepresentation.

Two Paradigms of Intelligibility?

If it was indeed Plato's intention to direct our attention to the possibility of a ground of intelligibility and of being beyond reason, then Jaspers's interpretation of the Good as transcendent truth and as "a being beyond the fullness of the world" (*Sein jenseits der Fülle der Welt*)[18] may well point in the right direction. On the other hand, Jaspers does not succeed in explaining the apparent paradoxical nature of the Good as something both determinate and indeterminate. On the contrary, he adds a few more paradoxes to our list by claiming that that which is beyond the limit of thought at the same time constitutes our ultimate guiding principle,[19] or that knowledge of the Good is fulfilled ignorance (*erfülltes Nichtwissen*).[20] The idea behind the latter paradox is expressed more clearly when Jaspers tries to characterize the central experience of Plato's thinking, namely, that all determination of truth is preliminary, that determinate truth is necessarily wedded to the finite, while truth as such is infinite, and, so we must conclude, therefore also beyond determinability.[21]

It is interesting to note that Heidegger's concept of truth is very similar to Jaspers's. Their divergence on the Platonic Good is quite accidental in this respect. It depends on the fact that Heidegger is subjecting his understanding of the history of philosophy to a particular agenda, while Jaspers has no such ambition. But both philosophers share in the conviction that the ground of all finite truth and understanding is beyond determinability. If it is intelligible at all, it must be so indirectly, through a signification that seems to point toward something by indicating a direction for thought. But no single point can be defined by indicating a direction only. Nor can the transcendent ground be identified in the manner of an intersection of two nonparallel lines, because their meeting point would fall within the confines of the finite.[22] If at all, the transcendent ground can be determined only through parallel lines that meet in the infinite. Thought, because it is assumed to be finite, does not reach closure. To use a Hegelian expression, thought in both Jaspers and Heidegger assumes the character of finite transcendence.[23] In Jaspers, this translates into the notion of an "immanent transcendence."[24] Human existence, and with it human thought, must first be distinguished from transcendent being and transcendent truth, or transcendence, for short. However, if transcendence had no reflex in this world of human existence and experience, this would create a "split" and open up "an abyss between unrelated separates." And again, "God and the world would face each other as strangers."[25] It is ciphers such as the Platonic Good that, although beyond (determinate) being, allow us to relate the two spheres and establish a connection, however precarious and indeterminate, between them. A similar move occurs in Heidegger, when he finds it necessary to undergird unconcealedness with a ground that, in the act of disclosing beings in their being, simultaneously conceals itself.[26]

Finite transcendence is Hegel's structural equivalent for finite thought that, despite or rather because of the acknowledgment of its finitude, experiences the need for a grounding beyond the relativity of determinate knowledge. The idea of a finite transcendence captures thought's act of *gesturing toward* its own ground without being able to encapsulate that ground in a definitive formula, an ultimate cipher, or a final word. Inasmuch as the philosophies of Jaspers and Heidegger give expression to this self-experience of philosophical reflection, they seem to respond to a philosophical *Befindlichkeit* predominant in the twentieth century. Viewing these philosophies as ciphers in their own right, we may say that they reflect a loss of faith in reason prompted, perhaps, by the experience of a profound discrepancy between theoretical and practical reason, an experience that found its philosophical expression in much of nineteenth-century philosophy.

However, the question remains whether finite or immanent transcendence is ultimately a satisfactory position to hold. What are we to make of an argument that urges us to think in the direction of an ultimate ground, if I may say so, but refuses to specify that ground in any way other than saying that it will forever recede before our probing thoughts? Are we really prepared to accept the implied paradox of an unintelligible principle of intelligibility? Do we really believe that concealedness is the truth of unconcealedness? As regards Plato, one needs to point out that, taken in conjunction, the Sun and the Cave similes allow us to avoid the paradox, if it is indeed the case that the ascent from the Cave will eventually end in catching a glimpse of the idea of the Good. As for Jaspers, we need to raise the crucial question of how we are to determine whether or not a cipher is genuine. Must we not possess a rather specific notion of the transcendent fullness of Being already, if we are to adjudicate the merit of a myth, a metaphor, or a philosophy? And how could we do this without some preconception of the nature of that ultimate ground? And is it not also the case that we find one cipher more illuminating than another? On what grounds do we do so?

Both Heidegger's and Jaspers's stances seem to be problematic at the very least. I do not wish for a moment to deny that their positions reflect a genuine disenchantment of philosophical reflection with the shortcomings of the idealist as well as the anti-idealist traditions in the history of philosophy. However, it may well be the case that the willingness to embrace the position of finite transcendence constitutes only an immediate, first reaction of thought's experience with its post-Hegelian development, and that more satisfactory conclusions will lie hidden in the future, conclusions that would be capable of maintaining the continuity with philosophy's idealist tradition while at the same time doing justice to its challenges from the various existentialist, hermeneutic, and language-oriented quarters.

It would be much easier to defend this prospect of a new post-

Hegelian faith in reason if Heidegger's strategy of fostering the notion of a radically new paradigm had not been so successful. Since he has explicitly rejected the idea that the new way of thinking could still be called philosophy, while at the same time holding on to the notion of Being as the ground for E*k-sistenz*, I find it hard to avoid the conclusion that what emerges in the late and very late Heidegger is a new form of mysticism. For that is what his interpretation of truth as *a-letheia*, or unconcealedness, amounts to. The idea here seems to be much more one of celebrating and heeding Being than of thinking and understanding. The later Heidegger's advocacy of the abandonment of philosophy as we know it and a return to the zero line of thought has resulted in the widespread acceptance within the philosophical community of a radical discrepancy between the parameters of philosophical and postphilosophical rationality. Jaspers's neoexistentialist position, it needs to be mentioned, never aspired to a claim of this magnitude, since he appears to have believed in a fundamental continuity of philosophical thought, of which he regarded himself to be a part.

However, before we accept the idea of two paradigms of rationality or intelligibility as a given, let us consider whether such a reading of the history of philosophy is a viable one. For our purposes, I shall distinguish between the position that advocates the possibility of complete determinacy of thought, and hence also of complete intelligibility, and the position that argues for the necessary incompleteness of the determinacy of thought and consequently for partial intelligibility. In my view, Aristotle's concept of *noesis noeseos* and Hegel's absolute Idea give expression to the former, while Kant's concept of an *ens realissimum*, Schelling's notion of a being beyond being (*das Überseiende*), and, say, Jaspers's transcendence represent examples of the latter. Let me say in passing that at least *prima facie* the defenders of the necessary incompleteness of determinacy far outweigh in number those that hold completeness to be possible. Our problem then appears to be this: Do we have persuasive, or even compelling, reasons to prefer the paradigm of incomplete intelligibility to that of complete intelligibility?

If we frame the question thus, it soon becomes obvious that in devising a possible answer to it, we have only two options. Either we accept the idea of a profound discontinuity between the two alternatives and thus regard them as two different paradigms of philosophical thought, or we subject both to one and the same paradigm and hence reject the idea of two paradigms of intelligibility. Now it seems to me that an argument can be made to show that the first option is undesirable at the very least, and perhaps even self-refuting. For if we accept the discontinuity option, then, for one thing, a choice between the two paradigms can be a rational choice, that is, one based on arguments, only if there is a possibility of appealing to a *third* paradigm that would allow us to compare the merits and demerits of either of them. It is, however, extremely difficult to see what that third paradigm might be. A third paradigm can be ruled out by drawing attention to the fact that the only logical third option to either complete or partial intelligibility would have to be *zero* intelligibility. This would make the task of justifying our preference obsolete. We would be reduced to saying, with Fichte, that the kind of philosophy one chooses ultimately depends on what kind of person one is. If this axiom is to be taken seriously, it must result in the termination of the dialogue among the proponents of the alternatives, and thus will lead to a fundamental split in the philosophical community. I take it that there is a consensus to regard this consequence as highly undesirable. But undesirable or not, the necessity of introducing a third alternative would also refute itself, because it stipulates the existence of a common ground between two allegedly discontinuous paradigms. We may therefore dismiss the first option as logically inconsistent.

This leaves us with the second option, the continuity or one-paradigm-only option. Here it seems immediately obvious that complete intelligibility is at least preferable to partial intelligibility. But can complete intelligibility be had? The answer to this depends in part on how defensible we think the Aristotelian and the Hegelian proposals are. Fortunately, however, we need not engage in an extended inquiry into the strengths and weaknesses of these philosophies here. Apart from this long answer, there is a short answer also. For if it can be shown that partial determinacy presupposes complete determinacy, the superiority of the complete-intelligibility position may already have been vindicated.

The defense of the nothing-less-than-complete-intelligibility position is simple, although it may not be obvious. The crucial point is to recognize that intelligibility presupposes determinacy. From this it follows that the principle of intelligibility, on which philosophical thought is predicated, ought to be fully determinate. Partial intelligibility can be defined only in opposition to full intelligibility. However, for any principle to be fully determinate, the principle of determinacy must be satisfied. What, then, does the principle of determinacy require? It requires that a fundamental concept such as being, or substance, or subject, *include its opposite*, that is, it requires the acceptance of the Hegelian principle of double negation. The reason for this is that a concept A that forms part of our framework of intelligibility, in other words, that is a category of being, remains undetermined as long as its opposite represents its simple negation, not-A. For as long as A has not been invested with determinacy, not-A will be as vacuous as A. Determinacy can accrue to A, therefore, only if not-A is itself a determinate concept. The fact that A and not-A are already determinate is what formal logical always grants as a matter of course, without realizing that when the problem is to determine the prerequisites for conceptual determinacy, this is precisely what cannot be granted as a matter of course. The critical point, then, is to realize that for A to be different from, or other than, not-A, the difference must be reflected in the very concept of A itself. What makes A different from not-A is, however, simply the supposed otherness of not-A. Hence not-A's otherness is a determinant of A itself, or A = not-A. On the other hand, A = A also holds true, and if so, then so does A is not not-A. We have derived a contradiction, but a contradiction that seems to be unavoidable, if the attempt to determine A is not to remain stuck with the empty tautology of A = A. Hegel's suggestion is that the contradiction can at once be acknowledged and removed by transforming not-A into a determinate B, and by viewing both A and B as determinants of a new concept, C. C is fully determined by including both A and B, but C also makes it possible for A and B to limit one another and thus to become determinate themselves. The partial determinacy of A and not-A is transformed into the complete determinacy of C. Without C, however, a mututal limitation of A and not-A would not be possible. Hence the partial determinacy of A and not-A presupposes the full determinacy of C. (This raises a circularity problem which, I believe, can be overcome.) Technically speaking, concept C allows us to integrate the opposition of *contradictories* (A and not-A) by reinterpreting it as an opposition of *contraries* that both limit and define one another—a process referred to by Hegel as *Aufhebung*.

Complete determinacy is equivalent to complete intelligibility. The position that claims that finite transcendence and finite thought, both of which need the transcendent, or not-A, to define themselves, is all we can hope for, cannot, it seems, be consistently maintained. I conclude that a strong defense of the one-paradigm-only option is possible, and that the Heideggerian strategy of advocating a discontinuity between two paradigms of intelligibility can be shown to be unsuccessful. But neither does Jaspers's position of partial intelligibility seem to be entirely consistent. If the position of partial intelligibility is to prevail, it will have to prevail by default of its opposite. So far, however, it seems to me that the principle of determinacy has not yet been successfully refuted.

NOTES

1. See, among others, Rafael Ferber, *Platos Idee des Guten* (Sankt Augustin: Hans Richarz, 1984); Hans Joachim Krämer, "*Epekeina tes Ousias*: Zu Platon, Politeia

509B," Archiv für Geschichte der Philosophie 51 (1969): 1–30; Gerasimos Santas, "Two Theories of Good in Plato's Republic," Archiv für Geschichte der Philosophie 67 (1985): 223–245; Nicholas P. White, A Companion to Plato's Republic (Indianapolis, Ind.: Hackett, 1979); and Wolfgang Wieland, "Platon und der Nutzen der Idee: Zur Funktion der Idee des Guten," Allgemeine Zeitschrift für Philosophie 1 (1976): 19–33.

2. "Platos Lehre von der Wahrheit" in the original. In the biographical appendix to Martin Heidegger, Wegmarken (Frankfurt am Main: Vittorio Klostermann, 1967), in which the essay was reprinted together with a number of articles on related topics, Heidegger informs us that "Plato's Doctrine of Truth" was first given as a paper in the winter semester of 1930–31. The essay therefore marks an important point in Heidegger's reevaluation of the history of philosophy after the publication of Sein und Zeit in 1927.

3. See Heidegger, Wegmarken, 109. Heidegger's distinction between the said and the unsaid in a philosopher's thought provides an interesting parallel to the well-known distinction between the esoteric and exoteric writings that Aristotle attributed to Plato, and the subsequent scholarly attempt in this century to reconstruct an unwritten Platonic doctrine.

4. Heidegger, Wegmarken, pp. 124, 133, 136–138.

5. Ibid., pp. 136, 138.

6. Karl Jaspers, Die Grossen Philosophen. Vol. 1, Die massgebenden Menschen: Sokrates, Buddha, Konfuzius, Jesus; Die fortzeugenden Gründer des Philosophierens: Plato, Augustin, Kant, Heraklit, Parmenides, Plotin, Anselm, Spinoza, Laotse, Nagarjuna (Munich: Piper Verlag, 1957), pp. 254–271.

7. See René Descartes, The Philosophical Writings, trans. J. Cottingham, R. Stoothoff, D. Murdoch (Cambridge: Cambridge University Press, 1984), vol. 2, p. 32.

8. See Ferber, Platos Idee des Guten, pp. 193–197.

9. Jaspers, Die Grossen Philosophen, p. 253.

10. Ibid.

11. Ibid., pp. 241–242.

12. Ibid., p. 255.

13. Ibid., p. 272.

14. Ibid.

15. Ibid.

16. Ibid., p. 269.

17. Ibid., p. 255.

18. Ibid., p. 311.

19. Ibid., p. 255.

20. Ibid., p. 311.

21. Ibid., pp. 242, 250, 254–255, 271.

22. Here I am expanding on a metaphor used by Kurt Hoffman in "Basic Concepts of Jaspers' Philosophy" in The Philosophy of Karl Jaspers, ed. Paul A. Schilpp (LaSalle Ill.: Open Court, 1957), p. 112.

23. See Hegel's Science of Logic, trans. A. V. Miller (London: Allen and Unwin, Press, 1976), p. 135.

24. See Karl Jaspers, *Philosophy*, vol. 3, trans. E. B. Ashton (Chicago: University of Chicago Press, 1970), p. 120.

25. Ibid.

26. See, e.g., Martin Heidegger, "On the Essence of Truth," in *Basic Writings of Heidegger*, ed. David Farrell Krell (New York: Harper and Row, 1977), p. 139.

8

The Space of Transcendence in Jaspers and Heidegger

Stephen A. Erickson

MY TITLE is thematically odd, and I will undertake the unfolding of the pathway it suggests in a somewhat unusual way as well. What follows are some relatively short, numbered sections, slightly reminiscent in format of portions of Nietzsche's writings or of Wittgenstein's *Philosophical Investigations*. These sections seek to reflect on Jaspers's and Heidegger's largely parallel concerns with Transcendence and our means of access to it. The sections are deliberately more disjoint than conjoint in their relation to each other. This is in order to suggest potential openings in what would otherwise be an ordinary expository course of things, gaps in the movement of philosophical discourse, spaces, as it were, through which issues of transcendence might be glimpsed as more than speculative possibilities, however premature it may be to suggest ways of experiencing transcendence itself, ways at least that would begin to be compelling. In saying this I imply alternative titles for this undertaking, for example, "Taking Transcendence Seriously," or, more boldly, "Touching Transcendence," or, even, "Transcendence's Touch." For each and any of these alternate titles, however, the subtitle would unavoidably be the same: "An Experiment in Thought." Without such an implied disclaimer one would inevitably be imprisoned in considerable presumption.

In what manner and to what degree is this, then, a philosophical undertaking? Jaspers tells us that philosophy itself falls short of being knowledge of something. But this claim is misleading, for in another sense, we are told, philosophy might be said to precede knowledge. Jaspers construes philosophy as a self-generating act of the thinker's nature. Philosophy's self-generation is the result of human nature touching upon Transcendence. Philosophy, thus, is more reactive or responsive than analytical. It might be construed in Heideggerian terms as our very openness to Being insofar as Being not only makes this openness possible, but also (and necessarily) emerges within it. In contrast, what is normally thought of as philosophical knowledge is the working out of positions or consequences, a highly analytical enterprise. Such extrapolation Jaspers and Heidegger both construe, in their time at least, as a deadening and misguided, if not pointless enterprise, an *Armutszeugnis*. Its poverty grows out of an underlying failure to be engaged by the fundamental issues. In fact, this common and highly critical conviction regarding the philosophy "business," particularly neo-Kantianism, formed much of the bond between Jaspers and Heidegger in the 1920s. Jaspers is most explicit in this regard: "Even our first talks inspired me. One can scarcely imagine the satisfaction I felt in having at least one person in the philosophers' guild with whom I could talk at all seriously. . . . Clearly, we were both opposed to the traditional philosophizing of academics. Less clearly, but somewhere deep down, we felt a vague certainty that something like a reversal was needed in the field of professorial philosophy, which we both were entering with the will to teach and be heard. We both felt the call not so much of renewing philosophy but rather of renewing the *Gestalt* of philosophy as it was then being taught at the universities."[1]

It is of more than casual interest to note that both philosophers, as Jaspers tells us, find great inspiration in Kierkegaard. As we know, Kierkegaard looked beyond the possibilities of strictly rational comprehension, and in so doing may have been more faithful to the fullness of Kant's philosophy than those early-twentieth-century neo-Kantians whom Heidegger and Jaspers so strongly rejected. Kierkegaard, Heidegger, and Jaspers all took transcendence seriously, an academically suspect, if not impossible, undertaking.

1

From the standpoint of an investigation into Heidegger and Jaspers "the space of transcendence" must sound puzzling. Though in differing ways "transcendence" has a place, even a profound one, in both their thoughts, the same is not so obviously true of "space." And what should be made of "the space of transcendence"? What might this phrase mean? After Kant, under whose influence both philosophers labor, is it not a virtual oxymoron? Are not space and transcendence definitively severed from each other? Does it not follow either that Transcendence has no space, or, less plausibly, that its space is inaccessible to human beings?[2] In pursuing these matters, my concern will be primarily with Heidegger and with Jaspers almost incidentally. For good or for ill this reflects the direction and apportioning of philosophical interest over the period succeeding the publication of *Being and Time*. In the course of these reflections, however, I shall suggest not only some reasons why this disproportionate dispensing of attention has occurred, but also some reasons why it may have been in some respects most unfortunate. I turn now, however, to Heraclitus. An attack on the contemporary outcome of the philosophical tradition is also, if only by implication, an attack on the tradition itself. Affirmation often requires an appeal to something or someone standing behind that tradition. In this regard Heraclitus occupies a special place.

2

It is more salutary for thinking to wander into the strange
than to establish itself in the understandable.[3]

Duly catalogued as FR50 in Heraclitus, this fragment is strongly (and not at all surprisingly) endorsed by Heidegger. Somewhat less strongly perhaps, Jaspers would endorse it as well. Some of the underlying motivations engendering their endorsements bear repeating: The understandable is understandable just because and only insofar as the domain of its residence has already entered into human presence, and has thereby already been sorted out and appropriated with respect to its features. The strange is *strange* because it has not yet achieved, and may never achieve, such a comprehensible presence. It may, in short, never achieve a contextualization that renders it appropriable. Terminologically the domain of the strange is largely coextensive with Jasperian transcendence. It lies beyond the boundaries, the *Grenzen*, in terms of which, and against which, one comprehends oneself in and as one's situation. In Heideggerian terms, and following Heraclitus, that strangest of all, Being, which "is the transcendence pure and simple,"[4] must be given precedence over entities, however much it eludes one's comprehension, for only in terms of an implied understanding of such Being, however dulled (*verhüllt*), is human life possible at all. This is poignantly so in a needy time such as ours, when the disclosure of Being has been largely foreclosed. In such a time, our thought can, for the most part, only approach Being (and then only anticipatorily) as the strange or, far more destructively because less obviously, as the obvious.

The strange, in short, deserves far more attention than does the comprehensible. Why? In part because in our time the comprehensible has been imprisoned by an algorithm of calculation for the purpose of its further production, consumption, or elimination. Approaches to it not only level, but deprive it of any otherwise compelling significance. The burgeoning technologies of contemporary life use up both the familiar world and our lives within that world. On this both Jaspers and Heidegger agree most decisively. What is then left is mostly leftovers, a wasteland filled with wasted materials or materials stockpiled for future wasting. Thought has become one-dimensional in this setting, merely a calculative device.

Should thinking successfully "wander into the strange," however, perhaps thinking's own ways will have been changed. No new things may come to be found or made, but many things may be made or found to be new, or at least re-newed. Re-turning to the familiar may come to involve genuine dis-covery, restoration and renewal as well, perhaps of the re-turning wanderer particularly. This, then, is the strategic gamble, and gamble it is, for in confronting the strange, thought may be undone rather than re-newed. This, for example, was Kierkegaard's fondest hope, and not just Kierkegaard's. The French of late seem to be making an obsession of this possibility.[5]

But let us consider the Heraclitean fragment prologue to another, more difficult, quotation, this one from the contemporary Czech novelist Ivan Klima and found in his novel *Love and Garbage*: "Perhaps, it occurred to me, I was in some new space. I'd entered the place where oblivion was born. Or despair. And also understanding. Or perhaps even love—not as a mirage, but as a space for the soul to move in."[6]

What would Heidegger and Jaspers say regarding these statements? Though no answer to this question is definitively available, reflection on the quotation itself is beneficial and almost curiously instructive. Not only does it shed further light on some of the pivotal dimensions of what Jaspers and Heidegger would have called the contemporary situation; such a reflection may even contribute to the finding of a pathway out, through, and beyond the confusions (and accelerating conventionality) of recent postmodernisms.

Consider the recent history of metaphysics—its history over the last few hundred years, that is. Kant understands metaphysics not only as science, but as a natural disposition of the human soul. The former is impossible, the latter unavoidable. Yet to ask such questions as metaphysics requires is to open oneself to a kind of emptiness, an oblivion, for the space of such questioning is one in which no encounter is possible and, thus, no supportable answer is to be found. To the degree that metaphysical answers are not only consolations, but supports themselves, their failure to establish themselves projects human existence into an abyss, an *Abgrund*. With his proclamation of God's death, Nietzsche would dissolve the space of metaphysical questioning, thereby closing a centuries-old wound inflicted in part by the unholy alliance of Athens and

Jerusalem, but for both Jaspers and Heidegger, the space of such unmanageable questioning remains: for Jaspers as a stimulant and limit to intellectual and scientific thought; for Heidegger as a residence to be cultivated which then nurtures its cultivators in their long wait for the not yet, the return of the gods or, perhaps, the arrival of new ones. Without encounter with this space and, in Heidegger's case, a dwelling in it, life is not quite human, however productive and even satisfying it might be. One is reminded in this connection of Nietzsche's wry observation that people do not seek happiness, that only the English do, and of course for Heidegger England extends metaphorically to encompass virtually the whole non-German world at one critical point in the 1930s.[7]

Kant could see ideas both as limiting concepts and as regulative ideals. In Hegel they become constitutive realities. Surely in this, Jaspers follows Kant, enriching Kantian ideas both by derationalizing them into unfathomable boundaries of Transcendence and by suggesting an unpredictably productive encounter with them, the productivity of which, however, is manifested not beyond, but within, this world in a myriad of enriching intellectual consequences and personal deepenings. We must never forget in this regard that Jaspers was close not only to philosophy, but to psychiatry. Sustained productive and stable relations to the world in which one finds oneself are matters of abiding concern to him. In this sense Jaspers is less than revolutionary.

Heidegger, on the other hand, is quite different, more Hegelian. In accord with Heidegger's spirit and stance, and reminiscent of Hegel, the "Ideas" come to be concretized in their uttermost reality, lived with and dwelled in. Since the "Ideas" in our time, however, are largely *Platzhalters* for vanished and vanishing significances, not embodiments of an explicable totality of reason, a realizing of them in Heidegger, following Hegel in this regard, but by no means adopting Hegel's rationally biased method and content, amounts to a sustained encounter with Nothingness, a solemnly preparatory one. The contrast with Jaspers is instructive. The world as it is is looked beyond, and the possibility of a coming radical transformation of that world, far more engages Heidegger than do notions of amelioration and enrichment.

Nietzsche and, more generally, the existentialists saw that, to be genuine, philosophy had to grow out of life and reflect back upon life, for it was life itself that initially engendered philosophical reflection and was therefore its unavoidable touchstone. In contrasting Jaspers and Heidegger we should keep in mind that language and geography are central ingredients in life and that language and geography most decidedly matter. Heidegger's is an obscure and contorting language, the challenging call of a Black Forest outsider who remains deliberately outside with respect to the far more cosmopolitan currents of establishmentarian philosophy. Though Heidegger did not always explicitly seek the overthrow of such thinking—in the thirties at times, of course, he did, and with vehemence—Heidegger had no sense of stake in its continuance and, in fact, disdained its cultural trappings. The advanced civilized world, in fact, as reflected in its cosmopolitan centers and in the Germany of Berlin, was something in which Heidegger not only had no stake, but which he largely deplored. For those who would follow his path, he sought to prepare a deliverance from that world, a dimension of which deliverance was projected as the crumbling of the older order, of the age of the world picture, in and through the emergence of a spiritual indwelling for which Heidegger himself was preparing the ground.

The remove from Jaspers is obvious. Jaspers is himself more urbane, conventional, and traditional. He is conversational as well, by which we must understand that ties with existent communities matter in his thinking. He seeks to cultivate, expand, and deepen those connections, however much he seeks to rethink them and engender in them more pervasively self-critical moments. As words, 'advance' and 'enrich' are more apposite in conveying Jaspersian strategies with regard to the cosmopolitan world than are 'escape' or 'holistic transformation'.

Of course, one can put too much on this, but Jaspers is more Aristotelianly in the world and Heidegger more Platonically, even Orphically, looking out beyond it. Jaspers, therefore, has far more to lose in any radical dislocation of the world order. His Kantian investment in that order, his regulatively guided craving for a civilized peace and an educated and communicatively engaged community, make him in many ways conservative as well as cosmopolitan. That which might in some sense supplant the world Jaspers is temperamentally more prone to co-opt and experience as significant supplement. His is more an Aristotelian synthesis of what has gone before with what impinges, however diversely and threateningly, in the present.

Heidegger, far more the prophet in the wilderness, is given to despise, even to despair over, the fruits of city life in its multiple engagements and communities—and city, of course, is a metaphor for Athens become Berlin, London, or Paris or, indescribably worse, New York or Moscow. The forest is a place of renewal, and if Babylon must be sacked and destroyed, or simply left to rot from within, and countless such Babylons, then let that be Being's righteous judgment on a weakened and neglectful people. In these matters Heidegger is far from compassionate. That such people didn't know, or couldn't sustain, German Idealism in the nineteenth century was but a harbinger of their ensuing twentieth-century fate: to be among the last of last "men," or, even worse, to swell the ranks of those unable to attain "spirit" in any meaningful way at all. And when we point out these tendencies in Heidegger, found, for example, in his *Introduction to Metaphysics*, it is not just Heidegger whom we bring into partial (and somewhat painful) focus, into troubled concern. Consider the following quotations: "Must the phenomenon of exploitation of the globe, the phenomenon of equalization of techniques and the phenomenon of democracy, which allow one to foresee a *diminutio capitis* of Europe, be taken as absolute decisions of destiny? Or have we some freedom against this menacing conjuration of things."[8] And "How is the spiritual figure of Europe to be characterized? . . . In a spiritual sense the English dominions, the United States etc. belong to Europe, not however the Eskimos or Indians of the annual fair menagerie or the gypsies permanently wandering all over Europe."[9]

The first quote is from Paul Valéry. The second is from Husserl, who is reflecting on the spiritual, and presumably superior, character of Europe. It was originally given as a lecture in Vienna in the thirties and later published as *The Crisis of European Sciences and Phenomenology*. I mention them both simply to place Heidegger within a larger and surprisingly diverse context of common concern, one with potentially destructive consequences, if picked up in the wrong way and by the wrong people. Clearly Jaspers not only was not such a person, but, much like Thomas Mann, took considerable aversion to all such statements, fearing their likely political applications in the uprooted and displaced world of the European thirties. Jaspers was far more given to prudence, caution, and tolerance.

Looking over our century, particularly the period in Europe from Versailles to Nuremburg and even to the crumbled, then walled, then crumbling-walled Berlin, deliverance, not supplementation, has been the underlying hope, the consolation, if not consummation, to be sought. Thus, Heidegger has been given precedence over Jaspers. An age seeking salvation will follow the religious more than the secular metaphor, even in the midst of its own secularity. And, of course, religions tend toward absolutism of commitment and effort and uncompromising negation of that which they would replace or supersede. Had the more tolerant, because less absolutistic, spirit of Jaspers been given more attention, much misfortune might have been diminished, but this was not the *Geist* of our time. And in saying this, I do not mean to attack Heidegger himself, but more to lament the underlying desperation that made the following of Heideggerian tendencies, and their reinforcement and nourishment, so destructive in the Germany of some fifty years ago.

Given the ascendance, if not strangulatingly pervasive reach, of technology, the more romantic and thus counterbalancing Heidegger, obscure in an age of transparent senselessness, has received further privilege. But, again, this is not to be taken as an attack. The obscurity is in large measure a function of the depth and radically fundamental nature of Heidegger's grand undertaking, one given further impetus (and emphasis) by that spiritual uprooting engendered by global communication and its constant companion, technology.

3

Heidegger's attack on the traditional conception of space goes by way of Kant. As should be familiar to us, Kant took issue with the Leibnizian attempt to construe the "in" of spatial "withinness" exclusively in logical terms and relations. For Kant an object *in* a room could not be understood spatially merely through describing it as residing logically *in* a class of objects, for any description of that class would either be insufficient to capture the given object's location or it would import nonlogically spatial notions into its descriptive activity.

Similarly, Heidegger found that even Kant's thicker sense of space, essentially Newton's made transcendental, was insufficient to circumstances as are captured in locutions such as:

George is in Art History.
Jane is in love.
Laura is in Political Science.
Bill is in trouble.

As we know from *Being and Time*, Heidegger is trying to make available the space of involvement and concern, a space that undercuts the traditional (encapsulated) subject and (external) object distinction. If successful, Heidegger will thereby have overcome epistemology—to the extent, that is, that epistemology is fundamentally grounded in the distancing, spectatorial dynamics of ancient philosophy, mentalized and interiorized in a decisive way by Descartes.

The manner in which Heidegger does this, the path he follows in *Being and Time*, is worth comment. On the one hand nature is stressed in an almost romantic way. Consider, for example: "Here, however, 'Nature' is not to be understood as that which is just present-at-hand, nor as the *power of Nature*. The wood is a forest of timber, the mountain a quarry of rock; the river is water-power, the wind is wind 'in the sails'. As the 'environment' is discovered, the 'Nature' thus discovered is encountered too. If its kind of Being as ready-to-hand is disregarded, this 'Nature' itself can be discovered and defined simply in its pure presence-at-hand. But when this happens, the Nature which 'stirs and strives', which assails us and enthralls us as landscape, remains hidden. The botanist's plants are not the flowers of the hedgerow; the 'source' which the geographer establishes for a river is not the 'springhead in the dale'."[10] Side by side with this, in fact embedded in it, is a practical world of tools and equipment, the materials requisite for what is essentially a rural life, referred to by Heidegger as the realm of *Zuhandene*.

The contrast with Kant is instructive in some further ways. For Kant, following the tradition, sensibility is a sense-bound faculty. Human receptivity is thereby restricted to the sensible world. Heidegger, however, with his notion of *Bestimmung* (attunement) and his phenomenological pursuit of *Angst*, opens the possibility of a more (or other) than sensible encounter with the world, thereby opening receptivity itself to a fundamental expansion and radical (in part, because utterly rooted) rethinking. The sensible world gets opened to the possibility, though not yet the reality, of a thorough recontextualization. Further, for Kant, the space of encountering, construed through the guidance of Newton and Hume, is three-dimensional in a way susceptible to measure by means of calculable coordinates. This space provides the ground and support, and even an expandable and refinable coordinate system, for technologically motivated mappings and, subsequently, manipulations. It becomes a ground floor for representational thinking (*Vorstellendes Denken*). For Heidegger, however, seeking ever after the ground from which any and all constructions arise, the underlying, and, because underlying, fundamental space is one of concern and involvement. Quantification is possible only through a somewhat misleading, because distancing and abstracting, mode of encounter. The more fundamental space of concern and involvement opens up a world of things as they are and, through this, provides an opening for a problematic, though now at least possible, encounter with transcendence. If not itself the space of transcendence, the space of concern and involvement is at least its antechamber. By the time On *the Origin of the Work of Art* is written in the thirties, we know that more is needed, or so Heidegger has come to think, if the space of transcendence is not only to be entered, but found substantial in content. With respect to access, that "more," of course, comes to vacillate between the problematic politics of an idiosyncratically ontologized National Socialism and the poetic avenue opened through reflection on Hölderlin. Soon the voice of Hölderlin comes to dominate, helped along by the haunting meditations of Trakl, and the more explicit and public agony of Heidegger's political misadventure is left behind. But in this there is considerable instruction. As I think is now clear, in ways terribly and even terrifyingly romantic, Heidegger sought total revolution, something Jaspers could not support.[11] In this Heidegger was relentless, and perhaps this very relentless-ness along with its often vague political implications was an element making Heidegger the far more studied philosopher of the two. Heidegger was also deeper, more profound, more knowledgeable of the philosophical tradition and more willing to break and then pursue new ground. These features, however, are frequently pointed out. In what I am now saying I wish to give some slight emphasis to a darker side.

4

Our relation to Transcendence is construed in subtly differing ways by Jaspers and by Heidegger, the differences grounded in large measure in differing conceptions of what we might provisionally call "human nature" and its attendant situation or condition. In what now follows I shall be broadly interpretive, weighting underlying resonances more than fixed and specific doctrines. These resonances, I believe, are most revealing. Consider two continua, one of which I shall call voluntarism/nonvoluntarism, the other separation/participation. On this account, a voluntarist believes not only that we must decide whether or not to become ourselves, but that we must also decide (not discover) what the self is that we must become. The nonvoluntarist, in contrast, holds to the view that though we are free to choose whether to become ourselves, the proposed self available for this act of choosing is itself in significant ways fixed regarding its nature. Kierkegaard, for example, construed the self in terms of a particular relation to a particular god, the Augustinian-Lutheran Christian one. However free we might be in undertaking the journey of self-discovery and development, its successful completion was possible only as defined by the metaphysical anthropology of a largely Protestant Christianity. Nietzsche, on the other hand, was far more the voluntarist. At best one's self was dynamically and artistically created, not metaphysically discovered. Not just the journey but the destination remained perpetually open to reformation.

I mention these two figures, Kierkegaard and Nietzsche, because, almost curiously, Heidegger is far more like Kierkegaard. As expectant receptacle of Being, human being, when all is said and done, is governed by Being's call. This call sets parameters within which full, and thus authentic, life is possible. Though the call may "withhold itself" for a time, Heidegger gives us every reason to believe its arrival will be marked with a definition, one defining us in our humanness. By way of contrast, however, no matter how much Jaspers may reflect upon and grant various biological constraints, a function in part of his medical background, his conception of the possible end results of strivings for human self-completion is far more open-ended. Were I now to transplant this distinction into the realm of culture and politics, I would be inclined to call Jaspers far more liberal-cosmopolitan, Heidegger more provincially conservative. But I hasten to add that provincialism is only pejorative for cosmopolitans, and there are those who would say that the so-called cosmopolitan resides, often self-deceptively, in what amounts to just another province. It is typically construed by its detractors as a shallow one as well.

Another way to contrast Jaspers and Heidegger is in terms of what I will call the desperation factor. I will introduce it by reference to the second continuum I mentioned: separation/participation. The tone of Jaspers's writing is detached. However much issues of striving and *Angst* enter in, their appearance is balanced, issuing forth from a self-possession at home in the world, however much "Transcendence" is acknowledged and valorized. Heidegger, on the other hand, is more evangelical, more in a condition of yearning. A few now-famous quotations will be helpful in this regard: "Not only have the gods and the god fled, but the divine radiance has become extinguished in the world's history. . . . There fails to appear for the world the ground that grounds it. . . . The age for which the ground fails to come, hangs in the abyss. In the age of the world's night, the abyss of the world must be experienced and endured. But for this it is necessary that there be those who reach into the abyss."[12] And, "To know how to question means to know how to wait, even a whole lifetime. But an age which regards as real only what goes fast and can be clutched with both hands looks on questioning as 'remote from reality' and as something that does not pay, whose benefits cannot be numbered. But the essential is not number; the essential is the right time, i.e. the right moment, and the right perseverance."[13]

Desperation might not be altogether the right word, though it is close. What one finds in Heidegger, particularly from the mid-thirties on, is an involvement, even in the face of some considerable spiritual emptiness into which that involvement had to project itself. Heidegger's resonances are more those of a voice in the wilderness than of a learned and cosmopolitan philosophical thinker. In the face of what was experienced by Heidegger as a dark night of the soul, he could not take distance, nor simply speak in a balanced and scholarly manner. Transcendence had become not just an object for study, but a goal of spiritual yearning. This may also have been true of Jaspers, but Jaspers was far more inclined to keep private and public separate and not make the private a foundation upon which to project the outlines both of the disease of our age and its spiritual prescription. To the extent he did this at all, it was as the describer, not the agonized evangelist.

We cannot but believe that Heidegger's audience was as much taken with his sound as with his content, and it may be that in its outlines the transcendence Heidegger pursued differed little from that sought by Jaspers. The difference may have been primarily in the manner of proclamation. But this surely we shall never know. It is in the nature of transcendence, particularly that elusive transcendence that both Heidegger and Jaspers sought, that such questions as are stimulated by a concern with content cannot finally be answered. But one thing seems certain: The space to which one would attain, if the pursuit of transcendence, even, were to become a reality, is resonantly both larger and more empty in Heidegger. Perhaps for this reason his sound has attracted more concern and a greater following, if only because the chamber in which it has echoed has allowed for greater movement and a more fulsome vibration.

5

I am now brought to a temporary closure, dictated by a different but equally demanding space and time, both of which are now nearly filled. I believe we are left, in a way in which both Jaspers and Heidegger would have approved, with questions. Can and should transcendence be an issue for philosophers, or "only" for people? If only for people, how, in our time, can any but philosophers suggest ways into the space within which transcendence can issue and become an issue? But how can philosophers accomplish this while still remaining philosophers? These are questions of no small moment. Earlier in this century, they were raised thematically but also existentially in the lives and the work of Jaspers and Heidegger. In the service of these issues the two thinkers were pulled apart both politically and philosophically, and one will have to wonder if any attempt to engage the space of transcendence seriously doesn't open destructive as well as healing possibilities. The space of transcendence? It may name a problem or set of problems for which not just solutions but approaches remain barely accessible. But aren't such *aporias* as mask these approaches the richest of soil from which the best of philosophical thinking has so far arisen? If so, then space travel is an unavoidable, however long delayed, undertaking, a journey toward (and into) the space of transcendence.

NOTES

1. Karl Jaspers, *The Philosophy of Karl Jaspers*, ed. Paul Schilpp (LaSalle, Ill.: Open Court, 1981), p. 75/2.

2. If Transcendence (Being) has a "space" in Heidegger's thinking, if, that is, space is applicable to Transcendence, the word for it is probably "Truth."

3. Heraclitus, FR50, in *The Presocratic Philosophers*, ed. G. S. Kirk and J. E. Raven (London: Cambridge University Press, 1960), p. 188.

4. Martin Heidegger, *Being and Time*, ed. John Macquarrie and Edward Robinson (New York: Harper and Row, 1962), p. 62.

5. See in this connection Jacques Derrida, " 'Eating Well,' or the Calculation of the Subject," in *Who Comes After the Subject?*, ed. E. Cadava, P. Connor, and J. Nancy (London: Routledge and Kegan Paul, 1991), pp. 96–119. See also in this connection the interview with Derrida that appears in *French Philosophers in Conversation*, ed. R. Mortley (London: Routledge and Kegan Paul, 1991), pp. 93–108.

6. Ivan Klima, *Love and Garbage*, trans. Ewald Osers (New York: Knopf, 1990), p. 56.

7. Friedrich Nietzsche, *Beyond Good and Evil*, trans. Walter Kaufmann (New York: Random House, 1989), p. 157.

8. This is from Paul Valéry's *Variété* (Paris: Gallimard, 1924), p. 32. It is quoted in English in Jacques Derrida's *Of Spirit, Heidegger and the Question*, trans. Geoffrey Bennington and Rachel Bowlby (Chicago: University of Chicago Press, 1989), p. 61.

9. Ibid., p. 120. The quote is, of course, from Husserl's *Crisis of European Sciences and Phenomenology*.

10. Heidegger, *Being and Time*, p. 100.

11. These issues are, in fact, pursued in a most illuminating way by Bernard Yack in *The Longing for Total Revolution* (Princeton: Princeton University Press, 1986). Though Yack himself only takes these matters up through Nietzsche and barely mentions Heidegger, I believe he articulates the fundamental dynamics of this attitude and approach to the world.

12. Martin Heidegger, *Poetry, Language, Thought*, trans. Albert Hofstadter (New York: Harper and Row, 1971), pp. 91–92. This is from "Wozu Dichter?" first appearing in *Holzwege* and originally given as a lecture in commemoration of the twentieth anniversary (1946) of the death of Rilke.

13. Martin Heidegger, *An Introduction to Metaphysics*, trans. Ralph Manheim (New Haven: Yale University Press, 1987), p. 206.

9

The Concept of Freedom in Jaspers and Heidegger

Krystyna Gorniak-Kocikowska

THE RELATIONSHIP between Karl Jaspers and Martin Heidegger is probably one of the most frequently discussed relationships between two significant philosophers of the twentieth century. With the present paper, I would like to contribute to this discussion by examining some aspects of the problem of freedom as understood by Jaspers and Heidegger.[1]

The problem of freedom was crucial for both Jaspers and Heidegger. However, their approaches to it show how different their philosophies were, despite the similarity of their general philosophical outlook. To see this difference is important, in particular because Heidegger and Jaspers are regarded as the two most significant German existentialists of the twentieth century. Their names are usually brought together in contemporary textbooks on existentialism, rightly or wrongly, and in such textbooks, similarities rather than differences in their philosophies are usually emphasized. There is also the tendency to think that what divided the two was politics, not philosophy.

This, of course, is a serious oversimplification. Both philosophers were conscious that there were significant differences between them. Jaspers's point of view on these differences is clearer thanks to the record of his *Notizen zu Martin Heidegger*. Heidegger's criticism of *Psychologie der Weltanschauungen*,[2] by contrast, is not as well known as the *Notizen*, and it deals basically only with one early work by Jaspers.

Usually Jaspers and Heidegger are compared with regard to their position toward Nazism. While this is a significant factor, especially in the light of the discussion that took place after the publication of Victor Farías's book about Heidegger's links with Nazism, the political aspect of the relationship between Jaspers and Heidegger has undeservedly overshadowed the philosophical one. On the other hand, both philosophers share complicity in the creation of such an image.

Hans Saner, the editor of Jaspers's *Notizen zu Martin Heidegger*, stresses very strongly in his foreword the initial closeness, mutual fascination, and friendship between Jaspers, already academically well established, and Heidegger, the philosophical "rising star," when they met for the first time in 1920 at a birthday party for Edmund Husserl. Saner also writes that the first mutual disappointment took place apparently as early as 1921. The cause of this was Jaspers's book *Psychologie der Weltanschauungen*, the book in which Jaspers moved from the field of psychology toward philosophy as the major arena of his intellectual activity. Heidegger criticized the book by his older colleague in ways Jaspers never forgot or, for that matter, "forgave."[3] When Heidegger published *Sein und Zeit*, Jaspers in turn found the book worth some words of veiled criticism. Probably at that time they became conscious of the fact that their spiritual farewell had already happened.

It is, of course, impossible to project what the relationship between Jaspers and Heidegger might have been in the absence of a Nazi regime in Germany. However, the fact that they stood on opposite sides of the political barricade made their philosophical relationship much more complicated, difficult, and delicate. Jaspers obviously had the benefit of being "on the right side" in relation to Nazism. Thus he openly and justly criticized Heidegger's political views, and his criticism must serve as the basis of serious argument in the recent debate on Heidegger.

The polarity of their political positions made it impossible for them to criticize each other's philosophical views openly and sharply. For many years after 1933, their positions within the academic world were diametrically opposed. As a matter of fact, if they wanted to play fair, neither could really seriously criticize the other's philosophical work. If Heidegger criticized Jaspers's philosophy before 1945, it would have been seen as his revenge for Jaspers's criticism of Heidegger's political activity. During that time, Jaspers could not speak openly while presenting his views in public. To criticize him meant to kick someone who was already down. After the war, the situation changed, and Heidegger was silenced for years, not without Jaspers' contribution to it. Indeed, to criticize Jaspers would have required Heidegger to break his silence on political matters. On the other hand, Jaspers obviously did not want to give the impression that he profited as philosopher on the basis of his political righteousness. For Jaspers to now publicly criticize Heidegger would be to reverse the situation in which he had found himself prior to the war, in other words, to kick someone who had already been knocked down.

Beginning with Hitler's 1933 victory, Jaspers and Heidegger had reasons to avoid open attacks on each other's philosophy. They were friendly and neutral and watched each other's moves closely. They sent their books to each other and maintained a correspondence. In fact, the published correspondence (*Briefwechsel*) between Jaspers and Heidegger consists of 157 letters and brief notes written in the years 1920–1963.[4] In this correspondence, however, one can feel the thin needles being pushed into each other's positions. Of course, they both play according to the rules, with Heidegger, especially in the earlier correspondence, self-portrayed as the eager disciple asking his mentor for opinion and acceptance, being endlessly grateful for every bit of advice. Jaspers, in turn, plays the role of the sometimes bitter, often sarcastic, but also congenial older colleague, encouraging with a certain irony his already successful partner, for Heidegger would eagerly share with Jaspers information about all the academic activities from which Jaspers obviously had been excluded: travel to Italy, participation in a commission for the publication of Nietzsche's work, and so forth.[5] He would also write in a rather bored tone about his lectures on Schelling's "Concept of Freedom" during the time when Jaspers was forbidden to teach, thus displaying a certain insensitivity to his friend's situation.

Jaspers, on his part, never granted Heidegger publicly the appellation of "great philosopher." He would say rather that Heidegger "is a significant potency." But a "great philosopher"? Not in the opinion of Jaspers, who viewed Heidegger as being "extraordinarily uncritical" and "far away from science proper."[6] He would not go further in his public criticism[7] on Heidegger as philosopher, nor would he enter into any philosophical polemics with Heidegger. Nevertheless, he would follow carefully the traces of Heidegger's criticism of his writings and react to them perceptively in his private *Notizen*.

While the personal and political aspects of the relationship between Jaspers and Heidegger are potentially illuminating, what concerns me in this essay is their philosophy. The philosophical differences between them are profound, and these differences were important to both philosophers, whereas their readers usually overlook or minimize them, preferring only to see similarities rather than differences.

But as I've already indicated, both Heidegger and Jaspers had reasons not to enter any open, sharp polemics,[8] even though both knew that what really separated them was philosophy and the problem of philosophical truth and how best to approach it. Jaspers thought that the similarity between himself and Heidegger was the result of the influence of the same philosophers, whether Kierkegaard, Nietzsche, Hegel, Schelling, Kant, or Meister Eckhart. But he was also aware that their "difference from the very beginning had to do with Heidegger's antique-scholastic training."[9] Conversely, what separated Jaspers from the full esteem of Heidegger (and a great many other German colleagues) was his professional education in psychopathology. They came to philosophy from two different worlds.

This problem was important not only for the personal relationship between Jaspers and Heidegger. Paul Tillich sees it as having to do with the problem of existentialism itself. Tillich claims that it is typical for the existentialist to ask questions, not to answer them. Moreover, he thinks that all the answers we can find given by the existentialists do not follow from questions asked within existentialism but from other sources. In other words, when the existentialists answer any philosophical question, they do not answer as existentialists since existentialism, rigorously understood, precludes of necessity all essentialistic answers. In such a case the existentialist must go back to the sources of his or her philosophical upbringing. What is decisive for Heidegger, says Tillich, is "the mystical tradition within which he lived as a Catholic seminarian." For Jaspers, by contrast, "the answers come . . . from the classical humanist tradition or, more precisely, German Idealism."[10] Jaspers understood this, and knew that the difference between himself and Heidegger was not just the problem of interpretation or of philosophical grandeur. They had their cultural roots in different social and religious worlds.

Both Jaspers and Heidegger worked with the same material and read the same philosophical books; but they saw in these works different problems—or, more accurately, they saw the problems differently. For example, the way Heidegger wrote about the problem of freedom was completely nontraditional, but it was also different from Jaspers's nontraditional approach. From Jaspers's point of view, the traditional understanding of freedom desperately needed revision, and Heidegger was of the same opinion. Thus, even though they shared the same cultural tradition, the same language, and wrote on similar subjects,[11] Jaspers could say, "Heidegger does not know what freedom is."[12]

Was he right? How did Jaspers understand freedom? He devoted significant attention to the problem of freedom in many of his written works, including his major philosophical work *Philosophie*.[13] According to the concept of the "encompassing" with its different modes, Jaspers claims that there are special kinds of freedom for different modes of the "encompassing." The true freedom is for Jaspers only the being (*Sein*) of existence in its being-in-time (*Zeitdasein*); nevertheless, this freedom is not possible without other kinds of freedom, in which freedom manifests itself. On the plane of world-orientation (*Weltorientierung*), that is, in the empirical world, there is formal freedom, which manifests itself in "freedom as knowledge" and "freedom as willfulness." Other kinds of freedom are transcendental freedom, which is self-confidence in obedience toward an obvious law (in Kantian sense); freedom as idea, which is life in a whole; and finally existential freedom, which is the self-confidence of the historical source of decision. Existential freedom includes all other kinds of freedom. However, existential freedom cannot be objectively conceived, according to Jaspers. One can be sure of it not in his or her thought but in existence, not in observation and asking about it, but in realization. "Freedom is not absolute, but is at the same time always bounded; it is not possession, but a gain. As freedom itself its becoming thought (*Gedachtwerden*) is only in movement."[14]

For a human being, freedom is the beginning sense of one's existence which, as a continuous "becoming" (*das Werden*), is the only absolute truth. However, this "becoming," this self-creation, even in relation to oneself is limited by numerous external conditions. For that reason Jaspers denies the possibility of absolute freedom. If such freedom did exist, a freedom that could only be the freedom of the "Single One," it would have to be the freedom of totality. Nothing could exist outside of it; all contradictions would necessarily be contained within it. Without contradictions, however, freedom is impossible, because freedom must develop itself in a process, and this process is a struggle.[15] We will see later that Schelling was writing about the contradiction of necessity and freedom as a "life-condition" for not only "philosophy but every nobler ambition of the spirit."[16] Heidegger gave this statement a key function in his lectures on freedom.

We will also see that this type of freedom, which Jaspers declares to be impossible, is as a matter of fact the only one that really interested Heidegger: "For freedom is here, not the property of man but the other way around: Man is at best the property of freedom." He repeats: "*Key sentence*: Freedom not the property of man, but rather: man the property of freedom."[17]

As the result of the perspective taken by Jaspers, freedom, although it exists, has no possibility of full realization. Jaspers says that on the plane of empirical being one uses the words "I can" or "I cannot." But these words refer to the physical forces of an empirical individual and to an area of power in a given situation, but not to existence, according to Jaspers. In the sense of transcendental freedom, one can use the sentence: "I can because I ought" (this would be the Kantian understanding of freedom), and in the sense of existential freedom: "I can because I must." According to Jaspers: "This ability no longer refers to the factual realization of one goal in the world, but to both inner and external action, even if I as an empirical being do fail. It is the unconditionality of ability, which knows no boundary in the consciousness of original freedom."[18]

The philosophical interests of Jaspers throughout the period of his intellectual activity were focused on the human being treated as a universe. There is a difference between Jaspers and Heidegger in this regard, the difference that has been described by Tillich in an almost aphoristic manner: "We can thus generalize by saying that Heidegger wants to know what it means *to be* whereas Jaspers wants to know what it means *to be a person*."[19] For example, the subject of Jaspers's book on Schelling *is* Schelling ("his greatness and fate," as the subtitle says), whereas when Heidegger wrote his book on Schelling's philosophy, he concentrated only on Schelling's *Of Human Freedom*. Jaspers is interested in the man who was the philosopher Schelling. He lays Schelling on the psychiatrist's couch first, and subsequently makes philosophical judgments about him. Heidegger analyzes Schelling's last significant work since what he is interested in is the problem "of the essence of human freedom that means, at the same time, the question of freedom" because for Heidegger this is "the innermost center of philosophy."[20]

Jaspers claims that the human being is free; however, according to him, the human being is not free on the empirical plane nor in the sphere of transcendence. "Transcendence is not my freedom," Jaspers insists, "but it is present in freedom."[21] Only existential freedom is the true freedom. In freedom, there is a movement that aims at transcendence, but freedom itself does not reach transcendence, "it is only as existence in *Zeitdasein*."[22] Therefore, "freedom is always just the being (*Sein*) of Existenz, not of transcendence; it is the handle with which transcendence grasps existenz, but only because this Existenz is itself [namely, freedom] in its independence."[23]

Jaspers applies his concept of freedom among others to the book on Schelling.[24] He begins with Schelling's biography, with the personal life of the philosopher. Then, he gives his answer to the question, what does philosophy mean for Schelling? The next chapter of the book is devoted to Schelling's concept of Being. The fourth chapter has to do with "The Question About the Substance of Schelling's Philosophizing," and the last chapter is about Schelling and his times.

Heidegger started his work on *Schelling's Treatise on the Essence of Human Freedom* where Jaspers finishes, namely with the description of the political situation in which Schelling wrote on freedom. Then he discusses Schelling's book chapter after chapter, but devotes more than half of his efforts to the foreword and introduction.[25] Schelling's book serves him as a point of departure and as a point of reference. On this basis, Heidegger really presents his own concept of freedom in these lectures, the clarity of which (astonishing for many readers of *Sein und Zeit*) helps to explain Heidegger's great popularity among his students.

But this was not the first time for Heidegger to philosophize about freedom. Although he did not devote directly any single paragraph to this problem in *Sein und Zeit*, he lectured on freedom in 1930 just prior to Hitler's rise to power.[26] But again, the text of these lectures, which has the subtitle *Introduction to Philosophy*, was published only in 1982 as volume 31 of Heidegger's collected works. Heidegger's 1930 lectures on freedom show a direct kinship with the spirit of *Sein und Zeit*, but also a strong relation to Kant. It is interesting to notice that Jaspers somehow overlooked Kant's influence on Heidegger, despite Heidegger's *Kant and the Problem of Metaphysics* (published in 1929) and regarded by many, including Tillich, as one of Heidegger's most successful books. Perhaps Tillich has given the proper explanation for Jaspers's behavior by reminding his listeners that "it is Heidegger speaking here and not Kant." Of course, it was Heidegger's intention to do so, as we know from his own preface; therefore, Tillich justifies Heidegger. But his explanation also contains insights regarding his conception of hermeneutics: "Interpretation, if it is to be creative and successful, must be more than repetition. True interpretation is always the creation of something new, something which emerges between the text being interpreted and the interpreter. This, Heidegger knows very well indeed, and thus he goes back to Kant in order to show the significance of time for his own work."[27]

We will see later that Heidegger also used Kant to explain his understanding of freedom. However, such an attitude has two sharp edges. The creative interpretation, if it is not understood according to the intentions of the interpreter, can be read as misinterpretation. Jaspers obviously regarded Heidegger's interpretation of Kant's philosophy in that way.

Jaspers was of the opinion that Heidegger, like himself, was much influenced by Schelling—although he thought that it was inappropriate to compare Heidegger with Schelling since "Heidegger has nothing from what can be called Schelling's nobility, neither does he have any impulses of that *Philosophy of Freedom*."[28] Jaspers once made a comparison of his contemporaries with "the greats of the classic time" where Heidegger was paired by him with Fichte and not with Schelling—for whom Jaspers found an analog in Klages. Of course, Jaspers saw himself as closely "following Kant's footprints," however humbly,[29] and he frequently stressed that Kant was the philosopher who influenced him the most. Overlooking Kant's influence on Heidegger, Jaspers somehow admits that the ways both of them understood Kant were very different—as different as their own philosophies were.

It is not my intention, however, to determine how and why it was possible that Jaspers did not see links between Kant and Heidegger. But I think that this question is important for understanding the philosophical positions of both Jaspers and Heidegger. In the lectures *Vom Wesen der menschlichen Freiheit*, Heidegger devotes much space to the problem of freedom by Kant, examining different aspects of that problem resulting from Kant's position. But we also have Heidegger's famous *Rektoratsrede* (1933) in which he defined, among other things, his attitude to the problem of freedom and realization of the idea of freedom by the university: "To make a law for oneself is the highest value. *Academic freedom*, praised so often, gets removed from the German university for this freedom was false, for this freedom was exclusively denying. It signified mainly light-heartedness, freedom of intentions and inclinations, no restrictions as to the manner of action. The notion of German student's freedom will now be again reduced to its truth."[30]

Heidegger was frequently criticized for this statement. I think that some mistakes in the understanding of what "freedom" is for Heidegger, have been made here. When Heidegger spoke about removing of "false freedom" from German universities and gave as a reason for this the statement that the student's freedom is "exclusively denying," he must have meant the "freedom from," in other words, a totally nonproductive notion of freedom. But the "freedom from" was not for him the "right" freedom since it belongs to the sphere of "non-authentic being." To be truly free, one must be able to be "free for" which is possible for an "authentic being." The realization of freedom as "freedom for" was directed by a "transformed"[31] set of values different from those that were accepted for the "public sphere" of the modern Western society—but this is a separate problem. When we remember what Heidegger thought about the "everydayness," we should not be surprised by his opinion about values accepted in that sphere (or about the interpretation and application of those values). And if we follow honestly, without preference for interpretations to which we are otherwise inclined, Heidegger's criticism of the "everydayness" as well as his argumentation, it is difficult to defend morally the kind of "everydayness" he criticized.

Not only Heidegger, but Marx and Nietzsche as well, state that human beings prefer the world of desire (the non-existing-*yet*-world) to the real one and that, being unable to create "just now" and "just here" the world in which they would feel comfortable, people are inclined to create an image of the world that they wish to be true, and then go on to claim that it is the true world. In Plato, the inhabitants of the cave not only mean that "it's not even worth trying to go up" to the light; they would also prohibit the person who wants to go out of the world of shadows from doing it: "And if they were somehow able to get their hands on and kill the man who attempts to release and lead up, wouldn't they kill him?"[32]

In a sense, Heidegger realized this in his speech regarding his postulate of a revival of the university and a revival of philosophy—and it was a postulate that Jaspers had already put forward immediately after

World War I, even though it was different from the realization Jaspers anticipated.[33] Nevertheless, what Heidegger said about freedom in his festive speech is, in fact, another form of Kantian categorical imperative: "This will [the will underlying the idea of the university] is a true will if the German student community starts working, through a new student law, to the cause of the university and thus draws limits to this idea. To be able to determine principles for oneself is the highest freedom."[34]

As in Kant, freedom is here regarded as the highest value, and as in Kant, it requires self-sacrifice. Heidegger's concept of freedom, like Kant's, must be restricted to be realized fully. Heidegger demands that the limitation of one's own freedom be done as work devoted to a cause—to an idea whose fulfillment is a realization of existential freedom. Here one can also make reference to Nietzsche, for when Nietzsche claimed that service to a genius is the highest happiness of the nongenius, he presented a concept of the self-limitation of one's own freedom according to an ultimate goal. This is not very surprising because there is close relationship (however paradoxical it may sound) between Kant's notion of ethics and Nietzsche's "immorality."

It needs to be emphasized that all this follows as the consequence of accepting the concept of individual "freedom for" chosen by the mentioned philosophers as a point of departure for their considerations. In my opinion, Heidegger had in mind the "freedom for" when he wrote, in *Being and Time*, "As understanding, Dasein projects its Being upon possibilities. This Being-towards-possibilities which understands is itself a potentiality-for-Being, and it is so because of the way these possibilities, as disclosed, exert their counter-thrust (*Rückschlag*) upon Dasein."[35]

It is interesting to see how the Kantian understanding of the role of the individual in society, which should serve the creation of the new "civil society" (of individuals having equal rights who should build the area of "public sphere" in order to create ultimately a happy world) was explained and used for gradual deprivation of the rights to decide what the shape of this world might eventually be. In that sense, Heidegger's explanation of "everydayness" and its pejorative evaluation *may* be easily understood as the exclusion from the "mature" society of those who are unable to reach the "higher level." In short, such "immature" people must have a leader(s) and be obedient!

Three years after his inaugural speech, Heidegger, no longer a rector, was speaking again to the German students about freedom. This time he was lecturing on Schelling, whom he called "the truly creative and boldest thinker of this whole age of German philosophy."[36] He was talking to the students about the concept of freedom which "is not just one concept among others, but the center of Being as a whole." Heidegger says, "The concept of freedom has reality when being free as a manner of Being belongs together with the nature and essential ground of Being. If this is correct, the concept of freedom is no longer an arbitrary one."[37] This is an important statement, because it prepares the listeners/readers for the explanation of basic questions connected with this lecture, questions such as "Why Schelling? Why this last great representative of German Idealism? The creator of the philosophical system?" We are used to thinking of philosophers from Heidegger's generation as anti-idealists and antisystemists. Nevertheless Heidegger answers: "For the thinkers of German Idealism . . . a system is the totality of Being in the totality of its truth and the history of the truth."[38] And he continues: "If the freedom of the individual really exists [and here we must remember that Jaspers said such freedom does not exist on the empirical plane] this means that it exists in some way together with the totality of the world. And just this existential coexistence, *systasis*, is what the concept and the word system itself mean."[39]

As we remember, Schelling's treatise deals extensively with the question of pantheism. Heidegger refers to this repeatedly quoting Schelling as follows: "In man there exists the whole power of the principle of darkness and, in him too, the whole force of light. In him there are both centers—the deepest pit and the highest heaven. Men's will is the seed—concealed in eternal longing—of God, present as yet only in the depths—the divine light of life locked in the depths which God divined when he determined to will nature."[40]

Heidegger insists that "to understand this passage means to comprehend the whole treatise."[41] Indeed, the remainder of Heidegger's book is really the explanation of the above-quoted passage by Schelling. In this process, Heidegger comes to the question of the relationship between freedom and necessity, and the role of philosophy. He summarizes: "Schelling wants to say we are not philosophizing *about* necessity and freedom, but philosophy is the most alive *And*, the unifying strife between necessity and freedom. He doesn't just *say it*, he enacts this in the treatise."[42] This, says Heidegger, is a totally new approach. Schelling replaced the traditional opposition between freedom and nature with the opposition between freedom and necessity. It was possible for Schelling, because before Schelling there was Kant. Heidegger then goes on to trace Schelling's thoughts regarding *necessity*. This necessity can only be God, he says.[43] This is why Schelling was so preoccupied with pantheism. Traditionally, nature was regarded as being characterized by the lack of freedom. But now the situation changes;[44] the pantheistic approach implies some questions: Does the divinity of nature extend freedom into the realm of nature? Or is no freedom possible? Where is the place of human beings? Heidegger writes: "Schelling had pointed out a new solution to the whole question by showing that man's most lively feeling of freedom placed him not outside of God and against God, but as belonging to the 'life of God.' Freedom demands immanence in God, pantheism. Now it must be shown on the other hand that pantheism correctly understood demands freedom. If this evidence is successful, the assertion set up as the key phrase—that pantheism as the sole possible system is necessarily fatalism—is refuted in every respect. Then the way is at least free for the possibility of a system of freedom."[45]

Heidegger, still tracing Schelling, makes the statement that there are two theses of pantheism: (1) Pantheism is not fatalism, and (2) God is man.[46] Heidegger makes the assertion that this thesis has to be correctly understood, and explains: " 'Correctly understood' means that the 'is' must be understood as real identity."

Following Schelling, Heidegger presents seven concepts of freedom,[47] and then he makes a statement: "The main concern of the introduction is to make clear the fact that not a step can be taken in the whole question of freedom and the system of freedom without an adequate concept of Being and without an adequately primordial basic experience of beings."[48]

This is a powerful statement since it justifies *Being and Time* as the necessary book to precede any subsequent works on freedom Heidegger might write after it. As a matter of fact, the above quotation says that *Being and Time* is a book about freedom. There is an anecdote that after Heidegger published *Sein und Zeit* one of his students asked, "Professor Heidegger, when will you write a book on ethics?" Heidegger answered "Why? *Sein und Zeit* is on ethics."[49] It seems to me that for Heidegger *Sein und Zeit* was already on freedom, too.

Jaspers did not understand *Sein und Zeit*—or better, he understood *Sein und Zeit* differently from the way Heidegger wanted it to be understood. He also did not see, or did not want to see, that not only was he himself "following Kant's footprints," but that Heidegger, from his own perspective, was also attempting to do this. It is not surprising, therefore, that Heidegger's understanding of freedom provoked Jaspers to say, "Heidegger does not know what freedom is."

NOTES

1. I presented a paper titled "Jaspers and Heidegger: Philosophy of Freedom, Freedom of Philosophy" at the session of the Jaspers Society of North America during the American Philosophical Association Annual Meeting (Washington, D.C.) in 1985. It has been translated into Croatian and published with the

title "Jaspers—Heidegger: filozofija slobode, slobode filozofije" in *Filozofska Istra-zivanja* 22, God. 7 (1987), Sv. 3, Zagreb, Yugoslavia, 1987, pp. 977–984. However, the present paper is not a repetition of what I wrote six years ago—it is a different approach to the question of freedom in both philosophers, to the importance of this question in their works and in their life. This time I investigate different texts.

2. See Martin Heidegger, *Anmerkungen zu Karl Jaspers Psychologie der Weltan-schauungen*, in *Wegmarken* vol. 9 of Heidegger's *Collected Works* (Frankfurt am Main: Vittorio Klostermann, 1976), pp. 1–44.

3. See Hans Saner's foreword to Karl Jaspers, *Notizen zu Heidegger*, ed. Hans Saner (Munich: Piper Verlag, 1978). Later, in lectures on Schelling, Heidegger refers to Jaspers's *Psychology of World Views* in a very neutral, matter-of-fact way; the reader is unable to say whether Heidegger likes this work or not. However, the reader who knows about Heidegger's criticism would have the impression that Heidegger is not necessarily enthusiastic about Jaspers's definition of the world-view he quoted. See Martin Heidegger, *Schelling's Treatise on the Essence of Human Freedom*, trans. Joan Stambaugh (Athens: Ohio University Press, 1985), pp. 18ff.

4. The 1926–1969 correspondence between Hannah Arendt and Jaspers, by contrast, consists of 432 significantly long and substantive letters. See *Hannah Arendt, Karl Jaspers: Correspondence, 1926–1969*, ed. Lotte Kohler and Hans Saner, trans. Robert and Rita Kimber (New York: Harcourt, Brace, Jovanovich, 1992).

5. See *Briefwechsel*, ed. Hans Saner (Munich: Piper Verlag, 1990), Letter 122.

6. Ibid., p. 271.

7. Even this was not really public, because the criticism quoted was expressed only in an official letter for the *Bereinigungskommission* after the fall of Nazism.

8. The very beginning of Heidegger's lectures on Schelling is interesting in this aspect, given the time Heidegger lectured. The philosopher speaks about the year of publication of Schelling's treatise (1809). This gives him the opportunity to remember the relationship between Goethe and Napoleon. Then he speaks about the break between the youth friends: Hegel and Schelling, a break that was caused by "a sharp denial of Schelling" (Heidegger, *Schelling's Treatise*, p. 2) by Hegel in the preface to "The Phenomenology of Spirit." It is easy to see in Heidegger's presentation a continuation of his dialogue with Jaspers. Heidegger leaves, of course, to his listeners the discovery of the similarity between "then" and "now."

9. See Jaspers, *Notizen*, p. 189. Jaspers stated also that Heidegger's thinking is theological, which for Jaspers means having a tendency to both dictate and obey, without Revelation. According to him, what Heidegger reaches is "not self-thinking (*Selbstdenken*), not freedom—but aesthetic perplexity" (p. 153).

10. See Tillich's comments in Chapter 1 of this volume.

11. Jaspers published his book on Nietzsche in 1936; Heidegger published his in 1961. In 1955, Jaspers published "Schelling." Heidegger's book on Schelling was based on his lectures from 1936, although it was published as late as 1971. But Jaspers, too, had become interested in that philosopher already shortly after World War I, as he claimed in the foreword to his book. Of course, there were other philosophers (Kant) and other problems (the situation of German universities)

they both worked on, but for this paper's sake, I will concentrate only on the problem of freedom.

12. Jaspers, Notizen, p. 77.

13. Jaspers presents his concept of freedom in an interesting way in "Philosophical Faith and Revelation" (esp. pp. 235–238). There are some differences between this presentation and what we can read in his Philosophie. Since it is impossible to deal with them in a short paper, I concentrate only on the concept of freedom presented by Jaspers in Philosophie.

14. Karl Jaspers, Philosophie (Berlin: Springer Verlag, 1956), vol. 2, p. 185.

15. See Jaspers, Philosophie, vol. 2, p. 194.

16. Schelling, Of Human Freedom, trans. James Gutmann (Chicago: Open Court, 1936), p. 9.

17. See Heidegger, Schelling's Treatise, p. 9.

18. Jaspers, Philosophy, vol. 2, p. 186.

19. See Tillich's comments in Chapter 1 of this volume.

20. Heidegger, Schelling's Treatise, p. 4.

21. Jaspers, Philosophie, vol. 2, p. 199.

22. Ibid., p. 177.

23. Ibid.

24. Jaspers's book on Schelling was written at the same time as he wrote his Philosophie.

25. Heidegger was of the opinion that "the true weight of Schelling's treatise . . . lies in introduction and the first four sections." (Schelling's Treatise, p. 162)

26. Jaspers published his own Introduction to Philosophy in 1950. The German subtitle of Heidegger's Vom Wesen der menschlichen Freiheit is "Einleitung in die Philosophie," whereas the German title of the book by Jaspers is Einführung in die Philosophie (Zurich, 1950), translated into English by Ralph Manheim as The Way to Wisdom (New Haven: Yale University Press, 1951). Einleitung and Einführung are synonyms. One could, of course, speculate about, whether the authors decided to use different words on purpose, or whether they did it unintentionally.

27. See Tillich's comments in Chapter 1 of this volume.

28. Jaspers, Notizen, p. 154.

29. Ibid., p. 101.

30. Martin Heidegger, Die Selbstbehauptung der Deutschen Universität/Das Rektorat 1933/34 (Frankfurt am Main: Vittorio Klostermann, 1983), p. 15. I offer my own translation of this passage because the existing English translation distorts the meaning of Heidegger's pronouncement. The English translation by Dagobert D. Runes runs as follows: "To give oneself a code of laws is itself the highest form of freedom. The much-sung academic freedom will vanish; it was false because it was only negative, implying uncommittedness in thought and act. The concept of the freedom of the German student will be brought back to reality." Martin Heidegger, German Existentialism, trans. with introduction by Dagobert D. Runes (New York: Philosophical Library, 1965), p. 15. Runes translated Heidegger's speech as it appeared in the Freiburger Zeitung, and it differs significantly from the text published by Klostermann.

31. This is not the same as Nietzsche's "transvaluation" of values.

32. See Plato's *Republic*, trans. Allan Bloom (New York: Basic Books, 1968), p. 196.

33. See Karl Jaspers, *The Idea of University*, ed. Karl W. Deutsch, Introduction by Robert Ulich, trans. H.A.T. Reiche and H. F. Vanderschmidt (Boston: Beacon Hill, 1959). Jaspers, in a sense, joined Kant (*Der Streit der Fakultäten*), Schleiermacher (*Gelegentliche Gedanken über Universitäten*), and Nietzsche (*Über die Zukunft unserer Bildungsanstalten*) in their discussion about German universities.

34. Heidegger, *Das Rektorat* 1933–34, p. 15. This passage is completely distorted in the text translated by Runes.

35. See Heidegger, *Being and Time*, ed. John Macquarrie and Edward Robinson (New York: Harper and Row, 1962), p. 188.

36. Heidegger, *Schelling's Treatise*, p. 4.

37. Ibid., pp. 20–21.

38. Ibid., p. 48.

39. Ibid., p. 49.

40. Ibid., p. 38.

41. Ibid., p. 53.

42. Ibid., p. 58.

43. Ibid., p. 162.

44. Ibid., p. 60f.

45. Ibid., p. 85.

46. Ibid., p. 88.

47. Ibid., pp. 88, 97, 102.

48. Ibid., p. 89.

49. Pawet Dybel, "Panie Heidegger, kiedy pan napisze etyke?" in *Aletheia: Heidegger dzisiaj* (Warsaw) 1, no. 4 (1990): 326.

10

Heidegger's Debt to Jaspers's Concept of the Limit-Situation

William D. Blattner

IN HIS DISCUSSION of death in Chapter 1 of Division 2 of *Sein und Zeit*,[1] Martin Heidegger refers us "especially" to Karl Jaspers's discussion of death in the latter's *Psychologie der Weltanschauungen*.[2] What does Heidegger's treatment of death in *Being and Time* owe to Jaspers's in *Psychology of World Views*? The debt is twofold. First, Heidegger's approach to death is to treat it as something very like a limit-situation. Like limit-situations, death is a condition in which one confronts the limits imposed on existence by an inherent tension within that existence; and like limit-situations, this confrontation gives rise to an extreme form of disquiet, characterized by Jaspers as a sort of suffering, and by Heidegger as a form of anxiety. Second, although for Heidegger death is not very much like the ordinary phenomenon of the ending of a person's life, still as the end of Dasein's ability-to-be, death marks out the limits of Dasein's existence. Both Jaspers and Heidegger take the discussion of death to have a significant role to play in the development of an ontology of human existence, because both take limit-situations to reveal the limits that define that existence.

I shall approach this issue in the following way. I shall first lay out the setting in which the issue of Heidegger's debt to Jaspers's concept of the limit-situation arises. Second, I shall develop an interpretation of Jaspers's concept of the limit-situation as it is found in his *Psychologie der Weltanschauungen*. Third, I shall describe Heidegger's interest in limit-situations. Fourth and finally, I shall state how Heidegger appropriates and redeploys the concept of the limit-situation in his discussion of death in *Sein und Zeit*.

The Setting of the Issue

The name of Karl Jaspers appears three times in *Sein und Zeit*, each time in a footnote. All three occurrences are primarily references to Jaspers's

Psychologie der Weltanschauungen. The first two footnotes (pages 249 and 301 of SZ) are references that involve the notion of a limit-situation among other things, whereas the third reference (p. 338) focuses on the concept of the Augenblick of human temporality. We know that Heidegger read Jaspers's Psychologie der Weltanschauungen carefully, and that between 1919 and 1921 he composed a lengthy review article on it. That review only appeared in 1973 in a collection of materials on Jaspers,[3] and later in the second edition of Heidegger's Wegmarken, under the title "Anmerkungen zu Karl Jaspers Psychologie der Weltanschauungen."[4] Although he never published the piece, as originally intended,[5] he thought well enough of what he wrote to send it to Jaspers (as well as to Husserl and Rickert).[6] That review and the scanty remarks on Jaspers in Sein und Zeit suggest Heidegger's debt to Jaspers's work, and in particular to the concept of the limit-situation.

The overriding theme of Heidegger's comments on the concept of the limit-situation is that it is an important clue to the ontology of human existence. Heidegger embraces the limit-situation as an ontological clue, even though as I shall argue later, he rejects Jaspers's ontology, and consequently does not find precisely the same content in the concept. The second reference to Jaspers in Sein und Zeit sets the general tone rather clearly. He writes in the main text: "The task of portraying factical, existentiell possibilities in their chief tendencies and contexts and of interpreting them according to their existential structure falls into the circle of tasks that belong to thematic, existential anthropology. The existential delimitation (Umgrenzung) of the authentic ability-to-be, which is attested in conscience from out of Dasein itself and for Dasein itself, is sufficient for the fundamental-ontological intention of the current investigation" (SZ, 301).

Here Heidegger contrasts philosophical anthropology's goal of describing some of the specific, yet basic, possibilities that confront human beings, with his own fundamental-ontological goal of laying out the essential structures of the being of any existent Dasein. In this context and concerning the notion of existential anthropology, he footnotes Jaspers as follows: "In the direction of this problematic, Karl Jaspers has for the first time explicitly grasped and carried out the task of a doctrine of world-views. See his Psychologie der Weltanschauungen, 3d ed., 1925. Here it is asked 'what man is,' and the answer is determined in terms of what he essentially can be (see the Foreword to the 1st ed.). In these terms the basic existential-ontological significance of 'limit-situations' is illuminated. The philosophical tendency of the Psychologie der Weltanschauungen is completely misunderstood, if one uses it simply as a reference book for 'types of world-views' " (SZ, 301, n. 1). Heidegger thus seeks to protect Jaspers from a vulgarizing reading of *Psychologie der Weltanschauungen*, namely as a catalog of worldview types, for in PW Jaspers attempts to interpret the basic human possibilities he discusses in light of the guiding conception of existence (*Existenz*). This ontological orientation gives Jaspers's work a special status for Heidegger.[7]

To understand Heidegger's interest in limit-situations in more detail, we must first examine what limit-situations are.

Limit-Situations in Jaspers

Limit-situations are situations in which the subject runs up against an antinomy in its existence. Limit-situations, according to Jaspers, are "decisive, essential situations, which are bound up with human being as such, which are unavoidably given with finite existence, beyond which one's vision cannot reach." Furthermore, "What is common to [limit-situations] is that—always within the objective world that is to be found in the subject-object-division—nothing firm is there, no indubitable absolute, no support that can resist every experience and every thought. Everything is in the flux of a restless movement of being put into question; all is relative, finite, split up into contraries, never the whole, the absolute, the essential" (PW, 229). What makes limit-situations distinctive is that in them the subject confronts an essential antinomy, that is, some real opposition between conflicting forces or goals or structures, which cannot be overcome or undone. In limit-situations one loses one's grip on what one is thinking about or valuing, because one is buffeted back and forth from one side of an opposition to another. Let me explain in more detail.

All limit-situations are based on an antinomy. An antinomy is a special sort of opposition. An opposition is any two contradictory or contrary propositions, forces, or phenomena—ranging from blue/green and animal/not-animal, to life/death and positive /negative electricity. An opposition is in turn an antinomy if it is (a) essential, (b) unresolvable, and (c) pervasive. Let me clarify these conditions by focusing on antinomies in valuing. (a) To say that an opposition is essential is to say that everyone must confront it, because it necessarily arises from the nature of valuation itself. One can try to deny or ignore the opposition, but this only covers it up. (b) To say that the opposition is unresolvable is to say that there is no stable standpoint from which either one side of the opposition wins out or some higher synthesis is achieved. These oppositions are "something final," in that there is nothing beyond them that clarifies, eliminates, or overcomes them. (c) Finally, to say that they are pervasive is to say that they are not discrete difficulties that stand on their own, but rather are difficulties that arise within the attempt to establish or realize *any* value. They are structural in nature, since they arise within, and apply to, everything attempted within their proper domain. "Real oppositions," Jaspers explains, "are antinomies, if they are grasped as something final (*etwas Letztes*), which from the standpoint of valuing appears essential and questionable, and if existence is grasped as in the end split into two, so that individual existence only arises if these opposing forces or phenomena are found together" (PW, 232). Any attempt to establish values necessarily runs up against the unresolvable opposition in question. The opposition defines the "limits" of valuation, since it constitutes a point to which all valuation is ultimately referred, and beyond which no valuation can advance.

Since the limits of valuation are defined by an opposition, rather than by some stable, unitary, highest good, the subject is pulled into an endless reference back and forth between the two poles of the opposition. This makes it impossible for the subject to arrive at a comfortable, valuative resting point. Jaspers's prime example of this is what he calls "essential guilt":[8] Essential guilt is the fact, according to Jaspers, that in every attempt to realize some value, the agent necessarily must will some subservient values that undermine or sully the end-value. "Values become actual through forces and conditions that themselves are valuatively negative: if one wants some value in reality, one must, on account of objective connections, unavoidably take negatives (*Unwerte*) into the bargain too" (PW, 237). All action misfires at some level, and this is simply part of what it is to be an agent in a real world. This throws the agent's values into question, or at least the attempt to realize them, since it sends one around in an endless reflection from the positive to the negative value, never being able to come to a rest with the one or the other.

This consequence leads in turn to an acute form of suffering. "What is common to all limit-situations is that they cause suffering" (PW, 247). Jaspers does not really say very much about this suffering, except to give a list of examples of what he has in mind. He includes on his list both "anxiety in the face of death" and "despair in the midst of unavoidable guilt" (PW, 248). One gets the general impression, though, that the suffering arises from the inability of the activity in question to achieve stability and satisfaction. One despairs because every value one attempts to realize is marked by, and thus drawn into question by, something negative, some disvalue. Or in the case of the limit-situation of confronting death, life is something that constantly strives to realize future goals, and reflection on its inevitable termination with death provokes an anxiety about the status and final disposition of one's goals and achievements.[9]

Now, Jaspers has a dual interest in limit-situations. First, he takes the description of limit-situations to help to define the subject, since it defines the limits of the subject's thinking, experiencing, valuing, or acting. He writes, "World-view psychology is a pacing off of the limits of the life of our soul, in so far as it is accessible to our understanding" (PW, 6). This pacing off of the limits of the life of our soul, delimits or describes that life: "A psychology of world-views . . . is the tracing out of the realm that we already possess conceptually" (PW, 6). In limit-situations the limits of the life of the soul are manifest, and thus we are able to fix the boundaries of that life. This is Jaspers's *ontological* interest in limit-situations.

But second, Jaspers also has a *classificatory* interest in limit-situations, since it is through one's response to limit-situations that one's "spiritual type" can be discerned. "These limit-situations are as such unbearable for life, and thus they almost never enter into complete clarity in the course of our living experience; rather as a matter of fact, we almost always have a foothold[10] in the face of limit-situations. Without such a foothold, life would end. As a matter of fact, man is relatively seldom in despair. He gains a foothold before he can despair at all; not everyone, but only the few live in limit-situations. We are asking what conditions men, so that they do not find themselves in limit-situations, or that they get out of them. Here we touch upon the center of spiritual types. What foothold man has, how he has, seeks, finds, and preserves a foothold; these are the characteristic expressions of the forces that live within him. If we ask about the spiritual type of a man, we are asking how he has his foothold" (PW, 229). By studying limit-situations and how people cope with them or avoid them altogether, the world-view psychologist can see how to classify people, can see to what "spiritual type" they belong.

Heidegger's Interest in the Concept of the Limit-Situation

Whereas Jaspers has both an ontological and a classificatory interest in limit-situations, Heidegger's interest is for the most part narrowed to the ontological alone. In *Sein und Zeit* and his early review article of the *Psychologie der Weltanschauungen* a clear demarcation between Jaspers's two interests is developed. In the midst of his discussion of death in Chapter 1 of Division 2 of *Sein und Zeit*, Heidegger makes his most important footnote reference to limit-situations. Heidegger writes, "For the following investigation, one should see *especially*: K. Jaspers, *Psychologie der Weltanschauungen*. . . . Jaspers conceives death by means of the clue of the phenomenon, set forth by him, of 'limit-situations,' whose fundamental significance ranges beyond all typologies of 'attitudes' and 'world-views' " (SZ, 249 n. 1). In this footnote Heidegger clearly indicates that he does not share Jaspers's classificatory interest. That interest is too ontical, too much concerns the way people happen to be, and does not directly touch upon the way all humans must be, the ontology of the human.

At the beginning of "Anmerkungen," Heidegger emphasizes Jaspers's ontological interest in limit-situations.[11] Furthermore, just as Jaspers argues that by pacing off the limits of the life of the soul, one can trace out the whole of that life, and thereby get a fix on what that life is, so in section 45 of *Sein und Zeit*, his introduction to Division Two of that treatise, Heidegger writes, "The end of being-in-the-world is death. This end, which belongs to the ability-to-be, that is, to existence, delimits (*begrenzt*) and determines the totality of Dasein that is in each case possible" (SZ, 234). Heidegger accepts the notion that by describing the limits of human existence, we can delimit and thereby fix what that existence is. This is something Heidegger owes to Jaspers's treatment of the limit-situation.

Although Heidegger does set aside Jaspers's classificatory aim in discussing limit-situations, it is worth noting that the idea is not entirely absent from *Sein und Zeit*. Heidegger argues that whether one is authentic or inauthentic is determined by one's response to the situation of anxiously confronting death. I shall shortly claim that this anxious confrontation with death is a limit-situation in an important sense. So, we see that Heidegger preserves the notion that fundamental distinctions between concrete ways of life emerge in response to limit-situations. Authenticity and inauthenticity are concrete, what Heidegger calls *existentiell*, possibilities of Dasein's being, and not essential, what Heidegger calls *existential*, features of that being. They are, however, first among equals, and worthy of treatment in *Sein und Zeit*, and for two reasons. (a) Although *existentiell*, that is, ontical rather than ontological, the choice between them that confronts Dasein is not optional, but forced. It is an existential fact about Dasein that it confronts this choice between these two modes of its being. This is unlike the distinction between being an American and being a German, which is *existentiell* but not forced in this sense. (b) This choice is ontologically significant, since in authenticity the proper ontology of Dasein is implicitly available to it, whereas in inauthenticity it is covered up. So, Jaspers's strategy for getting at the typology of worldviews by examining responses to limit-situations is not wholly absent in Heidegger, though it has taken on a purely strategic importance, and thus has been greatly slimmed down to the primary option between authenticity and inauthenticity. Jaspers's detailed discussions of pessimism, optimism, Buddhism, and so on are absent from, and irrelevant to, Heidegger's treatment in *Sein und Zeit*.

Beyond these connections between *Sein und Zeit* and *Psychologie der Weltanschauungen*, does Heidegger owe anything more determinate to the concept of a limit-situation? In particular, since Heidegger refers to the concept in the midst of his discussion of death, does Heidegger's treatment of death owe anything to Jaspers's discussion of limit-situations? The answer is yes—it is profitable to view the anxious confrontation with death in *Sein und Zeit* as a sort of limit-situation.

Heidegger's Appropriation of the Concept of the Limit-Situation

What Heidegger calls "death" is a condition in which Dasein confronts a tension in its existence, a tension that arises from the very structure of that existence. Though Heidegger does not characterize that tension as an antinomy, it is a tension that arises within, and constitutes a breakdown of, Dasein's existence. Like limit-situations, it also inevitably involves an acute form of anxiety. Finally, death helps to define the nature of Dasein's existence, because it reveals that existence's inherent limits. What Heidegger calls death is indeed a limit-situation. And it is for this reason that Heidegger refers the reader "especially" to Jaspers's *Psychologie der Weltanschauungen*.

Despite what I argue is Heidegger's debt to Jaspers's concept of the limit-situation, the details of Jaspers's treatment of death do not transfer to Heidegger's discussion,[12] because the two philosophers' ontologies of the human differ substantially. For Jaspers, death is the ending of a human life, and thus his discussion of it revolves around concepts such as mortality, immortality, and the afterlife. A central presupposition here, indeed throughout the *Psychologie*, is that the person is a sort of life. In his "Anmerkungen," Heidegger identifies this element of life-philosophy at the center of Jaspers's thinking.[13] Part of the burden of the review is to suggest that this residual life-philosophy ought really to be developed into an existential ontology. "It is worthy of note that the life-philosophy that has developed within an authentic orientation to intellectual history . . . tends towards the phenomenon of existence" in Heidegger's sense ("*Anmerkungen*," 14). This is a tendency that Heidegger finds and praises in Jaspers. It is not, however, until *Sein und Zeit* that Heidegger succeeds in developing a concept of existence that departs from the life-philosophical conception. Existence is not a form of life, but rather the ability-to-be someone. When he develops this notion in *Sein und Zeit*, death can no longer be the end of a life, but must rather in some sense be an end of this ability-to-be.[14] Recall that he writes, "This end, which belongs to the ability-to-be, that is, to existence, delimits and determines the totality of

Dasein that is in each case possible," (SZ, 234). This gives Heidegger's discussion of death a very different direction from Jaspers's.

Although the content of Heidegger's discussion of death differs substantially from that of Jaspers, nonetheless Heidegger deploys the essential idea that death can be considered a limit-situation. Let me argue first that death is a situation, and then ask in what way it reveals limits. The official definition of "death" (Ch. 1, Div. 2) is this: Dasein's "death is the possibility of no-longer-being-able-to-be-there" (SZ, 250). The commonsense way to read this definition is thus: Death, an always impending possibility for Dasein, is a condition in which it is no longer able to be, because its organic and mental functions have been brought to an end. But this cannot be what Heidegger means, for he interprets death not as an impending event that can and almost certainly will happen to Dasein, but rather as a possible way *to be* Dasein. "Death is a way to be, which Dasein takes over, as soon as it is," (SZ, 245). Death is not Dasein's being "at its end," but rather a condition or situation in which Dasein can find itself!

In a limit-situation, one runs up against the limits of existence. Since this existence is now considered an *ability*—Heidegger calls this fundamental ability Dasein's "ability-to-be" (*Seinkönnen*)—the limits of existence must now be the limits of an ability. In what ways do abilities have ends in the sense of limits? Abilities have limits in (at least) two ways. On the one hand, there are limits on the scope or range of an ability: One's ability to add may have its limit with ten digit numbers. On the other hand, abilities can be stifled (or *disabled*) in certain sorts of situations. So for instance, my ability to see is stifled in the absence of light, my ability to breathe is stifled by the absence of oxygen. Now, Heidegger characterizes the end of Dasein *qua* ability as a certain sort of *inability*: Death is the condition in which Dasein is no longer able to be Dasein. Let me suggest that the end of Dasein *qua* ability is a stifling situation in this latter sense: a condition in which Dasein is unable to exercise that ability that it is. Such a situation in which Dasein is unable to exercise its fundamental ability is a situation in which Dasein confronts the stifling limits of its ability-to-be; it is a limit-situation.

In order to develop this idea further, I must ask the reader to accept my rather unconventional interpretation of the concept of death in *Sein und Zeit*.[15] Death, as a limit-situation, is a condition in which Dasein finds itself unable to be. Recall that Dasein's "death is the possibility of no-longer-being-able-to-be-there" (SZ, 250), and this possibility is "a way to be" (SZ, 245). Now, this may strike one as not only scandalous, but also self-contradictory. If death is the possibility of Dasein no longer being able to be, then surely death cannot be a condition in which Dasein can find itself. After all, if in death Dasein is not able *to be*, then death is not a condition in which Dasein can find itself, because in that condition it cannot *be* at all. My solution to this apparent contradiction in Heidegger's account of death is to distinguish what I call "thin" and "thick" senses of Dasein's being, which I identify with Heidegger's notions of existence and understanding. For Dasein to exist, in Heidegger's technical vocabulary, is for Dasein's being to be at issue for it (SZ, 42). That is, to exist is to be confronted by the question, Who am I? Dasein has no essence, and so who Dasein is is determined only by its going about business in the world in some definite fashion. For Dasein to understand itself, Dasein must determine who it is by pressing ahead into some definite way to be Dasein made available to it by its culture (SZ, §31). In self-understanding, Dasein provisionally answers the question, Who am I? by giving its existence definite content. Now, this self-understanding is only possible, Heidegger argues, if possible ways to be Dasein already matter differentially to it in determinate ways (SZ, 144). This self-understanding is the way in which Dasein is its ability-to-be, because it is the manner in which Dasein is able to be some determinate answer to the question, Who am I? (SZ, 142).

Given these two senses of Dasein's being, the possibility emerges that Dasein might find itself in a situation in which although the question, Who am I? impends for it, it is unable to make an even provisional answer to this question. I do not have in mind here a situation in which one's ability to press ahead into some definite possibility is undercut by a definite failure of capacity to be *that* possibility. I do not have in mind trying to be something or other but failing. Rather, I have in mind a situation in which Dasein's ability-to-be is stifled by the absence of a condition necessary for pressing ahead into *any* possibility of its being. Recall that self-understanding requires, according to Heidegger, that possible ways to be Dasein matter to one differentially. Consider a condition in which no possible ways to be Dasein matter to one differentially, but rather all show up as equally irrelevant or meaningless. This is the condition Heidegger calls "anxiety," the condition in which "what stifles [one] is not this or that, but also not everything occurrent together as a sum, but rather the *possibility* of the available in general, that is, the world itself" (SZ, 187). The world is the domain in which possible ways to be are sketched out for one by one's culture. And in anxiety this world becomes "uniquely obtrusive," because everything that shows up in it becomes "totally insignificant" (SZ, 186–187). So, in anxiety Dasein is unable to be anyone, because it is unable to understand itself in terms of any possible way to be Dasein. Anxiety is the condition of no longer being able to be Dasein (in the thick sense), in other words, what Heidegger calls "death."

In this condition, Dasein is confronted with an inherent tension in its being. In death Dasein is confronted with a tension between existence and understanding, a tension opened up by anxiety: Although Dasein confronts the question, Who am I, it cannot answer it. The sense in which for Heidegger this tension is inherent is somewhat different from the way in which antinomies are inherent for Jaspers. Jaspers's account of the inherentness of the antinomies he identifies resembles closely the Kantian strategy on which it is modeled. The antinomies arise necessarily in any attempt to use certain human faculties, such as thought or valuation. But Heidegger's tension is not inherent in that sense: it *need* not necessarily arise in the attempt to answer the question, nor even in an honest attempt to answer the question. Rather, death is a condition that is always *possible* for Dasein. Despite this difference, it is nonetheless an inherent possibility. It is a possibility that arises from Dasein's very structure, and thus does not depend for its possibility on Dasein's being some specific sort of person. Anyone can suffer anxiety. Furthermore, Heidegger argues that anyone can suffer anxiety at any time. To make oneself impervious to anxiety, one would have to work certain definite structures of mattering right into one's essence, so that anxiety could not arise and defeat them. But Heidegger takes the thesis that Dasein has no essence to entail that no definite structures of mattering can be worked into an essence. Thus, anxiety is always possible, simply by virtue of being Dasein. It is, in this sense, an inherent possibility.

Both Jaspers's limit-situations and Heidegger's death are pervasive in the sense that both (can) affect all other attempts to use those faculties or abilities.[16] Limit-situations are not just several particular situations amongst others, but rather special sorts of situations that apply to and qualify the rest. The limit-situation of essential guilt in Jaspers is not some particular situation of recognizing some particular guilt one bears or even must bear for some particular action or even specific sort of action. In essential guilt one confronts a form of guilt that derives from the structure of any attempt to establish any value. Jaspers's essential guilt also reveals that any attempt to realize this value must be willing to take some negatives "into the bargain too"; it reveals a responsibility for the negative that arises in all cases. Similarly, Heidegger's anxious confrontation with death is not a response to some particular sort of human predicament or inability. Death is a condition that can break in upon the pursuit of any other possibilities Dasein has. In breaking in upon other pursuits, it undercuts them and renders them disabled, by throwing one into a condition in which they no longer matter. Thus, although (as pointed out above) death is only an inherent possibility, it is pervasive in the sense that it arises within, and applies to, all other concrete possibilities.

Finally, like Jaspers's limit-situations, death gives rise to an acute form of disquiet. Here is a point on which I find Heidegger's account decidedly more convincing. Jaspers's limit-situations do not arise simply in the attempt to use certain faculties, but rather in the attempt to use these faculties to completion. That is, according to Jaspers, suffering is caused by one's inability to complete the task set up for thinking, or to come to rest in one's evaluation of an action. Jaspers himself characterizes the limitation involved as the absence of an absolute. It is unclear why we should be quite so shaken as Jaspers suggests by the absence of an absolute (PW, 229). In Heidegger's case, however, anxiety is a condition not in which some ability cannot find consummation in an absolute, but rather a condition in which that ability is stifled altogether. This generates anxiety, because the ability in question is not some specific ability, but rather the ability to be anyone at all. As Heidegger argues, this stifling arises only when all the possible concrete ways to be Dasein that are available to one become irrelevant, and thus the world as a whole becomes insignificant, meaningless.

Conclusion

What does Heidegger owe to Jaspers's concept of the limit-situation? He owes a general strategy for approaching the task of defining human existence, namely by pacing off the limits internal to it. He also owes an orientation toward death as such a limit-situation, despite the significant differences in their respective treatments of the topic. This notion of the limit-situation is something Heidegger clearly owes to his intensive study of the *Psychologie der Weltanschauungen* around and about 1920. Thinking of Heidegger's discussion of death in this way also helps us, I think, to approach the darker bits of Chapter 1 of Division 2 of *Sein und Zeit*. If we approach death as a limit-situation, in this case a situation in which one's ability-to-be is anxiously stifled, rather than as the ending of one's life, we can make considerable progress with our interpretation of Heidegger's discussion of death. This also leads us to ask what Heidegger might have learned from Jaspers about the *Augenblick*, the topic of discussion that prompts Heidegger's other specific footnote to Jaspers. It also raises the question what Heidegger's discussion of guilt in Chapter 2 of Division 2 may owe to Jaspers's extended treatment of essential guilt in *Psychologie der Weltanschauungen*.

NOTES

1. Martin Heidegger, *Sein und Zeit*, 15th ed. (Tübingen: Niemayer Verlag, 1979), hereafter cited as *SZ*. The reference mentioned is found in note 1 on page 249. All translations are my own.

2. Karl Jaspers, *Psychologie der Weltanschauungen*, 6th ed. (Munich: Piper Verlag, 1985), hereafter cited as *PW*. The section on limit-situations is Section 2, Chapter 3, pp. 229–279. All translations are my own.

3. Hans Saner, ed., *Karl Jaspers in der Diskussion* (Munich: Piper Verlag, 1973).

4. Martin Heidegger, "Anmerkungen zu Karl Jaspers *Psychologie der Weltanschauungen*" in *Wegmarken*, 2d Edition (Frankfurt am Main: Vittorio Klostermann, 1978).

5. In *Die Göttingischen Gelehrten Anzeigen*. See *Martin Heidegger/Karl Jaspers, Briefwechsel, 1920–1963*, ed. Walter Biemel and Hans Saner (Munich: Piper Verlag, 1990), note 3 to Letter 1, p. 221. Perhaps the oblique reasons for not publishing it there are given in Heidegger's letter of June 25, 1921, Letter 5, pp. 20–21.

6. Heidegger sent a copy to Jaspers in June 1921. Jaspers acknowledges receipt of the document in his letter to Heidegger of June 28, 1921 (Letter 6, p. 21, *Briefwechsel*). The editor of Heidegger's *Wegmarken* argues that Jaspers responds to Heidegger's critique in the preface to the 3d Edition of *PW* (see editor's *Nachweise* to Heidegger's *Wegmarken*, p. 475). For the references to Rickert and Husserl, see Heidegger's letters of June 25 and August 5, 1921 (Letters 5 and 8, pp. 20–21, 24 in *Briefwechsel*)

7. This distinguishes Jaspers from Kierkegaard, of whom Heidegger writes that "he has most insightfully seen the *existentiell* phenomenon of the *Augenblick*, which does not yet mean that he has succeeded at the corresponding existential [i.e., ontological] interpretation. He remains trapped in the vulgar concept of time and determines the *Augenblick* with the help of the Now and Eternity" (*SZ*, 338, n.1). He then approvingly refers the reader to Jaspers's discussion of the *Augenblick* in PW (this is the third reference to Jaspers in *SZ*).

8. The term is used to contrast the antinomical structure essential to all attempts to realize values in the world with guilt for some particular action. See *PW*, p. 274.

9. I have here extrapolated somewhat from what Jaspers says in his discussion of death, because he does not state this particular thought very precisely.

10. "Wir haben faktisch fast immer angesichts der Grenzsituation einen Halt." A *Halt* in this context means something like a foothold or a support. The idea seems to be that *Grenzsituationen* are confusing, disarming, and unbearable, and thus that one must gain some grip when confronting one. It is unclear here whether Jaspers intends to characterize such footholds negatively as a sort of crutch, or whether he wants to claim that all attitudes are footholds in his sense here—even the wide-eyed recognition of *Grenzsituationen* and the empowerment he indicates one can find through such recognition (see his reaction to antinomical situations in *PW*, no. 3, pp. 241–242).

11. Heidegger, "Anmerkungen," p. 1.

12. The one exception to this lies in the thesis that the situation we are interested in is the individual's approach to his or her own death, rather than to the death of another. Heidegger's consideration of this point sounds strikingly

like Jaspers's, indicating that Heidegger had Jaspers clearly in mind as he wrote Chapter 1 of Division 2; see *PW*, pp. 260–261 and SZ, § 47.

13. Heidegger, "Anmerkungen," passim, but esp. pp. 13ff.

14. This is not to say that Dasein is not also alive, and thus that Dasein's life does not also end. Heidegger calls this phenomenon "demise" (*Ableben*; death is *Tod*). See *SZ*, p. 247.

15. I develop this interpretation further in an essay titled "The Concept of Death in *Being and Time*," forthcoming in *Man and World*.

16. I discuss the inherentness and the pervasiveness of death, to parallel the essentiality and the pervasiveness of limit-situations for Jaspers. I pass unresolvability by, however. Unresolvability is crucial to antinomies defining the limits of existence, because they define a point beyond which the faculties for which they arise cannot be used. But since the sense in which death defines Dasein's limits is somewhat different, unresolvability is not an issue for death.

Recent Publications on Heidegger

Bourdieu, Pierre. *The Political Ontology of Martin Heidegger*. Trans. Peter Collier. Palo Alto: Stanford University Press, 1991.

Derrida, Jacques. *Of Spirit: Heidegger and the Question*. Trans. Geoffrey Bennington and Rachel Bowlby. Chicago: University of Chicago Press, 1989.

Janicaud, Dominique. *L'ombre de cette pensée: Heidegger et la question politique*. Grenoble: Jérôme Millon, 1990.

Krell, David Farrell. *Daimon Life: Heidegger and Life-Philosophy*. Indiana University Press, 1992.

Neske, Günther, and Emil Kettering, eds. *Martin Heidegger and National Socialism: Questions and Answers*. New York: Paragon House, 1990.

Nolte, Ernst. *Heidegger: Politik und Geschichte im Leben und Denken*. Berlin: Propyläen, 1992.

Ott, Hugo. *Martin Heidegger. Unterwegs zu seiner Biographie*. Frankfurt am Main: Campus, 1988.

Petzet, Heinrich Wiegand. *Encounters and Dialogues with Martin Heidegger, 1929–1976*. Trans. Parvis Emad and Kenneth Maly. Chicago: University of Chicago Press, 1992.

Rockmore, Tom. *On Heidegger's Nazism and Philosophy*. Berkeley: University of California Press, 1992.

Rockmore, Tom, and Joseph Margolis, eds. *The Heidegger Case: On Philosophy and Politics*. Philadelphia: Temple University Press, 1992.

Rosenberg, Alan, and Gerald Myers, eds. *Echoes from the Holocaust: Philosophical Reflections from a Dark Time*. Philadelphia: Temple University Press, 1988.

Sallis, John. *Echoes: After Heidegger*. Bloomington: Indiana University Press, 1990.

Sallis, John, ed. *Reading Heidegger: Commemorations*. Bloomington: Indiana University Press, 1992.

Schalow, Frank. *The Renewal of the Heidegger–Kant Dialogue: Action, Thought, Responsibility*. Albany: State University of New York Press, 1992.

Scott, Charles E. *The Question of Ethics: Nietzsche, Foucault, Heidegger*. Bloomington: Indiana University Press, 1990.

Spanos, William. *Heidegger and Criticism: Retrieving the Cultural Politics of Destruction.* Minneapolis: University of Minnesota Press, 1993.

Thomä, Dieter. *Die Zeit des Selbst und die Zeit danach: Zur Kritik der Textgeschichte Martin Heideggers 1910–1976.* Frankfurt am Main: Suhrkamp, 1990.

Vietta, Silvio. *Heideggers Kritik am Nationalsozialismus und an der Technik.* Tübingen: Niemeyer Verlag, 1989.

Wolin, Richard. *The Politics of Being: The Political Thought of Martin Heidegger.* New York: Columbia University Press, 1990.

Wolin, Richard, ed. *The Heidegger Controversy: A Critical Reader.* New York: Columbia University Press, 1992.

Zimmerman, Michael. *Heidegger's Confrontation with Modernity, Technology, Politics, Art.* Bloomington: Indiana University Press, 1990.

About the Contributors

WILLIAM D. BLATTNER is Assistant Professor of Philosophy at Georgetown University. He received his Ph.D. from the University of Pittsburgh in 1989. Professor Blattner has published several essays on Heidegger's *Being and Time* and is currently finishing a book entitled *Temporality and Time in Heidegger's Early Thought*.

KLAUS BRINKMANN is Associate Professor of Philosophy at Boston University. He was educated at Bonn, Tübingen, and Oxford and taught at Bonn and Tübingen prior to joining the faculty at Boston University in 1988. He is the author of *Aristotele's allgemeine and spezielle Metaphysik* and has published several articles on Schelling and Hegel. Professor Brinkmann has recently published a review essay on new monographical studies of Aristotle's metaphysics and is currently completing a book on Hegel's concept of subjective spirit.

LEONARD H. EHRLICH is Professor Emeritus of Philosophy and Judaic Studies, University of Massachusetts at Amherst. He studied at Basel (where he was a student of both Karl Jaspers and Karl Barth) and received his doctorate at Yale in 1960. Professor Ehrlich has been a guest professor at Freiburg (1973/74), Kassel (1988), and Mainz (1990), where he was also a Senior Fulbright Research Fellow. He is the author and editor of several works including *Karl Jaspers: Philosophy as Faith* (University of Massachusetts Press, 1975); *Fraglichkeit der jüdischen Existenz. Philosophische Untersuchungen zum modernen Schicksal der Juden* (Alber, 1993); coeditor and cotranslator, with M. Ermarth and Edith Ehrlich, of *The Great Philosophers*, by Karl Jaspers, vols. 3 and 4 (forthcoming from Harcourt Brace, 1993–94); coeditor and cotranslator, with George Pepper and Edith Ehrlich, of *Karl Jaspers: Basic Philosophical Writings, Selections* (University of Ohio Press, 1986); and coeditor, with Richard Wisser, of *Karl Jaspers Today: Philosophy at the Threshold of the Future,* (University Press of America, 1988) and *Karl Jaspers: Philosopher Among Philosophers/Ein Philosoph unter Philosophen,* (Königshausen and Neumann, 1993).

STEPHEN A. ERICKSON is E. Wilson Lyon Professor of Humanities and Professor of Philosophy at Pomona College. His publications include *Language and Being: An*

Analytic Phenomeonology (Yale University Press, 1970), *Human Presence: At the Boundaries of Meaning* (Mercer University Press, 1984), and numerous articles and reviews in such journals as the *Review of Metaphysics, Man and World,* and *Philosophy Today.*

KRYSTYNA GORNIAK-KOCIKOWSKA is Assistant Professor of Philosophy and Religion at Southern Connecticut State University in New Haven. She received her Ph.D. in philosophy at Adam Mickiewicz University in Poznan, Poland, and is presently completing her second Ph.D. in religion at Temple University. Her first dissertation was on "Nietzsche's Philosophy of Culture" and her second is on "Karl Jaspers, Hans Küng, and the Idea of Global Ethos." Professor Gorniak-Kocikowska is the coauthor and/or coeditor of three books published in Poland, and she has also published numerous articles in English, German, Polish, Italian, and Croatian.

KARSTEN HARRIES is Professor of Philosophy at Yale University. He has also taught at the University of Texas (Austin) and the University of Bonn. He has published many articles on Heidegger, early modern philosophy, and the philosophy of art and architecture. His books include *The Meaning of Modern Art* (Northwestern University Press, 1965), *The Bavarian Rococo Church: Between Faith and Aestheticism* (Yale University Press, 1983), and *The Broken Frame: Three Lectures* (Catholic University Press, 1990).

JOSEPH MARGOLIS is Laura H. Carnell Professor of Philosophy at Temple University. His books include *Values and Conduct* (Oxford University Press, 1971), *Knowledge and Existence* (Oxford University Press, 1973), *Persons and Minds* (Reidel, 1977), *Philosophy Looks at the Arts* (Temple University Press, 1978), *Art and Philosophy* (Humanities, 1980), *Rationality, Relativity, and the Humane Sciences* (Nijhoff, 1986), *Pragmatism Without Foundations* (Blackwell, 1986), *Science Without Unity* (Blackwell, 1987), *The Truth About Relativism* (Blackwell, 1991), and *The Flux of History and the Flux of Science* (Blackwell, 1993). He edited, with Tom Rockmore, the English edition of Victor Farías's *Heidegger and Nazism* (Temple University Press, 1989) and *The Heidegger Case* (Temple University Press, 1992).

HAROLD H. OLIVER is Professor of Philosophical Theology at Boston University. He is past president of the Karl Jaspers Society of North America and, in 1963–64, studied with Fritz Buri and Karl Jaspers in Tübingen and Basel. Professor Oliver serves as a member of the editorial boards of *Zygon: Journal of Religion and Science* and *The Personalist Forum.* During 1971–72 he was a Visiting Fellow of the Institute of Theoretical Astronomy at Cambridge University. His books include A *Relational Metaphysic* (Nijhoff, 1981) and *Relatedness: Essays in Metaphysics and Theology* (Mercer University Press, 1984). He has recently completed for publication a translation of Fritz Buri's *The Buddha-Christ as Lord of the True Self: The Religious Philosophy of the Kyoto School and Christianity.*

ALAN M. OLSON is Professor of Religion and Associated Professor of Philosophy at Boston University and has served, at various times, as the chairman of both departments. His publications include *Transcendence and Hermeneutics* (Nijhoff, 1979), *The Seeing Eye: Essays on Hermeneutic Phenomenology*, coauthor (Pennsylvania State University Press, 1983), and *Hegel and the Spirit: Philosophy as Pneumatology* (Princeton University Press, 1992). He is also the editor of several collections including *Disguises of the Demonic: Contemporary Perspectives on the Power of Evil* (Association, 1975); *Myth, Symbol, and Reality* (University of Notre Dame Press, 1980), *Transcendence and the Sacred* (University of Notre Dame Press, 1981); and *Video Icons and Values* (SUNY Press, 1990). During 1986, Professor Olson was Senior Fulbright Research Fellow at the University of Tübingen.

TOM ROCKMORE is Professor of Philosophy at Duquesne University. His many books in philosophy include *Fichte, Marx and German Philosophy* (University of Illinois Press, 1980), *Soviet Marxism and Alternatives* (Reidel, 1981); *Hegel's Circular Epistemology* (Indiana University Press, 1986); *Habermas on Historical Materialism* (Indiana University Press, 1989), *On Heidegger's Nazism and Philosophy* (University of California Press, 1992), *Irrationalism: Lukács and the Marxist View of Reason* (Temple University Press, 1991); *Hegel: Avant et après* (Paris, 1992), *Antifoundationalism Old and New*, edited with Beth Singer (Temple University Press, 1992); and *The Heidegger Case: On Philosophy and Politics*, edited with Joseph Margolis (Temple University Press, 1992). Professor Rockmore serves on numerous editorial boards, including: Studies in Continental Thought (Indiana), Studies in Phenomenology and Existential Philosophy (Northwestern), Archives de philosophie, Sovietica (Reidel), Studies in Soviet Thought, and the Center for Advanced Research in Phenomenology.

PAUL JOHANNES TILLICH (1886–1965), in the view of many, is the most influential philosophical theologian of the twentieth century. He received his doctorate at the University of Breslau in 1910 and taught at Berlin, Marburg, and Frankfurt. When the Nazis came to power in 1933, Tillich was dismissed from his professorship at Frankfurt and immigrated to the United States, where he taught at Columbia, Union, Harvard, and Chicago. Paul Tillich has written some forty books, including his magnum opus, the *Systematic Theology*, 3 vols. (University of Chicago Press, 1951, 1957, 1963). His *Gesammelte Werke*, 14 vols., is published by the Evangelisches Verlagswerk in Stuttgart.

Index